THE
OTHER
EXILE

THE
OTHER
EXILE

*The Remarkable Story
of Fernão Lopes,
the Island of Saint Helena,
and a Paradise Lost*

A R AZZAM

ICON

First published in the UK in 2017
by Icon Books Ltd, Omnibus Business Centre,
39–41 North Road, London N7 9DP
email: info@iconbooks.com
www.iconbooks.com

This edition published in the UK in 2018 by Icon Books Ltd

Sold in the UK, Europe and Asia
by Faber & Faber Ltd, Bloomsbury House,
74–77 Great Russell Street,
London WC1B 3DA or their agents

Distributed in the UK, Europe and Asia
by Grantham Book Services,
Trent Road, Grantham NG31 7XQ

Distributed in Australia and New Zealand
by Allen & Unwin Pty Ltd,
PO Box 8500, 83 Alexander Street,
Crows Nest, NSW 2065

Distributed in South Africa
by Jonathan Ball, Office B4, The District,
41 Sir Lowry Road, Woodstock 7925

Distributed in India by Penguin Books India,
7th Floor, Infinity Tower – C, DLF Cyber City,
Gurgaon 122002, Haryana

ISBN: 978-178578-344-9

Typeset in Goudy Oldstyle by Marie Doherty

Printed and bound in the UK
by Clays Ltd, Elcograf S.p.A

Man is committed at birth to two journeys. The first he cannot escape, for this is the journey of action and experience as he travels down the stream of his own lifetime ... The second journey is upstream using time and locality only as starting points, leading beyond their zone. This is the journey described in countless myths and legends, the arduous, perilous way towards the centre of being, the passage from the ephemeral and illusory towards the eternal real.

CHARLES LE GAI EATON, *KING OF THE CASTLE*

To my parents,
To memories of Beirut
And above all to Inaam, in my heart forever.

ACKNOWLEDGEMENTS

So many people have contributed their thoughts, suggestions and help during the writing of this book and I am truly grateful to all of them. My lack of Portuguese meant I had to lean heavily on João Paulo Oliveira e Costa who kindly introduced me to João Luís Ferreira, who in turn laboriously scoured the archives in search of Lopes. Many thanks also to Ângela Xavier and to Hélder Carvalhal as well as to Annemarie Jordan Gshwend, who patiently answered my amateurish questions as I tried to get my head around a period of history I knew so little about. Thanks also to Simona Cattabiani, whose encouragement and faith in my early drafts will see this book appearing in Portuguese.

I was fortunate to have some conversations with Beau Rowlands, an expert on Saint Helena and one of the very few living people to have written about Lopes. It was Rowlands who pointed out some very interesting developments in Lopes' life which I pursued in my book.

A special mention has to go to my agent Isobel Dixon at Blake Friedmann, who was the first to read my initial draft. She saw the potential of the story and introduced me to Tom Webber at Icon Books. Tom's constant challenges, prodding and editing of the manuscript improved the work immeasurably.

Finally a mention to Moji, because Moji will always be Moji.

CONTENTS

INTRODUCTION

Solitude has its coordinates. At exactly latitude 15.25 degrees, 55 minutes South, longitude 5.25 degrees, 45 minutes West, 1,143 miles west of Angola, 1,800 miles east of Brazil, a remote rock lies in an endless ocean.

Once there had been a time when the English, not normally so careless, had allowed him to escape, but now they settled on a volcanic island, in the middle of the South Atlantic Ocean, a mere ten and a half miles long and six miles wide, so isolated that there was no need for a prison. From the moment that Napoleon set foot on Saint Helena he understood that his fate was sealed, but in so many ways, so was that of the island. Henceforth it was no longer possible to imagine the island *sans* Bonaparte as he raged and railed against his fate, a Corsican Lear on an empty stage. And yet if Helena, the saintly mother of Constantine the Great after whom the Portuguese, in 1502, had named the place, could somehow intervene to silence the Corsican, and to gently coax the island to tell its tale, perhaps it would choose to tell a different story: one not as dramatic, but in its own way more haunting and profound. It would tell the story of another, earlier, exile, but one of a different nature: not a forced exile but a self-imposed one;

not a recriminatory exile but a redemptive one. And in its strange and poignant tale of Fernão Lopes, the island of Saint Helena may just help us unlock one of the great secrets of life – the secret of solitude.

I first came across Fernão Lopes by accident and in the most unlikely of places. Researching a paper regarding hostage-taking in Beirut in the 1980s, I stumbled across a book written by a Frenchman, Jean-Paul Kauffmann, who had been seized by militias and held for three years in Lebanon, and had later travelled to Saint Helena to write a reflective book on captivity. The subject, naturally, was Napoleon, but halfway through the book Kauffmann mentioned that while on Saint Helena he had learned of another exile who had been there 300 years earlier than Bonaparte and who, he enigmatically noted, was a 'Portuguese Muslim' and the island's only living human inhabitant. It was a passing reference – a historical *amuse-bouche* – and Kauffmann's comment intrigued me, but not for long. At that time I had just been commissioned to write a biography of Saladin and for the next few years I immersed myself in the world of Sultans and Lionhearts. And that seemed that. Except that it was not. On occasion, as I was busy researching an arcane point on the Third Crusade, I would find myself wondering: what could possibly have brought a 16th-century 'Portuguese Muslim' to a deserted island in the South Atlantic? And could it really be true that he had been the only living soul there? The answer, astonishingly, was yes.

Saladin over, to satisfy my curiosity I briefly turned my attention back to this enigmatic Portuguese Muslim. Having spent years reading hundreds of documents on Saladin, I was dismayed to find that only a handful mentioned Lopes. I struggled with the sources: there were inconsistencies and gaps in the story, and I remained frustrated by my inability to read the original documents in Portuguese. But the more I read the more the story drew me in: it stretched from Lisbon to Goa, from the society of *fidalgos* to

Hindu dancing girls and from the most terrible torture and disfigurement to a redemptive and transformative exile on an isolated island. Above all and throughout it was the image of Lopes on a deserted island that haunted me from the first reading, and that continued to haunt me. I became determined that the story of Fernão Lopes needed to be written.

In *The Other Exile*, I chose to write the story of one man and his journey through life – a journey lived on many levels, worldly and spiritual – but I was not sure what kind of book would emerge. The reason was simple: though the adventure story of a real-life Portuguese Robinson Crusoe was undoubtedly intriguing, full of drama, treachery and heroism, I sensed that the real story lay elsewhere, and that its importance lay in what was unsaid. Ultimately it was not just a story about a man or an adventure or even an island. It was a story about us and what makes us human. But though one can write about the geography of Lopes' physical journey, how does one express the geography of his spiritual one? Words in themselves hold no power, spiritual descriptions offer no genuine or profound meaning. How does one express the mystical when by its own nature it cannot be contained in words? In many ways I chose to write the story of Lopes as an adventure story partly because I could not describe the spiritual journey, but also in the hope that the adventure will be an embarkation point from which the reader can enter into the drama of the soul.

This is Fernão Lopes' story. It was only later, after I first stumbled across him as a 'Portuguese Muslim' living in isolation on a deserted island a thousand miles away from anyone, and after I decided to write about him, that I began to understand I had unwittingly entered midway into his story. If to understand a man's life one needs to understand it in its totality, then in order to move forwards it was important to begin the journey by going backwards. Only this way could we attempt to answer the question of *why* Fernão Lopes was on the island with any sense of profundity. Today the story of Fernão Lopes is largely forgotten, even though there was a time when it was well known, and if this book aims to bring him back to life then it is for one purpose only: to allow him to tell *his* story. The Portuguese poet Fernando Pessoa, perhaps Portugal's most famous 20th-century literary figure, asks an astute question in his writings: who, he enquires, if they are Portuguese, can live within the narrow bounds of just one personality, just one nation, just one religion? Lopes was born in the Golden Age of Portugal, the age of explorers like Vasco da Gama and Bartolomeu Dias, but his life also bridged two seismic events which profoundly transformed and traumatised Portugal during this period. Both fundamentally challenged the very identity of what it meant to be Portuguese. In telling the story of Fernão Lopes, one is naturally drawn to telling the story of this remarkable period.

PART I

The First Journey

'My soul waits for the Lord more than the watchmen for
the dawn; Indeed more than the watchmen for the dawn.'

PSALM 130: 6

CHAPTER ONE

A Kingdom Far Away

As our story begins at the end of the 15th century, Portugal lay at the end of the world: a frontier to nowhere. Beyond its coast there was nothing but ocean, not even islands. There was a time when it had been one of the 'five kingdoms' in the Iberian Peninsula. Four were Christian: Portugal, Castile, Aragon and Navarre, and one was Muslim – Granada. At the beginning of the 16th century, Castile had conquered Granada and Navarre, and was united with Aragon, emerging as the great Kingdom of Spain. As for the fifth kingdom, Portugal, it was a land defined by what it was, but equally importantly by what it was not. It was not Spain – despite the logic of geography which dictated otherwise. There was no overwhelming reason why Portugal should be distinct from the rest of the Iberian Peninsula, a fact which led a contemporary Portuguese historian to describe its independence as a geographical absurdity. It was not Spain, even though matrimonial unions were so close and frequent that it is possible to claim that the kingdoms of Portugal and Castile were ruled by a single dynasty during the entire Middle Ages. Undoubtedly a distinct national language, which borrowed heavily from Lusitanian and Arabic, helped in cementing its separate identity. Similarly, a medieval Portuguese would recognise today's country, since even 500 years ago the land had already assumed approximately the political shape it retains today, by far the first European state to do so.

Although Atlantic in location, Portugal's soul was Mediterranean, its people closer in character to the Greeks than to the Bretons or Basques. In the North, rain swept across mountainous ranges and valleys of great beauty, rendering the landscapes green and the summers mild. Beer, not wine, was drunk and people cooked with butter and not olive oil, which was undoubtedly a Celtic legacy. Further south the mountains receded and the land was flatter, with fiercely oppressive, stifling summers. Here one found an abundance of grapes, citrus fruits and figs as well as wine, olives and cork. North or south, Portugal was an impoverished land, overwhelmingly rural, with small, heavily walled towns between which communications were so bad that only those with access to the rivers could export their produce. Roads barely existed and there were no coaches. People had to move by horse, mule or donkey. Many simply travelled on foot. Only the endless sea which framed the land offered an alternative, as fishermen trawled the bleak windswept shores and tributaries for sardines and explored its waters for cod and herring. The land was sparsely populated, and there was a terrible reason for this. By the time the plague, known as the Black Death, had run its course in 1352 it had taken more than 30 per cent of the population of Portugal with it. But still the plague was not satisfied and it returned again and again, consuming all those who crossed its path. Neither the wealthy nor the poor were spared its pestilence. Nor were the pious, who prayed fervently but in vain to Saint Sebastian to intercede, for neither supplication nor potion came to their aid. Sweeping through the monastery of São Pedro in the city of Coimbra, the plague killed every human soul inside. Even when it had finally eased its terrible grip on the country, further disasters were to follow: between 1309 and 1404, eleven earthquakes are known to have struck Portugal, and the region suffered 22 famines. By 1450, Portugal's population had declined from 1.5 million to about 900,000.

Born in the early 1480s in Lisbon, Fernão Lopes grew up during Portugal's so-called Golden Age, the most memorable period in the country's history, unmatched before or after. This was the age of Bartolomeu Dias, the first European to sail around the southern tip of Africa, of Vasco da Gama and of Pedro Álvares Cabral, the discoverer of Brazil. Portugal launched its empire like a drunken love affair: chaotic and random, impetuous and cruel. During Lopes' youth the Portuguese sailors, formerly impoverished fishermen who trawled for sardines, rounded the Cape of Good Hope and sailed to India, founding settlements and trading posts as far away as Brazil and Africa, the Malay Archipelago, Macao and Japan. An achievement of astonishing audacity, it was an empire which typified the Portuguese character. In parts it was the consequence of Christian otherworldliness but also of plundering piracy and the bounty of enterprising adventurers. It was an empire which saw gold pour in and then slip away. Portugal's overseas expansion was a confusion of plans: an unfolding saga of ambitious kings, rapacious merchants, political magnates, travellers and pilgrims, all searching for opportunities.

As a Lisboeta born and bred, Lopes was a native of the city the Portuguese knew as the '*Lady and Queen of the Ocean*'. Bathed on one side by the sea, Lisbon's three other sides were dominated by five hills, giving the city an irregular semblance, not completely level and not completely uneven. With a population of roughly 50,000, the city was the same size as contemporary Bruges, half that of London and only one-quarter that of Venice. Its natural environment, on the slopes of the hills overlooking the Tagus, with fertile land and a deep-water harbour, attracted merchants and traders from across Europe. In its streets English, French and

Flemings jostled for space with mariners, fishermen and Genoese. On its most prominent hill stood the royal castle. Below there were houses and monasteries on the slopes. It was a city packed with churches, which were used not just as places of worship, but also as meeting places, and even places of amusement where dances were held and troubadours and jesters were heard. People ate and drank and slept in churches. They also spoke and laughed and argued loudly, and they did so standing, since it was not until the middle of the 15th century that benches were introduced. At the foot of the castle there were three Jewish quarters whose gates shut at night, while the Muslims had their own living quarters near the city's fortified walls just below the castle. Opposite the castle stood a Carmelite monastery and on the same hill was the Monastery of the Friars, a building where the young Lopes, had he visited it, could have marvelled at the embalmed crocodile hanging in the choir. In 1492 Hieronymus Münzer, a cartographer and humanist from Austria, visited Lisbon as part of a tour of the Iberian Peninsula and remarked on the presence of the embalmed crocodile, albeit with no explanation of how it came to be there.

Throughout, the city bustled with activity. From the Alfama district, clinging to the slopes of the Monte do Castelo – where Lopes was most probably born – to the Baixa district, with its vibrant crowded streets and houses – some up to four or five storeys high – where all manner of luxuries from gold and spices to elephants and wild parrots could be bought and traded, to the Praça do Rossio where, as a young boy, Lopes could have watched horse racing, bullfights and public executions while munching on almonds and figs. Although there are no records of how Lopes lived in Lisbon, we do know that Portuguese houses were notable for being poorly illuminated and barely ventilated, and for having no privacy. Indeed most of the inhabitants stayed away from their homes all day. Houses were small, and those with more than four rooms were rare and only for the wealthiest. In many houses the rooms did not have any walls and were divided by curtains or wooden panels. Furnishings in the houses tended to be very austere, with woollen tapestries used as insulation against the cold and the heat. Carpets were put on the floor, with the less wealthy using mats. The prevailing building materials were wood, nails, rammed earth, tile, stone, clay, sand and lime. Again, only the wealthiest could construct using stone slabs.

On occasion Lopes would have visited the fish market where the smell of sardines was everywhere and slaves sat languidly near empty baskets awaiting the arrival of the fishing boats. Fish was consumed in great quantities in Lisbon, particularly on religious days. But it was not just the fishermen, for near them vegetable sellers, confectioners, butchers, bakers and pastry makers also jostled to sell their wares. Fruit was plentiful, but the oranges were bitter and were used as lemons, since sweet oranges did not come to Portugal until a century later. Though there were vegetables for sale – spinach, turnips, radishes, lettuce, carrots, cucumber, asparagus, mushrooms and pumpkins, for example – they were eaten only by the poor who could not afford meat. The wine Lopes would have drunk was normally diluted with water since that was the custom, and he would not have drunk tea or coffee, which was unknown. Like most he was likely fast developing a taste for sugar, which was considered a spice and which was, at 50 times the price of honey, prohibitively expensive. From a young age, like most Portuguese of his age, he would have adopted the Arab habit of washing his hands before eating, and he would only ever have eaten with the knife he carried. Indeed, no one would ever leave their house without a knife and even the priests were armed. Lisbon was a filthy city. Despite being situated on the banks of a river, no one had had the idea of digging a canal where the filth could be discharged. Instead slaves carried buckets of excrement to the sea during the day, invariably spilling a quantity onto the ground. As one Portuguese contemporary acidly noted, 'The wise men who devote their time to splitting hairs to make laws have not yet found a time to issue one ordering that this refuse be carried out during the night'. Musk, amber and gum all recently brought from India were burned constantly to disguise the odour. On occasion the stench was alleviated by a waft of cooked meat and roast beef coursing through the streets, from one of the street stalls.

The city in which Lopes was growing up was changing fast and there was no greater sign of this than on the Rua Nova, Lisbon's first named street. Its full name, Rua Nova Grande dos Mercadores, made explicit its purpose: 'The Great New Street of Merchants'. It cut a distinctive line across the Baixa district, linking the four directions of the city, and was situated between Lisbon's two richest parishes: the São Julião church with its three naves at the northern side and Madalena at the eastern end. More importantly, Rua Nova ran parallel to the Tagus waterfront where boats setting out for and returning from India docked. The street also lay a short distance from the riverside wharf near Rossio Square, where the market and public auctions of goods, furniture and slaves were held. In 1517 the dramatist Torres Naharro in his play *Propalladia* has a Portuguese shepherd declare that 'God is Portuguese, from the middle of Rua Nova'. Certainly an ambitious claim for a street, even if it lay at the heart of the capital of a mercantile empire. For the kings of Portugal, however, it was imperative that a New Jerusalem be built on the banks of the Tagus, one which befitted their claim to be Sovereign of the World, and at the heart of this city would be Rua Nova which would embody the architectural identity and reflection of the royal vision. For this reason João II decreed that the street should be meticulously measured in length and width, and the elevation of the buildings accurately recorded. And similarly, João's successor Afonso V was determined to introduce order and symmetry in place of the 'cluttered look', which was a reflection of the medieval organic Islamic city that the Alfama area of Lisbon represented. In 1500 Rua Nova received royal recognition when the King elected to relocate there from his medieval palace in Alfama. Lopes would have watched as the new palace was put up at what seemed to be a furious pace of construction. The palace was strategically positioned just a few steps from Lisbon's mercantile hub, and embedded within it on the lower floors were the custom houses of Africa and India, lying underneath the royal quarters. Just west of the palace was the shipyard, the *Ribeira das Naus*. The presence of the new palace meant that the Rua Nova now became the most fashionable location to live in Lisbon and properties and rents there were the most expensive in the city. It was here that one came to see and be seen, and where the richest merchants lived, many of whom were German and Flemish.

Almost daily as a boy Lopes would have traversed the Rua Nova and come across the merchants, seated on wooden benches in front of their shops deep in conversation, revealing little but listening intently to any gossip that could help further their profits. On that bustling street there was one magnificent house that stood out. The young Lopes may have been among those who stopped at its gates to gaze at its grandeur. He would not have needed to ask who lived there for it was well known in Lisbon. The Florentine merchant Bartolomeo Marchionni, now a Portuguese citizen, was an enormously wealthy man after having acquired a monopoly to trade from the Portuguese Crown. Indeed, he was considered the wealthiest man of his time, and he was a close confidant of the King, from whom he leased his property. It was hard to imagine that any man other than the King could possess such fabulous wealth and splendour, and during their daily errands many Lisboetas paused and, gazing at the house, asked themselves how it was possible to be so wealthy. But everyone who lived in Lisbon already knew that the answer was India. Fernão Lopes grew up in a Portugal gripped by an urgent and pressing question: why should Lisbon not replace Venice or Genoa as the commercial capital of Europe? For years the Portuguese could hardly have failed to notice that a quintal of pepper costing three *ducados* in Malabar could be sold in Lisbon for 40 *ducados*, nor could they ignore the fact that the lucrative eastern trade in gold and spices was an obvious source of prosperity to the Islamic countries and to the Italian maritime republics. The overland route to the East was, however, firmly in the hands of the Mamluk Muslim Sultanate – a slave dynasty which overthrew the Ayubids and ruled over Egypt until its defeat by the Ottomans in the early years of the 16th century. Indeed after the fall of Constantinople to the Ottomans in 1453, the routes of Syria and Egypt had gradually dried up for the non-Muslims. What was clear was that there could be no trade with India through the land route that did not go via Muslim lands. But what if there was a way to circumvent the land route, and to forge a sea route that could link Europe with India and the eastern territories; a route which would destroy the Arab trade monopoly? What if, in other words, there was a way to cut out the middleman and trade directly, and more profitably, with the producer? As early as 1291 two Genoese brothers – the Vivaldis – had tried to open a sea route to the East, sailing down the Moroccan coast. They were never seen again. But the idea did not die with the Vivaldis, rather it persisted and grew.

Young boys of Lopes' day idolised the great hero Prince Henrique, famous to us today as Henry the Navigator (1394–1460), and grew up enraptured by his stories. A royal prince and a patron of explorers, Henrique was convinced that India was closer to the east of Portugal than the west and he was determined to prove it. Before Henrique, sailors and navigators had sailed towards Africa with great fear and trepidation. No Portuguese sailor had ever gone south of latitude 27 degrees North, for beyond that lay the 'Sea of Darkness', where sea monsters and boiling waters awaited. But Henrique was curious to know how far the coast extended, and he sent fourteen expeditions into the 'Sea of Darkness' for a multitude of motives: to advance geographical and scientific knowledge, to spread the Christian faith and to search for the mythical Prester John – rumoured to be a potentate who held a great Christian empire which he ruled beyond Muslim territory in Ethiopia. Henrique also thirsted for Guinea gold, and wished to control its sources in the Upper Niger and Senegal Rivers, as well as to add to the lucrative slave trade. In 1424 one of his squires, Gil Eanes, rounded Cape Bojador in a *barca* – a small square-rigged craft – taking an enormous step forward. By 1441 Portuguese captains, braving a dangerous lee shore, contrary winds and adverse currents, had reached the white cliffs on the coast of Mauritania, and by the mid 1440s they were sailing in the waters of Upper Guinea. Progress, however, continued to be slow and dangers were everywhere, from the treacherous shoals to the poisoned arrows with which the Portuguese were welcomed by African warriors. The Portuguese learned quickly, and calculated that if they sailed away from the coast with the wind on their beam they would reach a zone of winds which would ease their journey. By 1460 they had gone as far as Sierra Leone and the Gulf of Guinea, which they believed to be the southernmost tip of Africa. One year later, however, Pedro de Sintra skirted the shores of Sierra Leone and made contact with the inhabitants of what is today Liberia. Then, in the 1480s, the Portuguese reached Timbuktu and Mali and in 1486 the Chief of the Ughoton in Benin accompanied João de Aveiro back to Lisbon, causing a sensation in the Portuguese court. Trade opportunities with West Africa had opened everyone's eyes. Soon it was not just the Crown or the nobility who were enriching themselves, but Portuguese of all classes who were supplementing the meagre returns they gained from the agriculture which had supported generations before them with various forms of trade. Fishermen, traders and shipbuilders all now looked across the sea.

In 1481 the great João II took the throne. It was João who truly launched Portugal's great age of exploration. Prior to his reign, Portuguese expansion and exploration along the coast of West Africa had been directed either by junior members of the royal family or enterprising merchants and traders. However, under João, the Crown for the first time took a leading role in the organisation and financing of Portuguese expeditions, putting into effect what Henrique had once dreamed of. In 1482, and again in 1485, João sent Diogo Cão, the first recorded European to see the Congo River, southwards along the coast of Africa. When in 1486 Christopher Columbus presented João with a proposal to seek a westerly passage to India, the King of Portugal rejected it, not because he was ignorant or uninterested, but because he was convinced that there was a more direct route. João had sent out emissaries over land to East Africa and India via the Mediterranean, and he was certain that a sea route was navigable. In the same year that he turned down Columbus, João sent out a fleet to find the end of Africa. Departing from Portugal in 1486, the navigator Bartolomeu Dias led his vessels far south along the coast, diligently recording and naming new points as he passed them. At one point very strong adverse winds blowing south-south-east prevented his ships from continuing, and he decided to turn away from the African coast, and sail west for fifteen days, then south, and finally east towards the coast of Africa once again. Pushing on, despite severe disapproval from his crew, Dias finally rounded a cape that the Portuguese initially named the Cape of Storms, ultimately marking the end of Africa. Later this cape was renamed the Cape of Good Hope. But then, although it finally seemed that the long-cherished prize was at hand, no further ships were sent out from Lisbon: João had more important things on his mind.

'The King is a man of simple habits, not at all prodigal, and who knows to make the best of everything', so wrote the cartographer Hieronymus Münzer in 1492 about João II, who was one of the most, if not the most, formidable European rulers of the time. For his rival, Isabella of Castile, he was simply 'The Man', and for contemporaries he was 'a man who commanded others and who was commanded by no one'. Over his Catholic kingdom, the King held authority. To all and before God his duties were clear: to ensure the fair pursuit of justice, to defend his territory and to preserve religious orthodoxy throughout the land. It was he who held the balance between opposing elements and ambitions, between those in the interior of the country and those on the coast, between those who favoured closer relations with Castile and those who opposed them, between the competing nobility high and low. But the throne of Portugal was not mandated from Heaven, nor was it an absolute monarchy. Whereas a strong tradition of sacred monarchy existed in England and France, where sovereigns were both anointed and crowned, this was not the case in Portugal where the principle of kingship in the late Middle Ages dictated that the King earn his right to rule. To win the crown he needed to be seen as being more than a first among equals. To retain it he had to convince the people – effectively the nobility – that he had the legitimate right to rule. The primary way this could be achieved was through the expansion of the royal household and by bringing a greater number of nobles into his service. So, despite the harsh economic conditions, the King could not be seen to have a small household, since that was a sign of both vulnerability and a lack of largesse. It also denigrated kingship – after all the King was God's representative on earth, and God was not poor.

Christian virtue and liberality were the key to good kingship, but so was wisdom. It was the Crown which awarded titles and granted seigneuries to the nobility, and the Crown could also rescind them. Lords of manors had the right to hold manorial courts and collect their rents, but if the Crown wished to collect taxes, the lords had to carry out the royal will. If the kingdom went to war, the lords had to raise an army. It was a social contract and a bond of trust: the nobles afforded great powers to the King to enable him to maintain order and justice, make law and coin money, and in return they expected the appropriate rights and privileges. The strength of a king depended on his ability to prevent the nobility from checking or even usurping his authority, and tension and conflict were inevitable, since a poor king was a weak king. João was said to have complained that he had been left as only 'king of the road'. Determined to stand up to the challenge to his authority posed by the powerful aristocratic families, João imposed an oath on his subjects by which they had to swear on their knees to deliver to him any castle or town they held on demand. The chief opponents to the King were the Duke of Braganza (who was also João's brother-in-law) and the Duke of Viseu, who was responsible for the border with Castile and had amassed tremendous wealth through monopolies. João knew that to assert his royal authority, his strength had to be on display, and he had the Duke of Braganza publicly beheaded for treason. Nor could he show signs of weakness, and shortly afterwards he personally stabbed to death the Duke of Viseu. Both acts were as shocking as they were violent, and it is possible João may have felt remorse, for he now summoned the Duke of Viseu's younger brother, Manuel, aged only fifteen, to appear before him. In a tearful audience João declared that he loved Manuel as much as his son and promised to make him his heir in the event that he should have no legitimate descendants. It was a grand gesture, and a public one. How the death of his brother at the hands of the King affected Manuel's feelings can only be guessed at for he wisely kept silent, and though he listened to João's tearful exhortations, he knew they were largely meaningless. There were six persons who had better claims to the throne, and in any case the King was in rude health.

CHAPTER TWO

'Well-greased and stowed away'

What history labels luck, man names providence. Remarkably, in 1495, when Lopes was around fifteen years old, Manuel I, Manuel the Fortunate, whose father had been stabbed to death by the previous King, ascended to the throne of Portugal. As one never destined nor imagined for power, Manuel had been expected to retreat from the matters of the court, and, given his nature, to take up Holy Orders. His rise to power was certainly wondrous, and he believed it to be predestined – when one ascends thus it is only natural to think that it is for a purpose. Deeply pious, Manuel had, since his youth, been a devotee of Joachim of Fiore, the 12th-century hermit who taught that the prophetic texts, and particularly the Apocalypse, were the keys to understanding God's purposes for mankind. The core of Joachimite belief revolved around a future ruler who was the *Restitutor Mundi* ('Restorer of the World') who would emerge to save his people and defeat the forces of Islam. At what stage Manuel began to see himself as being guided by the Holy Spirit, fulfilling a providential role to bring about the conversion of the world by conquest and proselytisation, is not clear; but it was beyond doubt that he was sincere in this belief. It was an extraordinary belief, but then again it was an extraordinary age. Eduardo Lourenço, the celebrated contemporary Portuguese essayist and philosopher, writes of how Portuguese identity possesses a 'sense of congenital weakness and a magical conviction of an absolute divine protection ... which is deeply imbricated in the notion of a special destiny'. This bewitching mixture was never more to the fore than in the reign of Manuel. In the two years between 1498 when Vasco da Gama rounded the Cape of Good Hope, and 1500 when Pedro Cabral landed in Brazil, Portugal succeeded in establishing a global maritime empire. Surely if this was not a sign of divine blessing and the fulfilment of biblical prophecies, then what was?

The Portugal in which Lopes grew up and over which Manuel now ruled was one where chivalric romances mingled with biblical prognostications, and ancient legends with Christian apocalyptic writings. Two legends in particular stood out as foretelling its divine role, and both involved Muslims. The first related the story of Afonso Henriques, who was to become Afonso I, the first King of Portugal. On the eve of a decisive battle with the Muslim armies in 1139, Afonso saw a great light in the sky which revealed the Cross, with Jesus crucified upon it, surrounded by angels. Afonso prostrated himself before this vision and the figure of Christ reassured him that he would be victorious and establish a kingdom which would be blessed by God: 'It is my will to build upon you and upon your descendants, an Empire dedicated unto me, so that my name will be spread to foreign peoples.' This legend became the founding myth of Portugal, a legend of both the divinity of its founding and the purpose for the kingdom. It was one that Manuel deeply believed in, for as soon as he assumed power he decreed the re-interment of Afonso Henriques' body in Coimbra. As for the second legend, I shall return to that later since it has a particular poignancy with regard to our story.

To dream well in Portugal was to dream of being a *fidalgo*. In

15th-century Portugal the term 'nobility' rarely appears, nor is it ever defined, other than in vague references to men who are 'well-born' or who are of *'boa linhagem'* – good lineage – or who through heredity or service were recognised as being 'noble'. Nevertheless, approximately one in ten of the population stood apart from the rest of society. They were the *fidalgos* – the sons of somebody (literally *filhos de algo*). The term *fidalgo* was not a title, rather it was a distinction which affirmed a certain privilege. But not all *fidalgos* were equal. Numbering no more than 50 families, the *grande nobreza* were the most privileged in the land, and they carried the title 'Dom', which was conferred by the King, before their names. They were the noblest men, who sat in the King's inner councils and in the Parliament (the *Cortes*) and had the King's ear. Next on the social scale were the *cavaleiros* (knights), followed by the *escudeiros* (squires), who were associated with the royal household and who aspired to a role in administration, or an appointment to a military post. Then there were the 'simple nobility' – the knights who owned little more than a horse, the judges, councillors and public servants – who 'lived nobly'. All nobles were considered vassals of the King, and all of them, from the high nobility to the simple nobility, were considered to belong to the company of *fidalgos*.

Since the whole essence of a *fidalgo* was that he was the son of 'someone', exactly who that someone was assumed critical importance. Quality of birth was more important than wealth and within the *fidalguia* (the community of *fidalgos*), those who were born into nobility were considered higher than those who attained that status through service to the King. In a society gripped by a collective frenzy of preserving and enhancing one's 'purity of blood', genealogical sleuthing became an obsession, as the names of new-borns were registered in a book so that they would not lose their social and political meaning. To aid families in registering their genealogical records, less scrupulous genealogists were plentiful, their quills ready to expand, elaborate and often simply to forge so as to allow a family to inherit a title of nobility that was not in fact theirs. This was not just a question of preening or of social climbing. For families, wealth, power and honour depended on who they were and where they stood socially, and so did abasement, disgrace and dishonour. It mattered, and it mattered greatly, otherwise why would the Counts of Pombeiro dispute in court, over generations, what they insisted was a genealogical error relating to an ancestor who had lived 300 years before? And why did André Amaral have to prove his great-great-grandfather had been a noble before he was permitted to add his coat of arms to the official *Livro do Rei d'Armas* in April 1515?

Royal proclamations of the late Middle Ages always addressed '*fidalgos, cavaleiros, escudeiros*', and Lopes belonged to the last category: an *escudeiro*, a squire. Initially, the squire's role was primarily to assist a knight, for example with his shield, hence the name in Portuguese (the Portuguese for shield is *escudo* and for squire *escudeiro*). However, by the time of Lopes the position of a squire was no longer simply viewed as a transitory or preparatory one and it had become established in its own right, entitling the holder to his own stable and retinue. Fernão Lopes may have been a squire, but he was not of noble blood. It was the privilege of the King to issue, on occasion, a charter to appoint squires who were not of noble birth. This was done largely for political purposes: to balance the power of the aristocracy and the feudal nobility who were forever challenging the King's authority. The opening formula used in most of the squire charters was 'We [the King] take [so and so] as squire, under our special guard and commendation'. Lopes was one of those squires, appointed by charter, and his status now qualified him to 'live nobly'. As a squire his name was registered in an 'Enrolment Book' which recognised his affiliation to the royal House and resulted in him receiving a *moradia*: a fixed amount paid by the King himself. This signalled that Lopes had become a servant of the King, with the first step in the social ladder being that of *Moço de Camara* – Chamber Boy – and it was under that designation that Lopes first appears in court records. Portuguese titles could grow increasingly complex and obtuse. There was for example the *Escudeiro Fidalgo* – Squire Gently Born – and the *Fidalgo Escudeiro* – Gently Born Squire – with the first title being considered as the higher grade, while the second was regarded as the lower. Lopes viewed himself, and more importantly he was viewed, as a *fidalgo*: and though the word technically means 'son of someone' with the assumed implication that this someone was a person of distinction, it was in many ways an informal label: a social group rather than a specific rank. Undoubtedly there existed a certain elasticity regarding who was a *fidalgo*, although a squire and a Dom were not on the same level, nor were those who were appointed squires (and hence *fidalgos*) considered to be the same as those born with noble blood. And yet it mattered greatly that he was recognised as a *fidalgo*. Indeed one can say it was all that mattered.

There existed a prevailing feeling that young nobles should be encouraged to pursue an education, and an ordinance dated 1500 stipulated that squires were not to receive their living allowance or *moradia* unless they had been given a note from their Master of Grammar, attesting to their attendance at lessons and their satisfactory progress therein. Consequently Lopes, who would have been in his early teens, was (one imagines to his consternation) put through the rigours of Latin grammar. He also studied classical works including Homer, Virgil, Ovid, Pliny and Cicero, and read the histories of great kings and leaders. In addition, he studied the Bible, astrology and planetary theory. It appears that the education of young nobles was undertaken by schools attached to the university, and by affiliates of the university who were attached to the royal chapel. This was not surprising, given the close proximity of the royal palace to the university. Lopes' thorough early education was in large measure attributable to the impact of print technology of the late 15th century. Whereas previously books were extremely expensive and difficult to obtain, now less wealthy nobles were afforded the opportunity of greater access to the written word. Printers made their money from mass production, printing editions of between 250 and 500 copies. One of the first printing presses in Portugal was set up in Lisbon where Valentim Fernandes and João Pedro de Cremona became primary printers for the Crown. Among their first printed works were books on grammar and breviaries or books of private prayer.

As a squire under the 'special guard and commendation' of the King – which effectively meant growing up under his tutelage and serving him – two career paths were open to Lopes: either a role in administration or an appointment to a military post. For Lopes, however, there was ultimately only one dream, and that was to become a knight. A knight exemplified honour, nobility and justice. For a young man of Lopes' time, a life of valour expressed on the battlefield was the one that counted, indeed the only one that mattered, and, as soon as he was appointed a squire, Lopes would have undergone rigorous military training. He was taught double-handed sword fencing, how to deliver fast and forceful blows, how to dodge and how to sidestep, above all how to block and strike at the same time. He also learned how to fight with a halberd, a pike fixed with an axe head. It was a formidable weapon, and Lopes would have had to train hard to handle it; how to thrust with the spike or smash with the hammer side or chop with the axe side, how to use the shaft to block, or even how to use it to unhook a rider. The training Lopes was subjected to was both fierce and thorough, for the Portuguese had acquired decades of battle experience. Since 1415, when João I had conquered Ceuta, they had fine-tuned their fighting skills in Morocco in a variety of ways, in small-scale skirmishes, siege warfare, sorties for plunder or the conquest of new cities. In many ways Morocco became the military schooling ground for the Portuguese, the place where the young and not so young nobility headed to practise and perfect the arts of war and combat.

There had been a time when knights derived their honour from hand-to-hand combat, and the cavalry charge was usually the most effective part of any battle. But that time was passing and the advent of gunpowder – whereby small firearms were largely replacing crossbows – was transforming traditional methods of warfare. However, as warfare changed, knights struggled to adapt, since for centuries they had been inculcated in the virtues of chivalry and taught to despise foot soldiers. The idea of killing someone from a distance appeared to the knight as cowardly and lacking in honour, but gradually they were forced to accept that these foot soldiers might replace them as the first arm in the field of battle. In other words, knights increasingly had to give up a way of life, and they did so with the utmost reluctance. Don Quixote is of course the most famous example of the desperate noble combatant who cannot accept that the world has changed. In a similar vein, Baldassare Castiglione, a contemporary of Lopes, wittily expressed the impact of these changes in a dialogue in *The Book of the Courtier*:

'But to come to specific details, I judge that the first and true profession of the courtier must be that of arms...'

'Well then,' the lady retorted, 'I should think that since you are not at war at the moment, and you are not engaged in fighting, it would be a good thing if you were to have yourself well-greased and stowed away in a cupboard with all your fighting equipment, so that you avoid getting rustier than you are already.'

As a squire Lopes was quick to discover that life at court did not come cheap. If he aspired to being a knight then military prowess would not have been enough: he also needed to dress well, serve a generous table and have a following. He needed to be literate and knowledgeable and he needed to be a patron to artists. There really was only one way he could afford all this: he needed to be as close to the King as possible to obtain patronage, and for that, a presence at court was vital, since a favourable position translated into both prestige and monetary rewards. In a court where there was a fine dividing line between the formal and the informal, being noticed by the King could lead to a rapid rise, and accordingly courtiers became more conscious of their outward image. Some curled their hair while others plucked their eyebrows. Some wore clothes made from velvet, satin and taffeta, while others adorned their clothing with jewels and precious stones. On one occasion when the King changed the style of his beard to a more modern French one, the barbers of Lisbon worked furiously as the whole court trimmed their beards overnight. But it was not just a matter of preening: being careless or negligent about one's clothing could lead to public censure from none other than the King. Elegant manners, fine clothes and witty conversations could not conceal the machinations of the calculating courtiers who kept a close eye on the King and a closer one on their rivals.

The court was an increasingly cultured place, with the King often being entertained by poets reciting songs whose roots lay in the Gallego-Portuguese tradition of troubadour poetry of the 12th and 13th centuries, and which were later collected in the *Cancioneiro Geral*. Every Sunday and on holy days the King listened to flutes, horns, harps, drums and fiddles. He also liked to listen to Moorish music while dining, and this was an occasion when squires like Lopes would be required to be present at court to dance. At court Lopes would have noted that Manuel had a demonstrable taste for Moorish things. Women and children sat not on chairs but on cushions, and Muslim dancers and musicians participated in court festivities. Muslim influence was also visible in the strict segregation of the living quarters of men and women, with spaces so strictly separated that men could not even pass by the threshold of women's apartments. Kingship in Portugal underwent a significant transformation during Manuel's rule. At first the steps were barely perceptible; the King's chair and his dining table were raised on a dais to set them apart. But it soon came to be that one could not be seated in the presence of the King nor retain one's hat when addressing him. Under Manuel the theatricality became more dramatic and pronounced; he was the first Portuguese King to be called 'Majesty', and when travelling he rode on horseback sheltered by a canopy of rich brocade. On special occasions, his cavalcade was accompanied by a range of his exotic animals: five elephants and a rhinoceros, as well as a Persian horse on which sat a hunting lynx.

It was thanks to Manuel that Lopes rose in society. We do not know how the young Lopes came to royal attention but from the moment of his proclamation as a squire, he owed his career to the royal House. He also owed the House his loyalty and fealty, for he was directly paid, promoted and honoured by the King. It was Manuel who was responsible for Lopes' education, for his upkeep, for his armour. It was normal for the King to bless marriages and though we have no record of it, we can assume that he would have blessed Lopes' marriage in Lisbon. In addition, it was the King of Portugal who would later send Lopes to India as an officer in his pay. The King more than anyone had seen how bloody the internecine struggles between the nobility could be, and he needed nobles who were loyal to him. Since Lopes was not originally of noble birth, his elevation to the nobility was based purely and solely on Manuel's prerogative. In return Manuel expected loyalty and obeisance from his squires. It was a bond they dared not break.

As the 15th century came to a close, the situation in Portugal was as stark as it was simple: the borders with Castile had been set, the Muslims had been expelled and there were no wars to be fought. If the King did not make war, then it followed that he could not grant the nobles lands, jobs or rents that matched their honourable status. Consequently many noblemen began to look elsewhere to prove their military capabilities and gain promotions and honour. Even though it was not fitting for noblemen to trade, doing it in the name of the King and dealing with a Crown monopoly was another matter. Many noblemen increasingly acted as factors – agents overseeing the sale of goods overseas – and were employed as administrative and trade officers. As noblemen began to head to the new settlements in the islands the Portuguese had discovered, they began to acquire land, and what had been impossible in the old kingdom now became possible abroad. Profits were to be made from the gold, slaves and ivory from the Guinea coast, from the sugar cane plantations in the Cape Verde Islands, and from the grain of Morocco. Service in North Africa could also be seen as a penance, an act of self-punishment which could help restore the blemished reputation of a nobleman. In 1513, Dom Jaime, Duke of Braganza, killed his wife, whom he erroneously believed to be unfaithful. Overwhelmed by remorse and in search of a deed as reparation for his guilt, the Duke personally raised an army of more than 4,000 troops to lead into the city of Azemmour. After all, what greater reparation could there be than fighting the Muslims?

As far as the King was concerned, external adventure and warfare were excellent ways to distract the nobility and provide them with a vehicle for social mobility, while still retaining their loyalty to the Crown. Overseas adventure gave the nobility a chance to live a life they could never otherwise have imagined and to obtain a social status they would never have achieved had they remained in Portugal. Above all it was the minor nobility (with whom Fernão Lopes identified) who sought to prove their military capabilities, win honour and acquire new properties or rents. Very few of the higher nobility, or at least the first sons, left Portugal.

Instead it was the lower nobility, the squires and the knights, who captained the ships: they were the warrior group of the crews, they were also the administrative and trade officers. Above all they were the ones who strove to show their capacity to serve the Crown as warriors. They were the young nobles. Their time had come.

CHAPTER THREE

The Lost Boys of Portugal

A king needs a queen, and since it was the custom for kings of Portugal to wed Castilian princesses, Manuel began negotiations for his marriage to the daughter of Ferdinand and Isabella, the Catholic monarchs of Castile. They, however, refused to countenance any proposal until Manuel followed their example and rid Portugal of its Jews. That was the price Manuel had to pay to secure this alliance and what followed is one of the most shameful and controversial episodes in Portugal's history. By and large, the Jews of Portugal, spread across the kingdom, from the border with Galicia in the North to the towns of the Algarve in the South, lived in *judiarias* (Jewish quarters) which had their own butchers, hospitals, schools, bathhouses and in some cases even brothels and prisons. Although all Jews were ordered to wear a distinctive red symbol on their clothing or a yellow symbol on their hats, their freedom to practise their faith was protected: they were governed by their own rabbis and magistrates, and forced conversions to Catholicism were expressly forbidden. In fact the free practice of Judaism (and of Islam) was not merely recognised, but also guaranteed by law. Thus, the first collection of codified Portuguese laws, the *Ordenações Afonsinas*, proclaimed by King

Afonso V in the mid-15th century, outlawed the forced conversion of Jews to Christianity. Jews had a virtual monopoly on financial operations such as the collection of state and seigneurial revenues and the administration of customs and excise. Nearly all the royal treasurers were Jews, as were the royal bankers, as were almost all the court physicians. The Jews were also learned: the first book printed in Portugal was the Hebrew Pentateuch and of the first fifteen books printed in Portugal twelve were Hebrew religious classics printed by Jews for a Jewish audience. The fact was, Portugal was a safe haven to which the Jews of Spain had been flocking in droves, especially after anti-Jewish riots had broken out in Seville in 1391 and spread across the Iberian Peninsula, leading to the massacre of thousands of Jews and the forced conversion of many more thousands. A century later, in 1492, with the Spanish Edict of Expulsion, which gave Jews four months to convert or depart, they once again fled to Portugal.

Nevertheless Ferdinand and Isabella were adamant; if Manuel wished to marry their daughter then the expulsion of the Jews was the price to pay for this alliance. Consequently in December 1496 the Portuguese Edict of Expulsion was proclaimed. It seemed a draconian measure, but most historians do not believe that Manuel intended to expel Portugal's Jews. In the words of a contemporary writer, 'When the King heard of their intention to depart, he feared that the kingdom would remain like an empty fishing net, for the Jews were extremely numerous, and they possessed most of the kingdom's wealth'. Certainly within a few days of the Edict, the King forbade any departure from the realm unless on ships under his command, and since no ships were provided, there was effectively no expulsion. However, that did not mean that the King did not have other plans. The first indication that Manuel intended to force the Jews into converting emerged when a decree was issued ordering the confiscation of all their books. One of the rabbis who lost his library was

Abraham Saba and the personal account he penned remains poignant:

> the crier went all about the country declaring that all the books must be brought to the Great Synagogue in Lisbon on pain of death. And they already took one Jew who loved his books and beat him severely with straps ... As I listened, I stood trembling, walking on with trepidation and fright, and I dug into the middle of a large olive tree which had extensive roots in the ground, and there I hid these books which I had written.

The vast majority of books seized by the Crown were publicly incinerated but it was the extraordinary fate of some of them to end up as far away as India. In 1505, Francisco Pinheiro obtained royal permission to sell a chest full of Hebrew books, seized from synagogues, to the Jewish communities residing in Cochin.

The confiscation of the books was a harsh blow for the Jews of Portugal but much worse was to follow, and in early 1497 Manuel took a step which landed on them like a hammer blow. In a decree biblical in tone and scale, he ordered that all Jews under the age of fourteen be taken from their parents and distributed across the land where they would be brought up as Christians. Within a few months, as stated, chillingly, by a municipal charter of the time, 'the Jews had been taken'. Records were kept, and though the vast majority of documents was destroyed in the Lisbon earthquake of 1755, we are afforded a glimpse of the human tragedy which Manuel's decree led to:

> Isaac de Ru and his wife Velide lost their son Jacob who was aged 8 and was given to Bartolomeu Afonso.
> Santo Fidalgo and his wife Araboa lost Abraham (8) and his sister Reina (2). They were given the names Goncales Dias and Gracias Dias and were brought up by an Old Christian.

Still Manuel of Portugal was not satisfied. By October 1497, he decreed that all Jewish adults had to convert, even if it meant priests throwing holy water over them. Within a few days the entire Jewish population of Portugal had been 'converted' and there were officially no longer any Jews in Portugal. Henceforth a Jew was a *Crista-Nova* (New Christian) and Manuel authorised that certain names hitherto used exclusively by noble families could be given to converted Jews. 'It pleases us that in all things [the New Christians] be considered, favoured and treated like the Old Christians and not distinct and separate from them in any matter'; so declared Manuel, and so a new life commenced for the Jews, with newly assumed names and with no legal distinctions made between Old and New Christians. To assist the process of assimilation, New Christians were forced to marry into Old Christian families, meaning no more segregation. It also meant the same food, the same clothing and the celebration of the same holidays. Manuel was true to his word and a further law declared that New Christians were not only allowed to keep all their goods, which were now exempted from the heavy taxes they had had to pay when they were still Jews, but by force of law all the educational opportunities, all the positions until then reserved for Christians were now open to them. What this meant was that in Portugal after 1497 a class of New Christian physicians, apothecaries, pharmacists, scribes and merchants arose and integrated themselves into the bosom of Christian society.

It was not just the Jews who suffered persecution under Manuel, for the December 1496 Edict of Expulsion was aimed equally at Portugal's Muslims. If the Jews endured great hardship at the hands of the Portuguese, it was less severe than the suffering inflicted upon the followers of Muhammad. Yet even today the expulsion of the Muslims from Portugal remains a perplexing affair. It was certainly unprecedented, since in the Iberian Peninsula, in Castile, in Navarre and in Aragon, the Muslims continued to live under Christian rule. When in the 1260s Alfonso X had expelled Muslims from Murcia and Andalucia, he had only targeted those who had rebelled, leaving those in other parts of his realm, such as Toledo, largely untouched. In any case his actions were determined by rebellion, whereas in the strange case of Manuel and the Muslims there was no insurrection or any provocation. It was the first time that a Christian ruler simply ordered all the Muslim subjects of his realm to leave. Unlike the Jews no Muslim children were taken from their parents and baptised. But then again the Jews were different from the Muslims. Jews may have been viewed as pariahs in Manuel's Catholic kingdom but they were useful pariahs who could be tolerated. They may have posed a theological threat but the Catholic Portuguese could by and large marginalise them. With the Muslims it was different. With the Muslims the Portuguese, and Manuel in particular, had an old score to settle.

There had been a time when all of Portugal had been under Arab rule. Although today there is some fleeting evidence of Muslim rule in Portugal, for hundreds of years Islam was at the heart of the land and the call to prayer echoed from north to south. Arabic was the language of government, spoken not just by the Muslims but by all the other communities, including the Christians who became known as Mozarabs. For the Catholic Portuguese kings, the 'athletes of Christ', the *Reconquista*, which in fits and starts ran from the aftermath of the Islamic conquests in the mid-8th century until 1492, was as much of a Holy Crusade as the liberation of Jerusalem. No greater praise could be bestowed upon a monarch than that he liberated Christian land from the Arabs and Moors, and one reads with increasing frequency in medieval chronicles the laudatory phrase: *recuperate fuit Hispania* – Spain was recovered. 'We seek only our lands which you conquered from us in times past at the beginning of your history', wrote Fernando I to the Muslims. 'So go to your own side of the

Strait [of Gibraltar] and leave our lands to us, for no good will come to you from dwelling here with us after today. For we shall not hold back from you until God decides between us.'

Characterised by a slow and intermittent advance from one river frontier to the next and accompanied by the repopulation of the people, the *Reconquista* was a war of both territorial aggrandisement and religious confrontation. Although today the term crusade has come to refer to the efforts to liberate the Holy Land from the Muslims, it also once applied to the Iberian Peninsula. Perhaps more accurately one can call the wars in Spain and Portugal substitute crusades. Knights unable to travel to Palestine were able to gain a dispensation from the Pope to fight instead in the Iberian Peninsula. The main purpose was not to convert the Muslims but to drive them out, in the words of a medieval chronicler, 'to expel the barbarians'. Though it is only natural to speak of the persecution of the Jews and Muslims in the reign of Manuel in one breath, in reality an important distinction separated the sad fates of the two faiths. The distinction is chillingly clarified in an original document detailing the compensation received by the dowager Queen Leonor in return for the income she lost in 1497, which states that her loss occurred 'because of the conversion of the Jews and the expulsion of the Muslims from our realms'. Different fates: for one conversion, for the other expulsion. It remains nevertheless an intriguing question: why were the fates different? One could argue that by forcefully converting the Jews, Manuel had cleverly appeased Ferdinand and Isabella while retaining the Jews' undoubted trading and professional skills within Portugal. But why then had he not pursued the same path with the Muslims? Why did he insist on driving them out of Portugal? This is a complex question to which one can only hazard a guess. Manuel knew that the number of Muslims was small and that they posed no threat to his kingdom. By expelling them he could boost his image among the Christian kings as a crusading king. He probably also reckoned that, had he forced the Muslims to convert, he would have faced a backlash from the Muslim sultanates which lay just across the Strait. The Jews, however, possessed no such hinterland.

Manuel granted all the communal buildings and property of the Muslims of Lisbon to the Hospital of All Saints, which in turn was quick to make a profit by leasing them out privately. As for the main mosque of Lisbon, it was leased out to a Garcia Fernandes. Not even cemeteries were spared; in 1497 the King granted the Muslim cemetery of Lisbon to the municipal authorities to use as a pasture for animals. Henceforth any Muslim merchant passing via a Portuguese port needed to wear distinctive clothing so as not to be arrested.

It took 200 years, culminating in 1492, to push the last of the Muslims back into North Africa, and the frontiers between Christianity and Islam gradually moved southward to the Mediterranean Sea, leaping across to the sands of North Africa and down the coast of West Africa before reappearing in the Indian Ocean. While in other regions of Western Europe the concept of the crusades had faded and Islam was a distant menace, to the people of the Iberian Peninsula (and for Manuel in particular), separated from the Muslim hinterland by no more than the Strait of Gibraltar, it continued to burn fiercely. Papal blessings continued to fan the flames and in return for the services they rendered to God, the King of Portugal and his successors were given a monopolistic charter to rule all new territories as their own, as well as the right to conduct exclusive trade with the inhabitants. For Manuel the spirit of the *Reconquista* had not abated, and an obsession with the crusade against Islam was a constant cornerstone of his reign, culminating in grandiose plans for an international crusade to 'liberate' Jerusalem and the Holy Land. Crusading, however, was an expensive enterprise which his nobles could ill afford.

The King had not forgotten the exciting possibilities that the rounding of the Cape of Good Hope had promised, and he now turned his attention to the route to India. In his mind faith and profit, religion and trade complemented one another. To a large extent Manuel was different from the other kings of Portugal. Like them he was aware of the riches that the Indian trade would afford to Lisbon and the profits that his merchants would make. Why should the Venetians profit when he could? Why should Lisbon not be the new Venice? And yet for Manuel the religious motivation of finding a route to India shone just as brightly. For him, and for a few in his court, the route to India was nothing less than the launch of a new crusade, one which aimed to win souls and ultimately to restore Jerusalem to the Christian fold. While some in Lisbon, aware of the dominance of the Ottomans, regarded Manuel's vision as a kind of apocalyptic folly, for the King it remained embedded at the core of his beliefs. 'If there were no merchants to go to seek earthly pleasures in the East', asked a priest at the turn of the 15th century, 'who would transport thither the preachers who take the heavenly treasures? The preachers take the Gospel and the merchants take the preachers.' Manuel was clear about the objectives of his expeditions: 'the principal motive of this enterprise', he wrote to the King and Queen of Castile, 'has been the service of God our Lord and our own advantage'. However, at the court in Lisbon there was apprehension; the enterprise to reach India from the Cape of Good Hope was too risky. Such a venture was sure to alienate the Venetians, who acted as Mediterranean middlemen in the lucrative trade (conducted mostly by camel caravans) transporting the spices and luxury products of India, China and the Far East to Europe. Any Portuguese attempt to circumvent the traditional trade route was sure to be resisted fiercely, and similarly, encroachment on the Red Sea, which acted as a transit route linking the Indian Ocean to the Mediterranean, was certain to meet military resistance by the Mamluk Sultan who jealously guarded access to it. Portugal, Manuel's advisors argued, was too small in population and militarily too weak to undertake such a venture. Manuel, aged 26, listened to the objections of those gathered in the council but was not convinced: 'I have inherited from my predecessors a sacred mission', he informed them, and he eventually got his way.

The command of the fleet was entrusted to Vasco da Gama, a Portuguese nobleman in his late 30s. Born about 1460, little is known about his early life. We know that his father, Estêvão, was an explorer and that Vasco learned to navigate in the navy, which he joined as soon as he was old enough. In 1492 he was dispatched to the south of Lisbon and then to the Algarve region to seize French ships as an act of vengeance against the French government for disrupting Portuguese shipping. Little else is known for certain, other than that he was the man chosen by King Manuel to find a maritime route to the East via the Cape of Good Hope. In so doing he would become the first person to sail directly from Europe to India. Thanks to Bartolomeu Dias, da Gama had new, and better, maritime technology at his disposal. Dias had recommended alterations to the Portuguese vessels he had sailed on a few years earlier when he first rounded the Cape, so as to allow larger cargo capacities and higher freeboards (the distance from the waterline to the upper deck level). It was imperative, Dias told the shipbuilders, that the vessel stood higher in the water while still being able to navigate along the coasts. Listening carefully, the shipwrights devised stouter, roomier craft with more hull capacity and crew quarters. The result was the Portuguese *nau*, with which they would build an empire.

On 7 July 1497 Vasco da Gama departed Lisbon with a crew of 148 men, sailing first to the Cape Verde Islands. From there, the ships travelled along the African coast, avoiding treacherous winds and currents where possible, bearing south-westward until they came within 600 miles of the South American mainland, then turning to the south-east and gradually beating back against the trade winds. By this stage da Gama had sailed 4,500 miles from the Cape Verde Islands without sighting land. Finally on 22 November, the fleet rounded the Cape of Good Hope. Battling scurvy, weathering harsh storms and making multiple stops along the way, da Gama and his crew at last reached the Island of Mozambique (off the coast of present day Mozambique) on 2 March 1498. Their reception was initially cordial, because the Arabs in Mozambique thought the European voyagers were actually Muslims. Da Gama knew that he could not reach Calicut (Kozhicode, in southern India) without an experienced pilot who could navigate the waters. He was therefore glad when the Sultan of Mozambique supplied him with two pilots, although one of them deserted when he discovered that the Portuguese were Christians.

One month later, in Malindi, in modern day Kenya, da Gama finally found an able Arab pilot who could take him to his destination. After an epic voyage of more than 12,000 miles, he and his men at last reached Calicut. This was the most important trading centre of southern India, and Calicut had attained a position of eminence in the trade of pepper and other spices including cardamom, sandalwood, arrack, nuts and coconut oil. With its secure harbour, it attracted the attention of merchants, traders, businessmen, mariners, adventurers and religious missionaries from various far-off lands. In 1342 the Muslim North African traveller Ibn Battuta noted that there were merchants from all parts of the world there, and at the beginning of the 15th century the Chinese Muslim traveller Mahuan remarked on the large presence of Arabs and Chinese, noting that what he called Ku-Li-Fo was the 'most important of all the maritime centres of trade'. Calicut was not an alien place to da Gama, who was already familiar with it from the descriptions of Nicolò de Conti, a Venetian who had visited in 1444 and described it as a 'a notable emporium for all

India'. Nevertheless the Portuguese were dumbstruck by the opulence they encountered. Called to an audience with the Zamorin
– the Hindu ruler of Calicut – da Gama presented his gifts: a
bale of sugar, two barrels of butter and one of honey as well as a
dozen coats and six hats, only to be met with dismissive laughter.
Even the poorest pilgrim, he was told, had more to offer. It was
clear what the Zamorin wanted: 'in my land there is much cinna-
mon, and much cloves and ginger and pepper and many precious
stones. And what I want from your land is gold and silver, coral
and scarlet.'

His vessels laden with spices gifted from the Zamorin to King
Manuel to sell in Lisbon, Vasco da Gama returned from Calicut
with a cargo worth 60 times what he had brought with him. Four
years later, in 1502, he returned to India. This time, however,
da Gama was at the head of a flotilla of 25 ships armed with the
most powerful cannons in the Portuguese inventory. Now his, and
his King's, intention was not simply to trade but to subdue, for
it had become clear that the Muslim merchants and rulers were
hostile to the arrival of the Portuguese on the scene. Da Gama,
on this journey, bombarded the city-states all along the East
African coast. Sailing to India, his fleet robbed a ship and the
Portuguese were delighted to discover booty of 30,000 *cruzados*,
the equivalent to a tenth of the annual income of the Portuguese
Crown. Da Gama's tactics were very effective, and further ships
were robbed and their crews mutilated – but he had not forgotten his crusading roots. As a young man he had been inducted
into the Order of Santiago, with its monkish white habit with
an embroidered red cross. The military-religious order had been
founded in about 1160 for the purpose of fighting Muslims and
the crusading zeal continued to burn fiercely in the hearts of its
knights. So when da Gama encountered a ship carrying over 700
pilgrims returning from Mecca to India, he did not show them
any mercy. Disregarding the plaintive pilgrims' pleas, da Gama

removed the goods on board, and burned the ship with all of its occupants, women and children included. A contemporary Portuguese source noted, 'All night long the poor unhappy Moors called on Muhammad to help them, but the dead can neither hear nor succour their votaries.' Manuel's crusade had reached the Indian Ocean.

CHAPTER FOUR

Waiting in Belém

On 6 April 1506, Fernão Lopes set sail from Portugal for India. He would not return to his native land for 24 years. It was barely eight years since the discoveries of Vasco da Gama's initial expedition had sent Lisbon into a state of frenzied excitement, after which other fleets had rapidly followed, dispatched by Manuel who now afforded himself the title of 'King of Portugal, Lord of Guinea, and Lord of the Conquest, Navigation and Commerce of Ethiopia, Arabia, Persia and India'. It was a remarkable title, one full of pomp and grandeur, but its most remarkable aspect was the fact that when the King proclaimed it he possessed no land at all in Ethiopia, Arabia, Persia or India. Evidently this title was meant to reflect a theoretical ideal, rather than being a realistic description of his authority, but it was certainly one befitting his messianic vision.

It soon became the Portuguese dream to travel to India. In his twenties, eager for adventure and wealth, having set sail Lopes would have felt that he was fulfilling his life's ambition. Although some *fidalgos*, motivated by an anti-Muslim zeal, were eager to bring the spirit of the crusades to the Indian Ocean, the majority were driven more by the desire for honour on the battlefield and the prospect of knighthood. But there was also trade to be had and wealth to be made. Certainly the names of their potential destinations, endlessly discussed in Lisbon, were as exotic as they were alluring: Sofala – where the source of East African gold could be found; Hormuz – the key to the Central Asian markets; Diu – where Gujarati cotton and silk textile were traded; Cochin – with its access to Malabar pepper; and Goa – the link in the maritime trade between the Deccan sultanates and the Middle East.

Aboard the fifteen-ship fleet which made up the Portuguese armada that set sail in 1506, two towering figures dominated the scene. The commander-in-chief of the fleet was Tristão da Cunha, a prominent *fidalgo* and a man trusted by King Manuel, who two years earlier had nominated him as the first Viceroy of Portuguese India. Intriguingly, the records show that, on the eve of his sailing, da Cunha had fallen ill with 'giddiness in the head whereby he finally became blind'. The blindness however was clearly a temporary blight, for da Cunha would sail to India, and go on to have a distinguished career history. Many years later, upon his return to Portugal, he was sent by Manuel as ambassador to Pope Leo X to present the new conquests of the Portuguese Empire. Determined to make an impact, Manuel instructed da Cunha to impress the Pope, which the Portuguese adventurer certainly did. He instructed his embassy of 140 to dress in Indian style, and in his procession he brought 43 different types of animals, including rare Indian horses, leopards, a black panther, some parrots and turkeys. At the heart of the procession and as a gift to the Pope, da Cunha led an elephant whom he named Hanno. On Hanno's back, da Cunha placed a silver castle containing a safe in which were pearls and gems, and gold coins minted for the occasion. The Pope could not fail to be impressed, and received the procession in the Castel Sant'Angelo, a mausoleum once constructed by the Emperor Hadrian which had been converted into a Papal fortress. Da Cunha was a man who clearly possessed a sense of humour and, according to an account written by his secretary Garcia de Resende, he now instructed Hanno, named with irreverence after the great Hannibal, to kneel down in front of the Pope. Then da Cunha instructed Hanno to spray the crowd and the cardinals (although not the Pope) with water from his trunk. The practice of elephants spraying people with water as a public spectacle was, it seems, common, for Lopes himself would witness a similar scene in Lisbon.

This was Tristão da Cunha, the commander of the fleet and the man tasked by Manuel to ensure its safe arrival in India. By da Cunha's side on this journey was his cousin, the formidable Afonso de Albuquerque, who would command a squadron of five vessels and who would one day have a devastating and terrible impact on Lopes. Manuel instructed da Cunha that, if the fleet was unable to make India before winter, it should take shelter on the island of Socotra off the southern coast of Arabia. Manuel instructed da Cunha to construct a fortress for the Christians who were thought to reside there, but above all he was to secure the island as both a winter base for future Portuguese fleets and a means to disrupt Arab trade with India. Tradition held that the inhabitants of Socotra had been converted by Saint Thomas the Apostle, who was once shipwrecked on the island, and that while his ship was repaired he taught Christianity to the local pagan tribes. After that the only contact with the island was via a few Arab traders and ship captains. In the 4th century, there is an account of missionaries arriving in Yemen from Socotra, suggesting the presence of Christians on the island, and in the 10th century, the Arab geographer Abu Zaid Hasan wrote that the majority of the inhabitants were Christian. The island was visited by Marco Polo, who also claimed that its people were Christian and that they had an Archbishop who was loyal to a Major Archbishop in Iraq; this led to many scholars believing that the Socotrans were Nestorian. Marco Polo also claimed that the inhabitants of the island had the power to control the wind. He wrote:

> These Christians are the most expert enchanters in the world. The Archbishop forbids and even punishes this practice, but without avail ... for instance if a ship is proceeding full sail with a favourable wind, they raise a contrary one, and oblige it to return.

Others recorded that the Socotrans protected themselves by using enchantments and spells to make the island disappear. On the island grew the dragon's blood tree, a mushroom-shaped growth about fifteen feet tall, with leaves spiky and green. It was born, according to legend, from the blood which was shed in a battle between an elephant and a dragon. Whether Socotra really had Christians on the island is, however, open to question, since when da Gama's fleet reached the island there was no sign of any Christian inhabitants, not even a church.

Fernão Lopes would have made his way to Belém at the mouth of the river Tagus in the late winter days of 1506. It was from there that the Portuguese fleet would set sail in a convoy system called the *Carreira da India*. The Portuguese had already learned that the fleet needed to depart Lisbon in late March or early April in order to round the Cape of Good Hope and reach Malabar by the end of September. The return voyage to Portugal, which also took around five months, began in late December or early January, arriving at Lisbon in June. This schedule had to be adhered to as much as possible as it was dictated by Indian Ocean weather patterns, and it was well known that between May and early September the south-west monsoons closed traffic to the harbours on the West coast of India. Of what lay ahead, of what the fabled lands of India were really like, Lopes cannot have had any real idea, and if it was understood by him it would have been in almost completely mythical terms. But he could have been under no illusion that the voyage was one of tremendous hardship. Enough people had suffered on that journey before for him not to realise this. Like all Lisboetas, he would have been horrified and fascinated by the story passed around the city that, on his return voyage from India in 1503, da Gama and his crew had had to resort to eating the ships' cats and dogs to survive. It was without any doubt a hard voyage; 'so hard', a contemporary had written, 'that you will run out of tears before you run out of reasons for shedding them'. Gonsalo de Silveira, a Portuguese Jesuit missionary who himself endured the voyage, noted that it was very much a journey to the unknown,

> as one cannot draw or paint a picture of death when a person dies, as only a person attending the dying could have an idea of it … In the same way one cannot say anything of the people sailing from Portugal to India nor could we understand; only the people who sail know about it.

It was a journey of immense, almost suicidal danger. Between 1497 and 1612, 806 ships left Lisbon bound for India and only 420 returned. Heavily loaded, they could not withstand the storms and their notorious structural defects were ill-suited to the sudden change in natural phenomena like winds and currents. Consequently, ships were often only good for one or two trips. The mortality rates were horrendous: in the early years of the India crossing one in every two who travelled died during the journey. Since an average ship carried around 600 crew that meant that, per ship, around 300 perished somewhere between Lisbon and India. The stark figures, recorded in the Portuguese logs, make for sombre reading. During his second voyage to India, Vasco da Gama lost half his crew. In the fleet commanded by Nuno da Cunha in 1528 over 200 died from fever, and in the fleet commanded by António de Noronha in 1571, 2,000 of the 4,000 souls who set sail perished on the way. Disease was the most common form of death: there was no obligation to maintain cleanliness on board and sick people were left wallowing in their own filth. Every ship did include one surgeon, although one wonders what he could possibly do. The three measures for treatment were bleeding, enema and trust in the mercy of God. Despite this, Lopes was among those prepared to make the sacrifices to voyage to India. By and large it was the second sons of the higher nobility and those from the lower nobility who embarked on this journey. The first sons and those who belonged to the highest nobility rarely ventured to India. This was partly due to the dangers involved, but also because they didn't need to. As a squire and the servant of the Crown, Lopes was being dispatched to India by the King himself, who was paying his salary and to whom he owed his advancement. Like many others, he was also leaving his wife and a young son behind – Lopes knew that India was a means to an end. After a few years overseas he could expect to return to Lisbon to be appointed to a position of command from which to further his career. This was the natural path for those who served the King. A typical example was that of one of Lopes' contemporaries, Duarte Coelho Pereira, who in 1509 voyaged to India and from there to China. He then returned to Portugal, where he was appointed ambassador to the French court, and was afterwards given a hereditary land grant by the King. As he waited for the fleet to gather, Lopes would have known that he was one of the fortunate few. Already many had left Portugal in search of fortune, and few had realised these dreams. The rest had died far from their places of birth, in places they had never thought existed.

In many ways Lopes was a symbol of the new vibrant Portugal which was emerging. Bartolomeu Dias and Vasco da Gama had heralded in a new and glorious age thanks to the empirical sciences of celestial navigation and cartography. They had demonstrated that no serpents lurked under the ocean, and no boiling waters awaited sailors who crossed the equator. Now young and ambitious Portuguese followed in their wake, hungry for fortune and adventure, armed with an indestructible optimism and the certainty that a new Portuguese age was dawning. They felt that they were the servants of God, chosen to undertake a divine mission and prepared to suffer its purifying consequences. It was both recognised and acknowledged that there would be suffering during the voyage, but this was tempered by the consolation of knowing that God had anointed the Portuguese as his new chosen people, the heirs to the covenant with Abraham. Yet despite the promised riches which lay ahead, Lopes would not have been able to shake off a sense of foreboding that in this heavenly Kingdom of Portugal all was not as it should be. To add to this foreboding, the plague had returned to Lisbon, and, for those who read signs in such things, this created a sense of disquiet and of an approaching storm.

Meanwhile in Belém, as the armada gathered slowly, Tristão da Cunha fretted. The news reaching him was alarming, for it seemed that the sleeping Muslim giant had awakened. The Portuguese atrocities against the Muslim pilgrims had not gone unnoticed and the Mamluk Sultan had written angrily to the Pope threatening reprisals against Christian pilgrims in return. A worried Pope Julius II had consequently forwarded the Sultan's letter to Manuel. The Sultan's concerns were equally pragmatic, for the Portuguese activities were threatening his revenues and the commercial prosperity of Cairo, and if he was concerned then so too were the Venetians who dominated the inland trading route. Things had changed too quickly for their liking. In 1498 there was so much pepper available in the markets of Alexandria that the Venetians could not raise enough money to buy it all. Just four years later, in 1502, there was not enough pepper to load their ships and they were forced to reduce the number of galleys in their merchant fleet from thirteen to three. This situation could not continue, and Venetian embassies to Cairo urged military action against the Portuguese, promising arms and men for the cause. Benedetto Sanuto, the Venetian envoy, badgered the Sultan on 'how important it was for his affairs that the spices should not make their way by the route to Portugal'. The Sultan as a result began to construct a fleet of twelve ships manned by 900 'Mamluks and Venetians, and Turks', whose task was to impose order on the increasingly chaotic conditions in the Red Sea. By August this fleet had reached Jeddah, the principal port linked to Mecca, and by 1507, it had entered the Indian Ocean. In reply and to counter the perceived Muslim threat, King Manuel decided to establish a permanent Portuguese presence in India – what was to become known as *Estado da Índia*. Manuel's decision was a truly remarkable one. The most striking aspect of this whole endeavour was that it was conceived as a royal enterprise. All those who went east – from the Viceroy down – were servants of the Crown. All payments and all commercial activities had to be accounted for in Lisbon and detailed records had to be kept of every item, ranging from the salaries paid to soldiers to the purchase of pepper and even the ceremonial furniture provided for the churches. It was effectively a militarised state paid for by royal bureaucracy, and it was as ambitious as it was extraordinary. Portugal, an impoverished and isolated country desolately clinging on to the Atlantic shore, was attempting not just to create a state several thousand miles away but to impose its will on distant, rich and populous kingdoms. And if that were not enough Portugal was claiming dominion over the sea all the way to India. Although the seas were theoretically open to all (according to the Papal bulls that legitimised the Portuguese missions) this only applied to Europeans and Christians, who were governed by Roman law – Muslims were excluded from such legislation.

For Manuel, the war might need to be fought at sea but its

ultimate triumph would be on land. He knew that, as well as being strategically important, their access to the Indian Ocean via the Cape of Good Hope was a source of tremendous pride for the Portuguese. But he also understood that it was neither faster nor cheaper than the traditional and superior transit routes through the Red Sea and the Persian Gulf, and could not replace them. By establishing a blockade of the Red Sea he hoped to deal a devastating blow to the Mamluks, which would allow him to launch an invasion of the mainland, seize control of Cairo and Alexandria, and ultimately liberate Jerusalem. On occasion Albuquerque had even boasted to him about the possibility of seizing Mecca itself. A Portuguese blockade of travel to and from the Red Sea however could not fail to inflame religious feeling in Muslim lands, since these were the traditional maritime routes used by Muslim pilgrims on their way to Mecca to perform the *hajj* – a mandatory ceremony for all adult Muslims. Since Mamluk (and later Ottoman) sovereignty in the region was based on the title of 'Defender of the Holy Cities', this meant that protect-ing Jeddah and the Holy Cities from Portuguese incursions and keeping the sea-lanes safe for Muslim pilgrims and traders was a religious duty. The Portuguese King's claim that he was 'the ath-lete of Christ' was now mirrored by the Muslim Caliph's claim that he was the 'Protector of the Holy Cities'. The Ottomans who brought Mamluk rule to an end in 1516 knew that geography favoured them, as they controlled the shortest and most direct routes to the Indian Ocean, ones that did not require naval block-ades, coastal patrols and garrisoned strongholds. This was a critical advantage, since what is favoured by geography is also favoured by the market. As the mid-17th-century English author Paul Rycaut lamented, 'God hath given the sea to the Christians and the land to the Muslims.'

In 1505, when da Cunha had been temporarily incapacitated by blindness, Manuel had appointed Francisco de Almeida as

Viceroy of India for a period of three years, and dispatched him with 21 ships to establish fortresses at key locations. Above all, Almeida was to deny Muslim shipping access to the Red Sea. Manuel insisted that this was 'so that they are not able to carry any spices to the territory of the [Mamluk] Sultan and everyone in India would lose the illusion of being able to trade with anyone but us'. Almeida, known as 'the Great Dom Francisco', had a distinguished military past and had fought at the siege of Granada, which ended in 1492 with the expulsion of the Muslims. Now he brought with him to the Indian Ocean the uncompromising attitude and the intractable hatred for Islam of the Christian *Reconquista*.

With the threat contained in the Sultan's letter to the Pope a constant presence, as da Cunha, now recovered from his temporary illness, waited for his armada to gather in Belém in the last days of March 1506, he had another reason to be worried. The ships with their massive triangular sails, on which white crosses with crimson edges had been sewn, certainly looked impressive, but the fifteen of them that were to make up his fleet were expected to carry 1,200 men and as things stood he was considerably short of that number. The armada should have set sail in February to catch the winds but with April approaching, the ships remained in Belém. Da Cunha was content with the *fidalgos* who had joined up and been assigned their responsibilities (among them Fernão Lopes, who was appointed as an officer) but it was the rest – the commoners and the soldiers – who alarmed him. Most of them were rural peasants and their navigational skills left a lot to be desired. Many did not know how to tell the difference between port and starboard and, dreaming of India, they appeared oblivious of the length of the journey and the hardships that it would entail. A priest, watching an India-bound ship setting sail, noted with astonishment the careless way that 'many embark as if they were going no further than a league from Lisbon, taking with them only a shirt and two loaves in hand and carrying a cheese and a jar of marmalade without any other kind of provision'. To make matters worse, the plague had broken out in Lisbon and da Cunha knew that this would make it even harder to find crew who were prepared to sail with seamen from that city. Already the plague had killed thousands, and the King had fled the city and taken residence in Abrantes, further up the Tagus. From there, Manuel had sent da Cunha a flag. Made of white satin, it had a prominent crimson cross, also in satin, in the centre. The flag was to be flown on da Cunha's ship, which was equipped with a banner of the Holy Relics to be displayed when the ship hit a storm. Da Cunha was not prepared to take any chances and when the armada passed through a severe storm he would request that the on-board Chaplain display the holy picture of the Virgin Mary on deck.

In the meantime, as crew were rounded up, da Cunha busied himself by stocking his ship, the *São Tiago*, with private trading goods which he intended to sell in India. Vasco da Gama had demonstrated that there were great riches to be had there and that the use of force was an effective tool in acquiring them. He had returned to Portugal in 1503, having amassed one of the largest fortunes in the country within one year. Some said it was as much as 40,000 *ducats*, at a time when the wealthiest kings of Europe would have possessed around 200,000 *ducats*. If da Gama could do this, why, da Cunha wondered, could not others? Almeida had continued in this tradition by looting and plundering indiscriminately although he was always careful to set aside a fifth for the Crown. Da Cunha had been personally granted private trading routes along the journey by the King and he fully intended to make a fortune for himself and his family. To his frustration the delay in setting sail meant that the fleet would not make it to India within the year and would have to 'winter' in Socotra, thereby diminishing his profits.

As for Afonso de Albuquerque, he had his own concerns. Although Manuel had selected da Cunha rather than Albuquerque to lead the armada, the King had done so with good reason: at the end of three years, according to the King's secret instructions, Albuquerque would get to assume the position of governor of Portuguese India, which was currently ruled over by the Viceroy, Almeida. Albuquerque would be governor, that is, but not viceroy, since in Portugal quality of birth was more important than wealth or even power and within the *fidalguia*, those who were born in nobility were considered higher than those who attained that status through service to the King. As a *fidalgo*, Albuquerque was of lower rank than Almeida who carried the title of 'Dom' as part of his name, a privilege afforded by the King and one that had not been granted to Albuquerque. Albuquerque was destined to be appointed as 'Governor' of India, instead of 'Viceroy', even though the duties and the powers of a governor or a viceroy were exactly the same. Even Albuquerque, the great Albuquerque, a man who would later gain fame as the Caesar of the East, had to understand his place in the complex echelons of the *fidalgos*.

Albuquerque had been brought up at the court of King Afonso V, where he had been a page. Educated alongside the King's sons, in his early years he became a friend of the future King João II. As a young man he served in Morocco where he remained for some years as an officer of a garrison, and where he developed a great hatred for Muslims, one which only increased when his younger brother was killed during a foray. Unlike da Cunha, this was not his first voyage to India and though he would not admit it, he had been scarred by his first trip there. Three years earlier, in 1503, he had commanded a squadron of three ships serving under his cousin Francisco de Albuquerque. His main contribution to the armada had been in building a fort at Cochin to defend the local Portuguese trading station (known as a 'factory' and overseen by a 'factor'); but he had also visited the seaport of

Quilon (now also known as Kollam) and appointed a trade overseer in that city. While in India he had quarrelled with his cousin
Francisco, and eventually, in spite of the King's direct orders to
the contrary, he departed without waiting for him. It was already
clear that he was headstrong, but equally Albuquerque possessed
an independent sense of adventure and self-assurance. Hitherto,
Portuguese fleets had always headed for the East African coast,
in order to make the passage across the Indian Ocean as short
as possible. Albuquerque, guided by an Arab pilot, chose not to
track the shore, and after a perilous voyage along the West coast
of Africa, he arrived at Lisbon in July 1504. It was only there that
he learned that his cousin, who had delayed his departure, had
been lost at sea with his squadron. Now, in 1506, Albuquerque
was returning to India, and soon he would be appointed as governor. Albuquerque wondered to himself how the current Viceroy,
Almeida, would respond.

For the time being, though, Albuquerque had more pressing
concerns. He had just learned that the pilot of his ship had fled.
Apparently he had quarrelled with his wife, killed her and escaped
to Castile. This was a serious development as, after the captain,
the pilot was the most important authority on the ship. It was
the pilot who navigated, since many of the captains – all *fidalgos* and recruited from the nobility – did not have any relevant
experience. It was the pilot who remained on the half-deck or
the quarterdeck, day and night, reading the compass. He was,
in a common Portuguese saying, 'as important to the ship as the
soul is to the human body'. Having failed to find one himself,
in vain Albuquerque petitioned the King to get him a new pilot
but it was too short notice. Men were committed elsewhere and
there were simply no pilots who were available, since it would be
eighteen months at the very least before the start of the return
journey. Meanwhile da Cunha, who did not want to have to
winter in Socotra and was doubtless keen to begin exploiting

his new trading routes, could not wait any longer. His patience finally ran out and though his ships were seriously undermanned, he determined to set sail. On 6 April, without any of the usual festivities traditional to a sending-off, without blaring trumpets or booming guns, without even a mass, Tristão da Cunha and his armada departed Lisbon. Albuquerque would just have to follow him when he could, when he had found a pilot and enough men.

Lodged on his ship the *Cirne*, Albuquerque was faced with a difficult choice. There was no knowing how long it would take to locate an experienced pilot, but dare he set sail without one? Finally consulting his chief officer, Diogo Fernandes, who had already been on two voyages to India, Albuquerque decided he could not wait any longer. He would sail without a pilot. As Albuquerque took his decision, a multitude of people gathered around the *Cirne*. These were the men who had been turned away by da Cunha for fear of contagion from the plague. Now, with his ship undermanned and with the men showing no visible symptoms, Albuquerque ordered their recruitment. He was under no illusion as to how arduous the journey ahead would be, for he had seen for himself the rate of fatalities that a voyage to India involved. Only time would tell how risky his decision to sail with potential plague victims was. For the time being the priority was to set sail and to catch up with Tristão da Cunha.

CHAPTER FIVE

'*The moon lies*'

*J*t was not very long before Albuquerque caught up with the armada, for it had been agreed with da Cunha that they would rendezvous at Angra de Bezeguiche (the modern day Bay of Dakar) which was Africa's most western point in the lee of Cape Verde, and the last calling point for fleets before setting out for the Cape of Good Hope. But when they met, a fierce disagreement broke out between them over the men Albuquerque had recruited in Lisbon. Da Cunha refused bluntly to take responsibility for them, fearing that they might be carrying the plague, and none of the other captains was willing to risk accepting them aboard. Eventually the men were put ashore at Bezeguiche and when, after a week or so, they showed no signs of the plague they were finally distributed among all the ships. A small vessel was then dispatched to Lisbon with a letter from da Cunha to Manuel informing him that the fleet was safe and that they would shortly be heading out into the Atlantic. The delay, however, exacerbated the tensions that were brewing between da Cunha and Albuquerque.

Once the Portuguese sailors had hugged the coast of Africa with daily, cautious reference to the shore, but gradually they learned to sail the high seas for weeks on end without sighting land. The intriguing question is: how did they know where they were and whether they were on the right course? The astonishing answer, to us moderns at least, is that they did not know where they were and that they did not much care. Today we think of navigation in terms of being able to plot a path between the location of a ship and its desired destination. This view was not widely accepted in the early 16th century. The purpose of navigation, pilots argued, was simply to get safely from one place to another. Whether one could locate a ship at sea actually had little effect on navigation. In fact the inability to do so was seen as more of a problem for the noblemen in Lisbon than for the pilots themselves. All that mattered to the pilots, who reasoned that they were not hired to explore new territory, but simply to guide the ship safely across the ocean, was that the proper course was known, that the ship was able to maintain that course, and that it sailed on until it reached land. Nor was there much advantage in travelling faster, as there was little to be gained by arriving earlier (it did not, for example, mean the return journey could start any sooner – it was the seasonal winds that would decide that, and not the pilots). The fact that there were shipwrecks did not alter that view; contemporary accounts blamed the weather, or piracy, or perhaps the pilot's ignorance of the peculiarities of ports and currents. In the 16th century 'lost at sea' referred to shipwrecks, not ignorance of precise location.

Things, however, were changing rapidly, not primarily due to navigation but to politics. A dispute had arisen following the return of Christopher Columbus. Although Columbus had sailed for the Crown of Castile, he had, on his way back to Spain, first reached Lisbon, where he met the King to show him the newly discovered lands, who then claimed all the land that Columbus had discovered for Portugal. A dispute was inevitable and it took the intervention of the Pope to bring both sides together, which, after many negotiations, led to the signing of the Treaty of Tordesillas on 7 June 1494. The Treaty divided the newly discovered lands outside of Christian Europe between Portugal and the Crown of Castile, effectively drawing a line in the Atlantic Ocean about 370 leagues west of the Cape Verde Islands, which were then controlled by Portugal. All lands east of that line (about 46 degrees, 37 minutes West) were claimed by Portugal. All lands west of that line were claimed by Spain. Spain was given exclusive rights to all newly discovered and undiscovered lands in the region west of the line. Portuguese expeditions were to keep to the east of the line. Neither power was to occupy any territory already in the hands of a Christian ruler. This new boundary enabled Portugal to claim the coast of Brazil after its discovery by Pedro Álvares Cabral in 1500. Today most Latin American nations are Spanish-speaking countries, for instance, but Portuguese is the leading official language in Brazil. This is because the eastern tip of Brazil penetrates the line agreed to in the Treaty of Tordesillas, and so the region was colonised by Portugal (the Treaty, of course, completely ignored the millions of indigenous people who now came under Spanish or Portuguese rule). The problem that followed was that ownership of a territory, such as an island, depended on defining its exact location in order to prevent others from encroaching on it or disputing that ownership.

This fundamentally altered the role of pilots, who were now not only expected to reach places safely but also to report the exact location of those places relative to a boundary line in a featureless ocean. It was argued in Lisbon that to be able to report back with the exact coordinate information that was necessary for updating the charts, the pilots needed to know at all times where their ships were – and the best way for this to happen was to use astronomical observations.

On the one side were the pilots. Trained primarily at sea, a pilot normally started his life as a ship's boy at eight years of age.

It was a low-status occupation and many died in poverty. Socially they were on a par with sailors. When Lopes went to sea, he went as a squire and a soldier – not a sailor – and a pilot would not have been permitted, unless invited, to sit in his presence; if a meeting took place during dinner then the pilot would remain standing. Nevertheless it was the pilots who asked, 'Why should the people in charge of navigation not be those who had learned their trade through lifetimes at sea?' For them what was important was knowledge of currents, headlands, ports and routes, of the winds and the feel of the ship. This is what mattered and this could only be learned through repeated voyages. They viewed charts and astronomical navigation with suspicion, and 'the moon lies' was a common expression among them. Naturally they viewed the nobles and cosmographers with barely concealed disdain: 'these gentlemen were also knights of the Order of Christ and they called themselves gods of the sea, and they always ran their ships aground'.

Ranged against them were men of a new learning, representing a new world. Educated in Latin and familiar with the basics of astronomy, hydrography and geography, they argued for the importance of theory. Against the experience and local knowledge that was favoured by the pilots, they put forth universal truths. They were the cosmographers. They believed that it was necessary to change the way that the pilots navigated. Rather than relying on local knowledge of winds and currents and the ability to keep a ship on course, pilots needed to use astronomical observations and celestial navigation, to do calculations and read tables, skills that stretched their educational abilities, as many of them could neither read nor write. Cosmographers argued that by forcing the pilots to determine their position at sea, navigation would become safer and more efficient. Ultimately the cosmographers were right: accumulated knowledge was no match for the Atlantic or the Indian Oceans. On the high seas where the only reference points were the stars and the sun, locations and courses had to be spatial and had to be calculated on a grid of imaginary lines of latitude and longitude. For them the pilots, sailors and mariners were the 'Scum of the Sea'.

The pilot's main guide was latitude, and his true friend was the North Star, Polaris. The Portuguese observed that Polaris maintained roughly the same height on a particular parallel of latitude and so a navigator observing the North Star each day at dawn and dusk could see both the star and the horizon and could, by noting changes in the star's altitude, calculate the changes in his position. The navigator who was planning to sail out of sight of land would simply measure the altitude of Polaris as he left his port: the easiest and most basic method was to use the width of a finger. When held at arm's length, the width of four fingers was considered to measure four *isba'* (*isba'* is the Arabic word for finger). In a 360 degree circle there were 224 *isba'*. By keeping the Pole Star at the same height, one could sail east and west on the same latitude; that height could be measured by the number of arm's-length finger-widths between the horizon and the star. It was roughly calculated that a day's sailing due north would raise the Pole Star one *isba'* from the horizon. To return after a long voyage, the navigator needed only to sail north or south, as appropriate, to bring Polaris to the altitude of the port from which he departed, then turn left or right as appropriate and 'sail down the latitude'. Soon lists of the altitudes of many ports were published in *roteiros*, Portuguese navigational routes compiled to aid sailors and pilots, which were carried on ships to guide them up and down the coasts of Europe and Africa. The quadrant refined their measurements to an even greater degree. Usually made of wood and hence light to carry, the quadrant was a very simple device: a quarter of a circle, with a scale marked on the curved edge. Along the straight edges there were two pinhole sights, and a plumb-line hung from the apex. The sights were aligned on the North Star and the reading taken from the point where the plumb-line cut the scale. Polaris' altitude in degrees gave the observer his latitude. If the navigator knew the star's altitude of a certain place then he could measure his distance from there.

The problem was that once the ships sailed south over the curve of the terrestrial globe, the Pole Star vanished and there was no other star with the same properties. The only alternative was the altitude of the sun, but naturally one could not study its position with the naked eye. This is where the cosmographers came in. In 1484 King João II created a commission of mathematical experts and astronomers to observe and measure solar altitude. It was understood that the sun was not as reliable a guide as the Pole Star since its path through the sky in relation to the equator changed on every day of the year. A navigator therefore had to take that variable into account and compensate for it. Before long, Portuguese astronomers figured out how to determine latitude using the position of the sun as it moved north and south of the equator with the seasons – what we now call its declination. This discovery was a major conceptual step forward in seagoing celestial navigation. Tables were drawn up which gave a figure for the declination of the sun on any given day and showed the navigators how to apply the figure to navigating the ship. Initially it was complex and obtuse, and one imagines many pilots chose to ignore these tables, but eventually they became invaluable.

The instrument for measuring distance from the equator was the mariner's astrolabe, which had been invented by the Arabs for travelling on land and to calculate the direction of Mecca for prayer, but which the Portuguese transformed into a tool for high-sea navigation. The astrolabe was a graduated brass disc, with a bar which was rotated until the point of light shining through the upper sight fell onto the lower one. As there were no accurate clocks, a series of readings had to be taken around what appeared to be midday, when the sun was at its zenith. As the distance between the equator and the sun changed from day to day and year to year, mariners needed accurate tables for measuring the sun's altitude. From around 1485 manuals were subsequently gathered in which estimates of the sun's declination were recorded and pilots were given information collected from previous voyages. From the 16th century on, all ships had to be equipped with astrolabes to measure the altitudes of stars or the sun, and pilots were only granted a licence once they could measure latitudes.

Having taken on board fresh supplies of water and meat at Bezeguiche, Tristão da Cunha now gave the order to set sail from the coast of Africa. With the fifteen ships carrying 1,200 souls fanning the horizon, the armada struck out into the Atlantic Ocean. 'Navigation on sea depends on the winds', so wrote Ibn Khaldun, the great Arab philosopher of history. 'It depends on knowledge of the direction from where the winds blow and where they lead.' By the time of Vasco da Gama, the Portuguese had begun to learn the wind patterns of the South Atlantic. They understood that they could not sail against the south-east trade winds and the north-going current, and that the only way to reach the Cape of Good Hope was to sail west into the Atlantic away from the African coast in order to pick up favourable winds, which would allow the ships to sail back in a counter-clockwise arc towards Africa. It was precisely this that the Portuguese navigator Pedro Cabral was attempting when he ended up sailing too far west and stumbled on the coast of Brazil in 1500.

Tristão da Cunha's pilots now set their course; the ships would sail west down to the latitude of 5 or 6 degrees North and, taking advantage of the trade winds, head for Brazil. The equator crossed, they would then pick up the south-east trade winds of the southern hemisphere until they crossed Cabo de Santo Agostinho, not far from modern Recife, which lay at 8 degrees South. From there they would sail south along the Brazil Current (a warm-water current, not unlike the Gulf Stream, flowing south from the equator along the Brazilian East coast), until at around 20 degrees South the winds would start to become south-westerly. Once they reached 36 degrees South, the pilots knew that it was safe to navigate east and head straight around the Cape of Good Hope.

On the ship, as he surveyed the men with whom he sailed, Fernão Lopes would have been struck by the large number who were not Portuguese, for it was full of men of different nations speaking different languages. There were Flemings, Germans, Sicilians and English and others he would not have recognised. Some had joined to fight, others to trade. Some, the quieter ones, were clearly running away from crimes they had committed while others were simply running away from their lives. More than half would die before they returned to Lisbon. Gradually Lopes adjusted to the daily routine of life at sea. He would have been constantly aware of the time, told with an hourglass. Every half hour of the day and night, the ship's boy turned the glass and the ship's bell rang. After eight bells those working would rest and the watch changed, and as the new team took over, an ancient ditty was sung:

'The watch is changed, the glass is running!
We shall have a good voyage if God is willing.'

At dawn the cabin boys, tasked with the menial jobs, sang a loud sea-orison. This song mentioned the ship and all the people on board, with their duties. As a squire, Lopes would not have joined in the back-breaking work of pumping out the water or swabbing down the salty decks or repairing tears in the sails, but he did help in cleaning the *bombarda* which was the main cannon on the ship, fashioned from a tube formed of wrought iron bars welded edge to edge and strengthened by iron sleeves until a tight cylinder was formed. The *bombarda* was lashed to a simple cradle of wood positioned on the deck of the ship and Lopes would help in testing it, firing stone, iron and lead projectiles into the open ocean. He was also familiar with the smaller types of iron breech-loading guns which were available on the ship. These rapid-firing weapons could be mounted in boats during exploratory forays up rivers or estuaries. During the voyage Lopes would also have practised on the *berqo*, a lighter swivel gun. Occasionally when the cabin boy was busy, and to pass the time, he shined his weapons and armour in readiness for the battle ahead. These included a sword (*espadas*), a dagger (*dagas*), a pike (*pica*) and a javelin. He also had a round shield worn on the arm, as well as his helmet and breastplate.

Daily religious rituals dictated his life on board as regularly as the hourglass, for the age in which Lopes lived was above all else an age of faith. Every morning he attended morning prayer and every evening the ship's master blew a silver whistle which hung around his neck, and Lopes and all those on board said a *Pater* and an *Ave*. Every evening on Mondays, Wednesdays and Fridays he said a rosary and on Saturday evening he recited the *Salve Regina* in honour of the Virgin Mary. Immediately following the *Salve* a loud exorcism was uttered against the evil spirit. This was done to keep away any possible danger to the life of the people on board. The *Salve* was not performed when land was in sight or when the ship was nearing the shore. No sacraments were administered on board during the voyage. The only sacrament that was allowed was confession, which was obligatory, and had to be made to the Chaplain. The use of holy oil was not allowed. Deaths were expected and frequent: the master (a nobleman with seafaring experience partly responsible for the navigation) announced the death of a person by blowing his whistle, and all on board were expected to offer their prayers for the dead. Burial, naturally, was at sea.

From the start it was clear that the armada was travelling too slowly. One ship in particular, the *São Tiago*, was losing speed, which was of particular concern as this was the flagship. The ship was heeling, and the waves were causing it to lean over to one side. The reason perhaps was that de Cunha, eager to make a profit, had overladen it with trading goods, but the result was that the rest of the fleet, to Albuquerque's great frustration, had to slow down to wait for the *São Tiago*. Then, early in the crossing and already delayed, an Atlantic storm struck the fleet with such great venom that the priests came onto deck and prayed on their knees. Some even went about the ship with a vase of holy water, spilling it all over the decks and into the sea while invoking blessings. After a couple of days of buffeting, the fleet managed to regroup only to discover that one of the ships, under the command of Job Queimado, was nowhere to be seen. It was now nearly the end of June, almost three months since the armada had set sail and the winds, now contrary, had turned. Although the fleet was tantalisingly close to Brazil from where the south-east trade winds could be picked up, it was clear that no further advance could be made. There was no option but to sail back towards the Gulf of Guinea and try to work their way to finding the trade winds from there.

Daily, an itinerary of the voyage, a *roteiro*, was written by the navigator, mentioning the route, distance, astronomical observations and calculations, and descriptions of lands. What was not written down was the hardship and suffering endured by those on board the ships. As a squire, Lopes would have fared better: the below space was reserved for him, where he slept on a mat under the quarterdeck. During the day he rolled up his mat and stowed it away and as he did so he would have had time to reflect on the fact that, were he to die, the mat he was rolling would be the shroud in which his body would be wrapped before being released into the sea. As a squire he was allowed to bring on board his own stock of food which would have included chickens and sheep, wine, vinegar and foodstuffs such as figs, oil, honey, sugar and salt, as well as cakes and biscuits. The remainder of those on board, however, fared less well. Their diet was limited to biscuits, and dried or salted meat and fish. The dried fish was inedible and the biscuits were often a year old and rotting. Due to the heat around the equator, butter, figs, raisins and oil quickly spoiled. Maggots, cockroaches and *gorgojos* (weevils) competed with the men for the food. Even the water spoiled and became contaminated with scum, bacteria and algae. Parched with thirst, all the men on board would have found that the only way to drink the water was by shutting their eyes and closing their nostrils. Astonishingly, each sailor was supposed to take care of preparing his own food. Naturally the kitchen was overcrowded, with about 80 or 100 pots on the flames simultaneously, causing small fires to break out all the time.

From the Gulf of Guinea the fourteen ships (for there was still no sign of Job Queimado's) gradually worked their way south, approaching the equator. As they passed Ascension Island the stifling heat rendered life on board intolerable. Summer was now upon the men and a terrible ordeal was about to befall Lopes and others who had not sailed these waters before. The lower decks were like an oven and Lopes and the other noblemen were forced to sleep on deck, but no place on the ship was spared the heat and the stench. There were no toilets on board so men relieved themselves over the side, but during storms they often simply relieved themselves on the spot. Soon the seawater on the decks was sloshing with vomit, urine and faeces. Men worked and slept in their clothes for months and never washed, since sea water was so briny, and fresh water far too precious. Nor did they cut their hair, which was soon teeming with lice. Throughout there were rats which became so bold that they ran across the sailors' faces even when they were awake. Some noblemen kept cats and dogs aboard to help hunt down the mice and rats but to little effect. Daily the scorching sun of the equator beat down on the men, and its oppressive heat did not differentiate between noble and commoner. Then, just when those on board had reached the limits of their suffering, the wind dramatically dropped and the ships were caught in a dead calm which lasted for days. Paralysed and debilitated with thirst and starvation, the crew began to die off on a daily basis. Those more experienced knew that the ships were traversing what today we know as the doldrums, a region near the equator, but this knowledge would not have eased their suffering nor brought much comfort. Once the still seas had sapped the energy of the sailors and lulled them into a fatal lethargy, the ships were caught in sudden storms and powerful gusts which made those on board violently sick. Then hot rain began to fall in sheets drenching everyone, and their wet clothes became infested with worms carried by the rain. Many died – mostly of scurvy, beriberi and high fever. The symptoms of scurvy were horrendous: teeth falling out, bleeding gums, putrefying sores, swollen legs and thighs. Beriberi was caused by malnutrition, and high and infectious fevers broke out rapidly and frequently, often causing delirium. In one case some of its victims tried to throw themselves overboard and had to be restrained and tied to each other to prevent them from doing so. And every morning and every evening, amidst the lamentations and groans, prayers were recited in a loud voice. And throughout there was a nauseous smell which reached every part of the ship. And the ship's bell rang.

Once in the open South Atlantic the ships picked up speed. Disease and sickness had left many dead but now the frequent rain squalls allowed the men to top up their casks. Some fished with hooks and nets and harpoons, others hummed or sang a sea shanty. On occasion a pod of whales could be spotted, which was taken as a good omen. Cooped up so long together, it was inevitable that indiscipline and discord were common and misunderstandings frequent. As an officer, Lopes would have helped maintain order on the ship, and punishments were harsh. Throughout the ship there were stocks in which men were locked by their neck or legs and left in the sun. For more serious offences there was keelhauling, where the victim was tied to a rope and lowered into the sea, and under the ship, before being pulled back on board. But the *fidalgos* also fought, and with them things were worse, for *fidalgos* travelled with their swords and one can imagine how in the confined and cramped environment, among the heat and hardship, slights or perceived slights could lead to violence and the shedding of blood. For this reason it was strictly forbidden to swear any oaths on board. Priests preached sermons attacking the practice of swearing oaths and if any *fidalgo* was found violating this order he was fined, while a commoner found himself in the stocks.

As the ships sailed south, a chill began to be felt in the air which soon turned into a freezing cold. Having endured the suffocating heat of the equator, it was now wind chill that became the biggest killer on board. Many men had not brought any winter clothing, either out of poverty or ignorance, and they were the first to die. The further south they sailed the colder it got, and the men endured and shivered. Soon it was no longer possible to light the on-board fires for hot food due to the cold and stormy weather. Eventually the pilots realised that the fleet had crossed latitude 36 degrees South and so, to the relief of everyone, the ships turned eastwards.

On the ship on which Fernão Lopes sailed the captain was Rui Dias Pereira, a *fidalgo* of high standing. As was the custom when a captain went to India, he was accompanied by some of his relatives, who sought their fame and fortune in his wake. Accompanying the captain was his nephew Manuel de Lacerda, who would establish himself in India as one of Portugal's greatest generals there, as well as a younger relative, also by the name of Rui Dias. It was during the voyage that this younger Rui Dias and Fernão Lopes first became acquainted, and a friendship grew between the two men which bonded closer with the slow passing of the days and weeks. Daily they would meet in the ship's stern gallery where they would chat. On occasion they strolled with others on the upper deck between the main mast and the foremast. *Fidalgos* were allowed games as entertainment, which often involved gambling, but prior to playing it was customary (sometimes even enforced by the captain) to make a donation to charity. Commoners playing anything other than board games or card games found themselves in the stocks. Entertainment was strictly forbidden after nightfall as this time was fixed for evening prayer. Among the board games, chess was very popular, although it would have been known as *xadrez* (pronounced *she-dres*), from *ash-shatranj* which was an Arabic derivation from the Indian *chaturanga*. Had Lopes been asked where the game had originated, he would have replied with assuredness that its origins were in Troy, for that is what educated Portuguese believed. In fact the game had originated in the land towards which his ship was heading, so that had he arrived in India during a game, a local notable would probably have been able to continue the same game, although only after overcoming some initial confusion, since the Portuguese would have been playing a much faster version of chess. The Europeans, finding the game too slow, had made some fundamental changes to the pieces which helped transform it into the game played today.

It was a bitterly cold Sunday morning in October and the fourteen ships had been ploughing through seemingly endless miles of ocean. They were sailing in sight of each other and this meant that when they saw it, they all saw it at the same time. First to emerge from the ocean, through the clouds, was a volcanic island crowned with a snow-capped peak. It was an astonishing sight, as unexpected as it was dramatic. As the ships approached this scattering of tiny isolated islands, Albuquerque sent a message to da Cunha that they should land somewhere to investigate this new discovery. As they approached the main island, the sailors saw thousands of sea birds whom they called 'sea crows'. In fact what they had seen were petrels and albatrosses. But there was no landing on the island as a sudden westerly gale scattered the ships, and by the time they had re-gathered a rapidly descending cloud layer, a tempestuous sea and the absence of a natural harbour made any landing hazardous in the extreme. And so the ships sailed away, though not without Tristão da Cunha first naming the islands after himself: a name which has endured, in an anglicised form, to the present day.

CHAPTER SIX

'I will build walls of Muslim bones'

When asked about their ordeal, those who made the voyage from Lisbon to India often spoke about the three stages of the journey, on which death was a frequent visitor. The first was the crossing of the equator when the stifling heat carried many deadly diseases, the second stage arrived with the bitter cold of the Cape when men succumbed meekly to pneumonia and fever. And then there was Mozambique. With its malaria and cholera, the little Island of Mozambique became a tomb for the Portuguese, and it was estimated that in the 30 years prior to 1558, 30,000 men died there en route to India. And yet a way station where ships could be repaired and supplied was absolutely necessary, and the Portuguese quickly realised that the Island of Mozambique was ideal. The island's Mossuril Bay provided a good natural harbour, where ships could find shelter while they awaited the right monsoon winds. It was also close to the mainland, where vegetables and fruits could be grown. In addition, the Island of Mozambique was a base from which the Portuguese could patrol the seas.

In December 1506, eight months after having set off from Lisbon, the fourteen ships of da Cunha passed the Cape of Good Hope and reached the Island of Mozambique. By then it was apparent that the north-east monsoon winds were not in their favour and that the fleet would have to winter on the island. Although initially disappointed, da Cunha knew that this had always been a possibility and he now turned his attention to executing Manuel's order to capture Socotra, which lay off the coast of modern day Yemen, thus helping to secure the entrance of the Red Sea. When Vasco da Gama had first sailed up the East African coast, he had discovered a string of trade ports, all Muslim, competing with each other from Sofala in the South to Mogadishu in the North. This was the fabled 'Swahili Coast' where slaves, ivory and gold were traded for textiles and beads. A Portuguese scout, Pedro da Covilhã, disguised as an Arab merchant, had travelled the length of the Kilwa Sultanate in 1489–90 and visited the ports of Malindi, Kilwa and Sofala. Da Covilhã assured all those who listened that Kilwa, founded on an island on the coast of present day Tanzania, was one of the most prosperous cities in Africa, and Mombasa one of the two most important trading cities on the East African coast. Da Covilhã also noted that the trade on the Swahili Coast was in the hands of the Arabs, who had succeeded in spreading their Islamic faith. What he probably did not know was that the word 'Swahili' was derived from the Arabic word meaning coasts, and that Swahili culture had developed as the result of the intermarriage between the Africans and the Arabs, producing a civilisation which borrowed heavily from both cultures but became firmly rooted in Islam. Running for about 1,900 miles of coastline between Mogadishu in present day Somalia and Sofala in present day Mozambique, the East African coast attracted Arab traders, largely from Yemen and Oman, from an early age. For them the coast offered a panoply of goods: slaves, gold, ivory, animal skins, glassware, beads. In addition it had good natural harbours with plentiful fresh water that favoured the anchoring of merchant dhows, the lateen-rigged ships with one or two masts which crisscrossed the Indian Ocean. The Arab traders had discovered the monsoon winds which between November and April would blow their ships westwards towards Africa and safely home again between May and October. As the years passed many Arab merchants settled in various places on the coast and intermarried with the locals, and Islam spread as the Africans were introduced to the Arabic language and culture. Certainly by the time that the Moroccan world traveller Ibn Battuta visited East Africa in 1331, the main coastal city-states of Mogadishu, Mombasa and Kilwa were all embedded within the Islamic orbit. At Mogadishu, where he stayed for three days, he attended Friday services and lived with the local religious judge, noting approvingly, 'the inhabitants are pious, honourable, and upright, and they have well-built wooden mosques'. At the time of Ibn Battuta's visit, Kilwa was the dominant commercial entrepôt on the coast, its wealth based on its control of the gold trade of the Zimbabwean Plateau, which had its outlet at Sofala.

In March 1500, Pedro Cabral was sent out with orders to make military demonstrations at Kilwa and to conquer it. Cabral failed to make an agreement with the local Arab ruler, the Emir, although he returned with a report of having seen beautiful houses made of coral stones. Two years later, in 1502, da Gama was ordered by Manuel to force Kilwa to pay him tribute for not answering Cabral's request. Certainly da Gama's words to the Emir of Kilwa this time left no room for any doubts:

> Take it for certain that if I so decide your city would be grounded by fire in one single hour, and if your people wanted to extinguish the fire in town, they would all be burned, and when you see all this happen, you will regret all you are telling me now, and you will give much more than what I am asking

you now, it will then be too late for you. If you are still in doubt, it is up to you to see it.

But the Portuguese knew that in order to trade on the Swahili Coast, they first had to conquer it. It was clearly understood that duplicity was to be a fundamental part of this strategy: the *Regimento* (Instructions) given to Almeida by Manuel in 1505 stated:

> And using this pretence [of peace] you shall leap ashore there from your longboats and using such dexterity as you may, you shall take all the Moorish merchants who may be there from foreign parts and all the gold and merchandise you find upon them ... we do so by reason of their being enemies of our holy Catholic faith.

Almeida's task was to capture and fortify Kilwa and Mombasa, and build fortresses at selected spots along the coast between the Cape of Good Hope and India to serve as way stations, fortified trade factories and secure havens for provisions and rest. Subsequently when his fleet stopped in Mombasa, one of the principal trading towns on the East African coast, Almeida sacked it and put it to the torch, killing 1,500 people and plundering great quantities of cotton, silk and gold-embroidered textiles as well as carpets. The words of the King of Mombasa to the King of Malindi following Almeida's visitation warned of this new and terrible terror:

> This is to inform you that a great lord has passed through the town, burning it and laying it waste. He came to the town in such strength and was of such cruelty, that he spared neither man nor woman, old nor young – nay, not even the smallest child ... Nor can I ascertain nor estimate what wealth they have taken from the town. I give you this news for your own safety.

When the King spoke of this new and terrible terror one imagines he must have been referring as much to the arms and gunfire the Portuguese had brought with them, and against which he had little defence, as to the cruelty and brutality shown by the soldiers.

By 1507, Kilwa, Mombasa, Malindi, Pate and Lamu had all been sacked by the Portuguese, and now that da Cunha and Albuquerque were tasked with securing the island of Socotra, after months of being cooped up on ships and buffeted by boredom and waves, Lopes would finally have had an opportunity to seek both plunder and honour. As they made their way north along the African coast, da Cunha and Albuquerque came across the city of Angoja which, according to the history written by Albuquerque's son, was ruled by a 'Moorish merchant who came from abroad but as he was very rich he had made himself lord of all that land'. Angoja was sacked and burned to the ground. A few weeks later the fleet proceeded to Barawa where the full fury and violence of the Portuguese was unleashed upon its people. The scenes of cruelty dealt out to the Muslim inhabitants were described by a Spanish eyewitness, Martín Fernández de Figueroa:

> The Portuguese entered the city by force of arms, killed many Moors, and carried off great riches which their owners had not thought to save, in the belief they could defend the town. They could not even save their own women, very rich and beautiful with seven and eight bracelets on each arm and just as many thick and valuable on their legs. This was an occasion for severe cruelty, for the men, blinded by avarice rather than mercy, in order not to lose time, cut off the arms, the legs, and the ears which bore the jewelry without pity.

The attack and pillaging of Barawa was probably Lopes' first serious engagement on the battlefield. As the violence raged, da Cunha was wounded, and what followed was a remarkable scene. Once the fighting ceased, in recognition of his bravery, da Cunha insisted that he be knighted. Albuquerque, as the most senior nobleman (other than da Cunha), performed a ceremony in which da Cunha, his son and many other participants in the action were honoured by being made members of the Order of the Knights of Santiago. Lopes was not among those knighted even though he had knelt, as all others had done, in obeisance to da Cunha. His time was yet to come.

From Barawa, da Cunha set sail for Mogadishu, which was the richest city on the East African coast, with the determination to sack it. But Mogadishu was well fortified and its men, aware of the horrors that the Portuguese had already visited upon the inhabitants up and down the coast, were determined to fight. Albuquerque knew of the fortifications, and urged da Cunha not to attack; when his words fell on deaf ears, he summoned the *fidalgos*, including Lopes, to persuade him. Finally da Cunha agreed to Albuquerque's advice and ordered the fleet to make straight for Socotra. There, he sent a message to the ruler of Socotra to inform him that he had a choice: to become the vassal of the King of Portugal or face the same fate as Barawa. The reply was as defiant as it was unambiguous: if the Portuguese felt so brave, they should land and take the fortress, for they could not have it any other way. Once again Lopes put on his armour and readied himself for war. The Portuguese charge was fierce and in the very first skirmish one of the sons of the Emir of Socotra was killed by Albuquerque. But the Muslim garrison of around 150 men did not buckle against the onslaught, standing their ground. For seven hours the Portuguese charged the fortress, during which time Albuquerque himself was wounded, his leg cut by a sword gash, until one by one the Muslim defenders fell. Infidels they may have been, but the courage of the Muslims that day could not fail to earn the respect of the Portuguese. In view of their unexpected bravery, after the fortress had finally fallen da Cunha ordered that the main town not be sacked. Perhaps, though, this Portuguese magnanimity needs to be interpreted in a different manner: they were initially confounded when, on approaching Socotra, they were confronted by a Muslim force as they genuinely believed (as Manuel, too, believed back in Lisbon) that the island was inhabited by Christians. Their sparing of the town may have been borne from a fear of unknowingly killing fellow Christians. This triumph, however, proved to be a fleeting one. The infertility of the land led to famine and sickness in the garrison, and the lack of a proper harbour for wintering led to the loss of many moored Portuguese ships. Four years later, the Portuguese abandoned the island. Writing about their departure, the Portuguese historian Castanheda cryptically noted that 'The people of the country were generally more friendly to the Moors than to us and often revolted when the Moors made war.' It seems that the 'Christians' on Socotra were not as unhappy with Muslim rule as the Portuguese believed them to be.

Socotra had been conquered for Portugal, and da Cunha now prepared to sail to India, but without Albuquerque. Whether it had been agreed upon in Lisbon, or whether it had been an impetuous decision, Albuquerque now announced that rather than sail immediately to India, he would raid the Arabian and Gulf coasts. Above all he had his eyes set on the capture of Hormuz, an island in the Persian Gulf off present day Iran, which was described by early travellers as 'the richest jewel set in the ring of the world'. Writing about Hormuz in 1580, the Italian Gaspardo Balbi described it as 'the most barren place I have ever seen. One can find there only salt and wood. Everything else required for food is carried from the Persian mainland.' But Hormuz was important: it was a key centre in the international maritime trade, where ships from India and South-east Asia made landfall on the Persian and Arabian coasts before sailing up the Red Sea to Egypt, from where the goods were transported overland to Alexandria and on to Venetian ships. In addition, the Persian Gulf at its narrowest point in the Strait of Hormuz is only about 30 miles wide. By taking control of Hormuz, Albuquerque knew that he would effectively close the Strait to everyone but the Portuguese. There was no doubting Albuquerque's courage or his fortitude, nor could one question his spirit, but he was the type of man who tried to bully his enemies, and he made many.

His decision to set off on his own had angered three of the captains who sailed with him: António do Campo, Afonso Lopes da Costa and Manuel Teles. They resented his authority and sneered at his decision to cruise the Arabian coast rather than trade in India. But none of them resented Albuquerque more than the captain João da Nova, who would become his implacable enemy. Da Nova had not even intended to be with the armada. He had sailed with Almeida's fleet in 1505, and when homeward bound had had to put in at the Island of Mozambique for repairs. While he was there, da Cunha and Albuquerque had arrived and the latter pulled rank and forced Captain da Nova's ship, the *Flor de la Mar*, to join his squadron. Perhaps that was the cause of the resentment, or perhaps it was the fact that da Nova, having previously served under Almeida, now resented having to take orders from the brusque Albuquerque. Was it possible that he had got wind of the decision to replace Almeida as Viceroy with Albuquerque? Whatever the reason, once da Cunha departed, da Nova became the leader of a group of dissenters against Albuquerque, and Fernão Lopes joined this group. To understand the cause of Lopes' turning against Albuquerque (which would later lead to such grief), we need to return to the men whom Albuquerque had rounded up for his ships. In Lisbon Albuquerque had turned a blind eye towards those who had clambered aboard, many of whom were criminals released from jails on the condition that they joined the fleet sailing for India. Now these men were let loose on the ports of the Omani coast which they ravaged and terrorised, looting and burning indiscriminately. At their head was

Albuquerque, commanding six ships carrying 400 men and driven on by a sense of divine mission. At the port of Qurayat, which lies around 50 miles south of modern day Muscat, he ordered that the place be set on fire, and 'the fire was so fierce that not a house, not a building, nor the mosque, one of the most beautiful ever seen, was left standing'. Then, to send a chilling message to Hormuz in case it chose to resist him, he dispatched a group of Muslim prisoners, though not without first ordering that their ears and noses be cut off. It was an act of barbarity which served no strategic purpose and which demonstrated little more than the hatred Albuquerque carried for the Muslims. This deep and vitriolic hatred of Islam was one of the constants in his life, a fact remarked upon by a contemporary:

> There were two actions which he was determined to perform. One was to divert the channel of the Nile to the Red Sea, thereby to render the lands of the Grand Turk sterile; the other to carry away from Mecca the bones of the abominable Mafoma [Prophet Muhammad], that, these being reduced publicly to ashes, the votaries of so foul a sect might be confounded.

The Portuguese it seems were under the impression that Mecca and not Medina was where the Prophet was buried. To Lopes and to the other *fidalgos*, seeing the violence and senseless torture being unleashed was shocking. They also did not understand why they had not sailed to India where there was trade to be made. After all, they had suffered such hardships during the crossing. Who cared about Hormuz?

On 25 September 1507 Albuquerque appeared with his six ships, carrying around 400 men, off the island of Hormuz. At that time it was under the control of a regent whom the Portuguese called 'Cogeatar' (a corruption of Khwaja Atta), acting for the young King of Hormuz, whose kingdom on the mainland stretched up the Persian Gulf. Cogeatar had evidently been made aware of the atrocities committed by the Portuguese to date and in the *Commentaries of Albuquerque* we read that 'Galleons and galleys between 150 and 200 in number were in the harbour, whilst ashore there were 20,000 men.' Nevertheless Albuquerque, despite his inferior strength, brusquely demanded tribute from the regent and when his *fidalgos* later chided him for his undiplomatic words, his reply was typical: 'Gentlemen, I am not the man to achieve so important an affair as this is with dissemblings and sentiments.' After three days of fruitless negotiations the Portuguese attacked the ships in the harbour and bombarded the city until the regent relented and promised to pay a tribute of 15,000 gold *xerafins* a year, to make a gift of 5,000, and to allow the construction of a Portuguese fort. Once again the heavy use of cannons and artillery by the bombardiers, unmatched by the ships of Cogeatar, led to a devastating victory. The tone of the Portuguese account of the battle reveals the vast superiority of their firearms: 'although the Moors endeavoured to avenge themselves our men were so well fortified with their defences that they did them no harm, except on the upper deck with their arrows they wounded some people'. However, not all the *fidalgos* were pleased by this Portuguese victory, and felt that Albuquerque had forced them into fighting. This is reflected in the *Commentaries of Albuquerque* in an oblique way, when it is mentioned that some of the captains and *fidalgos* made it clear that

> they had much reason to complain of him, for his coming to Hormuz had not been by their advice nor of their will, but as they were now there they would have to make some kind of convention [i.e. accordance] by reason of the quantity of soldiers and ships which were in the port, but they did not doubt that they would all be undone.

In fact they were not undone and Albuquerque was triumphant in the engagement, but a festering anger was on the verge of erupting among some of his *fidalgos*.

The news that instead of heading to India they were now expected to construct a fort on the island of Hormuz further exacerbated the tension among the *fidalgos* and once again a protest was made to Albuquerque:

> it would be of more service to the king for them to make their
> way and lie in wait for the ships coming from India with spices
> for the Strait than to stay building a fortress which, as soon as
> they left, would be taken by the Moors.

As tempers frayed more damaging accusations were made: Albuquerque was building the fortress not for the King but for himself, for he was not planning to return to Portugal. Then there was the question of the tribute paid by Cogeatar: why was it not distributed among them, why did Albuquerque retain it and spend it on the fortress?

It was at this point that four Portuguese sailors decided to abandon ship and flee to the Muslim side. The records do not mention their names and we know that they were not *fidalgos*. They had almost certainly fled because they were about to be punished for some petty crime, but when news reached Albuquerque his mood darkened and he flew into a rage. He at once dispatched his interpreter Gaspar Rodriguez to Cogeatar with the message that 'four Christians whom he had arrested for punishment for certain crimes had fled to his camp and he desired, as a favour, that he would deliver them up'. Cogeatar replied to Rodriguez that he knew nothing of these men and that he would return them the moment he knew what had happened to them. Cogeatar of course knew where the men were, but for the time being he was not prepared to hand them over. A few days later another angry message was delivered to him from Albuquerque demanding the return of the men, and this time Cogeatar replied that they had been located on the mainland, had been tied hand and foot, and were being sent back to the island where they should arrive in five days. But the five days passed and there was still no sign of the men, and the next message from Cogeatar was more ominous for he now demanded the release of Muslim prisoners in exchange for his returning the men. Albuquerque's interpreter, Rodriguez, had spotted the four men in Cogeatar's camp, and he now informed Albuquerque that the 'fugitives, clothed in the habit of the Moors, with their swords in their belts, appeared very happy like men who felt sure they were not going to be delivered'. It is a very intriguing sentence, for clearly the four men had been welcomed into the Muslim camp, but why would they choose to wear Muslim clothes?

By now the captains in his fleet, led by João da Nova, were speaking openly about leaving Albuquerque and sailing to India by themselves. They felt that he was following his own whims rather than the King's instructions, and they believed that his violence was bound to exacerbate the situation. In January 1508, Albuquerque was presented with a letter signed by da Nova and the three other captains, but reflecting the opinion of many others, including Lopes, in which a formal objection to his policies in Hormuz was spelled out:

Sir, we do this in writing, because by word of mouth we dare not, as you always answer us so passionately; and for all that you sir have frequently told us that the King gives you no orders to take counsel with us, yet this business is of such great importance, that we consider ourselves obliged to offer you advice.

The diplomatic tone of the letter barely concealed the animosity felt towards Albuquerque. Many *fidalgos* were aghast at his tyran-nical actions and, according to the historian Gaspar Correia, some believed that Albuquerque 'was damned and had the Devil in him'. In particular they strongly disapproved of his decision to spend half of the tribute from Hormuz on the building of the fort, which clearly signalled Albuquerque's intention to maintain permanent outposts, in direct contrast to the policy of Viceroy Almeida, who sought to focus solely on naval trade. Two camps now emerged: those who supported Almeida and those who stood by Albuquerque. The fact that Albuquerque had secretly been promised the position of governor further complicated the situation. Matters worsened rapidly among the men and on one occasion, in the presence of Lopes, Albuquerque drew his sword on da Nova and even had him arrested for insubordination, but he had to release him a short while later. However, the damage had been done and the resentment reached boiling point when Albuquerque dispatched a warning message to Cogeatar: 'If you interfere with me in any way', Albuquerque warned, 'I will build walls of Muslim bones, I will nail ears to the doors and erect the flagstaff on your skull.' He then, to the horror of his captains, ordered that they go ashore, poison the wells, bombard the walls and 'kill every living thing'. The *fidalgos* despaired of this com-mand and even petitioned Albuquerque to rescind the order, but he took no notice. Increasingly Lopes and the rest of the men did not wish to obey a commander who they thought had lost his senses and 'was not fit to command a rowing boat, let alone a fleet', and the rebellious *fidalgos* now departed on their own ini-tiative and set sail for India. Confronted by the departures, an enraged Albuquerque, since he no longer had enough men to build the fort, had no choice but to abandon Hormuz and return to his newly conquered outpost of Socotra. Before doing so, how-ever, he wrote to Manuel informing him of an interesting visit he had observed while at Hormuz:

Thirty pack animals arrived on the mainland from Shiraz ...
The people of this country are called the people of the red
caps. They are people of a Turkish race and are great horsemen
... they all wear red caps with Moorish turbans ... They are
good of character and are as fair-skinned as we are. They are
said not to believe in Muhammad but in his son-in-law Ali,
and this is a separate sect.

The Portuguese were rapidly beginning to differentiate between
the Sunni and Shi'ite Muslims.

Fernão Lopes was one of the handful of *fidalgos* who abandoned
Albuquerque to sail to India. With hindsight we can perhaps
point to this incident as explaining what was to follow, but we
need to be cautious about this. Noblemen fell out often, occasionally leading to bouts of great violence. Albuquerque as we
have seen had fallen out with his own cousin while sailing in an
earlier armada, and he had clashed with da Cunha as well. The
disagreement between Albuquerque and João da Nova may have
been a personal one, or it may have concerned the direction of
Portuguese policy in the Indian Ocean, but what was certain was
that the confrontation at Hormuz was just the beginning of their
open enmity. As for Lopes, he remained largely in the shadows,
playing a supporting role to the main protagonists; his significance
would emerge later.

João da Nova is of great interest for another reason. In 1502 he
had been dispatched by Manuel with four ships to India, and on
the outward leg he had unexpectedly come across an island in the
South Atlantic. The location of the island appeared providential;
as a contemporary Portuguese historian wrote:

God appears to have created this island in that very location, in order to nourish all those who come from India ...
for it offers the best water on the whole journey or at least

the most necessary, which one requires on the return voyage from India.

Some reports claim that the Portuguese built a chapel there, although no concrete evidence exists of it. Certainly they chose not to fortify the island, nor did they establish a permanent set-tlement there. It seems that there was no need to do so, since for them the island served no purpose other than as a stopping point on the return from India. As was customary, the island was named by the captain who discovered it, and since the day of discovery coincided with the feast day of the mother of Constantine the Great, João da Nova had called the island Santa Helena.

Now, five years after that discovery, João da Nova and Fernão Lopes sailed to India. Unknown to either man a strange bond tied their fates together: one would find fame as the discoverer of an isolated island in the middle of nowhere, while for the other that island would prove to be his destiny.

PART II

The Second Journey

'There is the heat of Love, the pulsing rush
of Longing, the lover's whisper,
Irresistible – magic to make the sanest man go mad.'
HOMER, *THE ILIAD*

CHAPTER SEVEN

An Islamic Lake

𝔍n writing history only inexperienced historians welcome facts. Seasoned scholars, on the other hand, while navigating its oceans, approach them in the same way that captains approach icebergs: with caution and wariness, for they know what damage a stubborn fact can do to a story. In the earlier chapters we have told the story of the great Portuguese navigators and of the Portuguese audacity, courage and fortitude which led to the rounding of the Cape and the opening of a new and uncharted route to India that heralded a new age.

But now it is time to tell a different story, one perhaps more dramatic, and this particular story begins with a fact. When Vasco da Gama and his men had arrived in India in 1498, after an epic voyage of more than 12,000 miles, they were greeted in Calicut's harbour (in the modern day state of Kerala) by two North Africans who could speak Spanish and Genovese. The fact is that when da Gama rounded the Cape and sailed up the East African coast he was a visitor to a known world, not a discoverer. When he sailed to India from East Africa, he was sailing in a part of the world that had long been settled by Arab traders. And not only by Arabs: nearly a century before da Gama set off from Lisbon, the famous Chinese Muslim admiral Cheng Ho had mounted seven naval expeditions, with up to 100 ships and 30,000 men, to reach East Africa, the Persian Gulf, Egypt and Ceylon. In the sense that the discovery of 'the Indies' heralded a new age it was only new for the Europeans, who were still to some extent physically and intellectually isolated. Perhaps one of the reasons why European exploration was so dynamic was because the Europeans still had so much of the world to explore. As for the Muslims, they could not discover 'the Indies' in the same way Western Europe could, because they had already known about them for centuries.

The Portuguese knew Muslims, and they knew that they did not like them. For centuries, they had read their own history as one of confrontation with Islam, and their colonial ventures as an extension of the crusades. Papal bulls legitimised the actions of the Portuguese kings and the Order of Christ instilled the spirit of the Holy War in the hearts of their nobility. Now, having expelled the weary and broken Muslims from the Iberian Peninsula, having wrought savage depredations and punishments upon their men and women on the golden Swahili Coast, the Portuguese, on reaching India, discovered a vibrant and thriving commercial society there, which turned in prayer towards Mecca, and where the *dinar* was the dominant currency. Everywhere the Portuguese looked there were Muslim traders: in Malacca with its connections to Gujarat, on the Malabar coast, in Bengal and in Burma. But also in the Persian Gulf, southern Arabia, the Red Sea, the Maldives, the coast of East Africa and in the ports of Calicut, Cambay, Hormuz and Kilwa. Muslims, it seemed to them, were everywhere, 'as numerous as the Fez in Tunis', commented a contemporary Portuguese, not without humour. Writing in the early 16th century about the Indian Ocean, a Portuguese chronicler noted that: 'People use it more often than all the seas of the world because of the "Ancient house" [referring to the Kaaba in Mecca] and the pilgrimage of the Prophet.' And the Muslims sailed that ocean with aplomb; the 12th-century geographer and traveller Ibn Jubayr was astonished by the navigational skills of sailors:

> We observed the art of these captains and the mariners in the handling of their ships through the reefs. It was truly marvellous. They would enter the narrow channels and manage their way through them as a cavalier manages a horse that is light on the bridle.

If Paul Rycaut had thought that God gave 'the sea to the Christians and the land to the Muslims', he may just have had the Arabs of the desert and their camels in mind, for as the Umayyad Caliph Umar II had succinctly put it: 'Dry land and sea belong alike to God.'

Before the arrival of the Portuguese, the Indian Ocean was essentially a *mare clausum* from which Hindus were virtually excluded, since Hinduism imposed restrictions on members of higher castes travelling by sea, and a Brahmin who did so would be excluded from the religious festivals. And so it was the Muslims who moved around the Ocean and their trade, carried on the monsoon winds, achieved a soothing symmetrical unity as gold from Zimbabwe was carried to the coast at Sofala, and where honey was produced in Bahrain for the Chinese (date honey was a much-coveted commodity in China, and was very popular with Buddhist pilgrims travelling to India). Hormuz was connected by trade to Tabriz and the Central Asian markets, a point remarked on by both Marco Polo and Ibn Battuta; the Indian city of Diu opened the door to the cotton and silk textile-exporting area of Gujarat, while Cochin provided access to Malabar pepper, and Malacca (in modern Malaysia) was the key to the markets of South-east Asia. A merchant in Yemen, writing 200 years before the Portuguese arrived in India, noted that he had 150 camel load of wares and 40 slaves and that he wished to carry Persian saffron to China where I understand it has a high price, and then take the dishes from China to Greece, Greek brocade to India, Indian steel to Aleppo, glass of Aleppo to Yemen and the material of Yemen to Persia.

By the time of Fernão Lopes, this was a world where the sharpest traders came from Gujarat. 'We believe ourselves to be the most astute men that one can encounter, and the people here surpass us in everything', wrote a merchant from Florence in 1510. 'They can do better calculations by memory than we can do with the pen.' The Portuguese physician Tomé Pires, a contemporary of Lopes and the author of the *Suma Oriental* – a landmark first-hand account of trade, geography and botany of the Indies – clearly advised that 'those of our people who want to be clerks or factors ought to go to Gujarat and learn, because there the business of trade is a science'.

Islam was of course not unfamiliar to the Portuguese. The first Portuguese code of laws, promulgated in 1438, had contained a full section on inheritance rules for Muslims according to their respective schools of law. In 1529, the word *Sunni* first appears in Portuguese, and although the word *xia* (Shi'a) is not recorded in the language before 1553, as early as 1508 Albuquerque was writing from Hormuz that 'People say they do not believe in Mohammad, but in "Ali, his son-in-law".' And yet the Portuguese rhetoric of Holy War against Islam, the *Reconquista* and the tenaciously held aspirations to liberate Jerusalem could not conceal the reality that they were both ignorant about and largely indifferent to the religious and cultural lives of the Muslims they now encountered in the Indian Ocean, who had become a strangely unfamiliar enemy. This was largely due to the fact that the Portuguese had done so little to preserve any knowledge of their own Islamic heritage. Although some Arabic speakers continued to be found in Portugal, it appears that by the middle of the 15th century a sort of collective amnesia regarding Islam had descended upon the Portuguese. When the Flemish scholar Nicolas Cleynaerts, who was living in Portugal in the early 1530s, wished to learn Arabic he was unable to find a teacher and it seems that the only group which continued to pursue studies in the language was that involved in the medical profession. It is an ironic fact that during the period of Portuguese expansion in the Indian Ocean, there were more Arabic and Islamic manuscripts in Italy than in Spain or Portugal. What this meant was that the Portuguese were unprepared for the linguistic complexity which greeted them in the Indian Ocean, the key to which was Arabic, the *lingua franca*; but that key required old skills that had been largely forgotten and arrogantly unlearned.

When Christopher Columbus travelled to the Americas and landed in the Caribbean in 1492 he was convinced that he had arrived in the Far East. When Vasco da Gama landed in Calicut in 1498, however, he knew that he had found India. But da Gama's India was deeply inspired by the classical images of Herodotus and Aeschylus, a land characterised by an abundance of gold and a preponderance of monstrous people such as pygmies, troglodytes and Amazons. This was an India which lay at the limits of the world and of human imagination. Lopes, like many Portuguese, had avidly read Marco Polo, and had based much of his knowledge of the land which lay ahead on his fantastical imaginings. For Lopes the attraction of India would not just have been down to its reported abundance of spices but also because there one came across valleys of diamonds, gigantic birds and serpents which guarded untold riches, and humans with tails. In this India one found pearls the size of pigeon eggs, and rubies so large that it took four men to carry one, and so shiny that once placed on the posts of a bed they eliminated the need for candles. It was the land where sailors were able to stay underwater for three hours so they could repair the keel of their ship and where some boats were not constructed with iron nails because the bottom of the sea was made of magnetic stone.

On the cusp of the age of Renaissance humanism, empirical information and scientific rationale, poised to benefit from the works of geographers and cartographers, the Portuguese still held firm to their medieval cosmology and their attachment to myths and legends. For them the India which lay on the other side of the world was the India of Sindbad and *The Thousand and One Nights* (there had been Spanish translations of the stories of Sindbad as early as the 1250s). And yet it is hard to explain away this ignorance, since despite its multiple gods, colourful myths and countless rebirths, India was never a closed country like, for example, pre-Meiji era Japan. A Venetian account of India written in 1444 is surprisingly accurate, describing the priestly class of the Brahmins, the Malabari matriarchy and polyandry, the Kingdom of Vijayanagar and its polygamous ruler, the custom of *sati* (the tradition whereby widows immolate themselves on their husbands' funeral pyres), and elephants and mangoes, besides other matters of commercial interest. Nevertheless, when da Gama and his companions were taken to a Hindu temple in Calicut they thought it was a church, and they offered prayers before an image which they took to be that of the Virgin Mary. 'Many other saints were painted on the walls of the church, wearing crowns', the writer noted. Some of these saints had 'teeth protruding an inch from the mouth, and four or five arms'. Even then the Portuguese, it seems, did not suspect that anything was amiss. They had arrived in India convinced that the population was composed of Muslims and Christians and had assumed that the Hindus were Eastern Christians, even if their rituals, like the practice of *sati* and their vegetarianism for example, must have appeared rather odd. 'The city of Calicut', Vasco da Gama wrote with supreme confidence, 'is inhabited by Christians.' It wasn't of course, but it should also be noted in passing that the Indians themselves were equally puzzled by the unexpected arrival of the Portuguese, and had initially assumed they were foreign Muslims who somehow could not speak Arabic. It was not until a second expedition in 1501 that it dawned on the Portuguese that the majority of the population of India were neither Christian nor Muslim. And since they were clearly not Jewish (at least that much was obvious), the Portuguese labelled them *gentios* – heathens, 'who worship the sun, the moon and cows'.

≈

When the final word came to be written about Dom Francisco de Almeida, the first Viceroy of India, it was in the form of a simple and poignant sentence, '*Here lies Dom Francisco de Almeida, Viceroy of India, who never lied or fled.*' By all accounts Almeida was incorruptible – presumably this was the reason Manuel appointed him as his first Viceroy in India. A member of the high nobility, he was a wealthy widower of 55 when he set off for India, a relatively old age at which to undertake such an arduous journey. For many Portuguese the attraction of India was the promise of wealth, but for Almeida it was the promise of honour. The King had instructed him to first gain control of the Swahili Coast and build forts at the cities of Cannanore, Quilon and Cochin. But Manuel had also given Almeida a further instruction: 'Wage war and total destruction, by all means you best can by land and by sea so that everything possible is destroyed.' Almeida had declared that the Empire was his ship and though he has been proclaimed as the founder of the *Estado da Índia* the Viceroy would have been surprised by that claim, since he had no great vision of establishing a land empire nor even permanent posts for the Portuguese in the interior. Except for some occasional diplomatic missions, the Portuguese under Almeida confined themselves to the coastal regions, trading where they could, limiting themselves to buying and lading spices, without bothering to explore the rest of the

Indian Ocean or to engage in local trade. Perhaps that is why Manuel, who was notorious for changing his mind, had gradually turned against Almeida and appointed Albuquerque to replace him.

When Fernão Lopes and João da Nova abandoned Albuquerque on his mission to subdue Hormuz, and sailed for Cochin, where Almeida was based, they knew that they would receive a warm reception and a receptive ear. Although it is uncertain whether Lopes knew Almeida in Lisbon, what is certain is that da Nova knew him well, for he had sailed to India with the Viceroy in 1505. However, the Almeida who welcomed da Nova and Lopes upon their arrival in Cochin was grief stricken, for a horrible calamity had just befallen him. A few weeks earlier the Mamluk fleet, mentioned earlier, which had been making its way down the Red Sea, had inflicted a terrible defeat on a Portuguese force off Diu (near present day Mumbai), during which Almeida's son Dom Lourenço de Almeida had been killed. The news of the death of his son struck Almeida as a lightning bolt, and for days he locked himself in his chambers, refusing to see or speak to anyone. When finally he did emerge, though, his countenance and demeanour were calm. Lopes and the other *fidalgos* present would not have failed to notice that the Viceroy's words carried a cold warning of his vengeance: 'He who ate the chick', he informed the men, according to Gaspar Correia, 'has to eat the rooster, or pay for it.' At the heart of his grief a fire burned, fanned by his hatred of Muslims and his desire to wreak a bloody and pitiless revenge. Almeida began preparing for a new battle which would decide the fate of the Portuguese in India, a battle for which he was prepared to die. However, the monsoon season had arrived, and so during the wet season he commanded that the ships be readied for the following year. It was during this time of preparation for war that da Nova and Lopes spoke to Almeida about Albuquerque, and about the folly of his fort in Hormuz. They also spoke about

Albuquerque's brutality and his needless punishments. As the men talked, bravado and wine flowed, and the stories grew wilder. 'In my opinion', one of the men ventured, 'India is now in greater peril from Afonso de Albuquerque than ever from the Turks', while others swore that they would leave India rather than serve under him. Almeida listened to all this but unbeknown to the men, his mind was elsewhere and he could not help but wonder: would his son have been saved had Albuquerque not insisted on building his fort at Hormuz and set sail instead to confront the Mamluk fleet? And when the *fidalgos* had finally taken their leave, the idea remained and festered in Almeida's mind.

A few months later, in late 1508, with the monsoon winds abating, Almeida finally gave the command to sail but, soon after, Albuquerque's ships were sighted approaching Cochin. Albuquerque's own ship, the *Cirne*, which had left Lisbon in pristine condition two and a half years ago, was now so waterlogged that fish were swimming in the hold. Albuquerque, brusque by nature, was a man of few words: he greeted Almeida and immediately presented him with Manuel's letter of authorisation and claimed the governorship for himself. Almeida knew that he could not disobey the King's orders, for he had no valid reason to do so, but neither could he leave India without first avenging his son's death. The following morning, Almeida slipped anchor at the head of eighteen vessels carrying 1,500 men, Fernão Lopes among them, and set sail to hunt the Mamluk fleet, leaving Albuquerque behind. Almeida knew that he had disobeyed Manuel's orders but the vengeance which now impelled him forward was too powerful to be contained. Previously he had been accused of being too cautious by none other than the King, but now he had decided to take the law into his own hands. Albuquerque could wait. Even Manuel could wait. Almeida sailed north, expanding Portuguese influence as he did so by demanding submission from the trading towns he passed, and by December 1508 he had reached Dabul, a wealthy Muslim trading port. Here was an opportunity for Almeida: to both train his men for the battles ahead and send a message to the enemy. He instructed his men: 'instil terror in the enemy that you are going after, so that they remain completely traumatised'. What followed that day was horror upon horror. Dabul, despite being defiantly defended by 6,000 men, was never going to be able to withstand the charge of the Portuguese soldiers, and the slaughter which followed was indiscriminate. Men and women were killed, old people cowering in fear were slain and children were dragged from the frantic grip of their mothers and dashed against the walls. And when all the Muslims had been slain, their corpses piled one on top of the other in grotesque bloated, distended forms, the animals – the dogs and cows, the sheep and goats – were then all killed. On that day Lopes, with the scent of blood in his nostrils and his armour reflecting in the sun, charged the inhabitants of Dabul and killed on a massive scale. But still this was not enough to sate the Portuguese, and Almeida's men urged him to torch the town, for in the words of Henry V, 'War without fire is like sausages without mustard.' Fire raged in Dabul until the smell of burning flesh made the men retch, and all that remained was ash and madness.

The ferocious assault launched in Dabul was a favoured Portuguese war tactic, by which they aimed to catch the enemy by surprise and subdue them as quickly as possible. The attacks themselves were largely disorganised: each man simply charged the enemy, lashing out at them with little concerted tactical coordination. The soldiers would rush in, motivated largely by the lure of loot, but there was also the desire, mainly among the nobility, to engage in acts of bravery and risk so as to be honoured. If their individual bravery outdid that of others and stood out, their boldness would be rewarded. Often the assaults succeeded in terrorising the enemy, but their disorganised nature also led to military disasters. On one occasion in 1510, during the attack on Calicut led by Fernão Coutinho, the disorganisation of the Portuguese, who were distracted by their desire for plunder, led to many deaths when the Indians launched a counter attack. On another occasion, in 1513, their scaling of the walls of Aden was so frenetic and frenzied that the wooden ladder broke and the assault collapsed. It was certainly *magnifique* but whether it was war is another matter.

For Lopes, chivalry had to be gained on the battlefield, and it had to be earned by performing heroic feats of arms under not only dangerous but even rash conditions. It was necessary to risk losing one's life, for chivalry was even greater than wisdom, which taught that one should not take unnecessary risks, or even rash ones. This led young noblemen to fight heroically against impossible odds, and to undertake almost suicidal feats in the heat of battle. It also led to furious killing and pillaging, for those twin feats were marks of the highest chivalry. As well as a code of behaviour, chivalry was a code of violence. Violence was considered not just a necessary part of life, but also moral, and needed in order to uphold the truth and to root out heresy. Suppose a man had gangrene in his leg which was spreading, and he was about to die, argued Saint Augustine. And suppose that the only way to save his life was to amputate his leg. Thus the man would have to be strapped to a table and the leg sawn off. This was an act of violence. But did that make the violence evil? Saint Augustine argued that it did not, and if that were the case and one exception could be found to the idea that violence was evil, then violence itself could not be intrinsically evil. Lopes' world was dominated by this Augustine concept. Violence could be evil but it could also be a force for good. In this way a famous French medieval magistrate was known to have lamented his leniency when, instead of having young children accused of witchcraft burned, he had sentenced them only to be flogged while they watched their parents burn. Violence also needed to be understood within a culturally constructed boundary which separated one group from the other – either on religious grounds, as for example the Christian from the Muslim or the orthodox from the heretic, or on economic or social grounds, such as the aristocrat from the peasant. As well as carrying out these feats, it was equally necessary to record them in written form. It is for this reason that Portuguese chroniclers took such pains to narrate details of gruesome violence, often, it must be said, exaggerating it. Such details, which culminated with the dubbing of the particular knight, were read out as part of the entertainment at the King's palace or in the palaces of great lords.

In February 1509, two months after the battle of Dabul, Almeida gained his revenge on the Mamluk fleet when he crushed it in a huge battle at Diu. It was an important victory – a historic one indeed which signalled to the Muslims that the Portuguese were there to stay in the Indian Ocean – but it was also a victory which was followed by a great shedding of blood, for Almeida now ordered that the captured Muslims have their hands and feet cut off and be burned alive on a great pyre. Some, for amusement, were tied alive to the mouth of cannons and torn apart from the blast. Others were lynched and their corpses were left hanging from the masts as the ships sailed back to Cochin. When victory was secured, feted and celebrated, Almeida knighted those who had fought bravely: among them Fernão Lopes, who had sailed for India with the hope of attaining such a title. Almeida's victory had cemented Portuguese power in the Indian Ocean, but in the process his *fidalgos* had shed much blood, and shed blood never sleeps. It would be remembered by the Muslims for a long time with grief, and would haunt the dreams of some of the Portuguese until their dying days.

In bloody triumph, with trumpets blaring, Almeida returned to Cochin where he found Albuquerque awaiting him on the beach to both congratulate him and finally assume command. But, perhaps fortified by his devastating victory, and with the blood coursing in his veins, Almeida not only brushed past Albuquerque, claiming that it was too late in the season for him to depart from India, but he went directly against the directives of the King and commanded that Albuquerque be indicted for mis-governance and placed under house arrest. In reality the confinement was hardly one of hardship, and remarkably Albuquerque, renowned and feared for his fiery temper and rage, accepted it with equanimity. One imagines that Albuquerque must have been told to stay at home for a while until Almeida had calmed down and come to his senses. There was no real chance of Manuel's orders not being carried out but the pride and egos of these two *fidalgos* must have been immense. During this period of confinement, an incident took place which demonstrated that although Albuquerque was quick to anger, he had an undeniable greatness and a magnanimity in his soul. One afternoon he was visited by Lopes, who informed him that João da Nova, the man who had caused him such disobedient hardship in Hormuz and who had then deserted him, had died in poverty. For a few minutes Albuquerque remained silent and then, tears welling up in his eyes, he paid for the funeral expenses.

But the man destined to be the next governor of India could not be confined for long; after all he carried with him a letter of appointment from Manuel, and Almeida soon came to his senses, having been counselled about the folly of his stubbornness. Handing over the governorship to Albuquerque, Almeida returned to Lisbon. He would never reach home, as he was killed in a skirmish on the West African coast, still rashly chasing honour and glory, just after he had rounded the Cape, and was buried in an impromptu grave on the African sea shore. 'They were killed by sticks and stones', so wrote the Portuguese historian Barros, 'hurled not by giants or armed men but by bestial negroes, the most brutal of all on that coast'.

The death of João da Nova had obviously reconciled Fernão Lopes with Albuquerque for, following Almeida's departure, he now served under the new governor. The past it seemed had been forgotten, but it would not be long before the tensions between them would erupt again, and this time in the most brutal form.

CHAPTER EIGHT

'Out of stubbornness he wanted to die and kill them all'

It was Timoji the Hindu who first planted the thought in Albuquerque's mind. Prior to the arrival of the Portuguese, Timoji had earned his fortune as a pirate, attacking merchant fleets that traded pepper with Gujarat. His fame had brought him followers, with 2,000 mercenaries under his command, but when he offered his services to Vasco da Gama in 1498, the Portuguese suspected him of being a spy and turned him down. By 1505 however it seems that Timoji had succeeded in embedding himself as a useful ally to Almeida, earning his trust when he warned him of the siege of Cannanore by Calicut forces. In 1510 Albuquerque was determined to return to Hormuz, but it was Timoji who advised him to look elsewhere. If, he argued, the governor wished to establish a Portuguese monopoly over the trade of India, then a secure base from which to patrol the western Indian waters had to be found. Goa, a city lying about 250 miles south of Bombay on the western coast of India, midway between Malabar and Gujarat, and situated on a fertile island between two rivers, was the ideal location at which to establish the capital of Portuguese

India, the seat of its viceroys and governors and the administrative centre of all its possessions east of the Cape of Good Hope. In addition, Goa lay between the Muslim-controlled North and the Hindu-controlled South, and its two rivers, the Mandovi and the Zuari, served as natural barriers guarding the city and making it defensible. Whether it really took a Hindu pirate to convince Albuquerque of the merits of Goa is unlikely since the Viceroy had already done his reconnaissance of the area, but Timoji did offer one piece of important information: the time was right to seize Goa, for the city was ready to fall.

Long before Goa came under the Portuguese it was a flourishing centre inhabited by the Hindus, under the rule of the Vijayanagar Empire, with a number of temples dedicated to various Hindu gods, Shiva being the most prominent. In 1472 however the powerful minister of the neighbouring Bahmani kingdom, Mahmud Gawan, captured Goa and converted it to a Muslim city, destroying all the Hindu temples. In 1500 Goa fell again, this time to Yusuf Adil Khan of Bijapur. The city was now absorbed into the Sultanate of Bijapur, which lay in the Deccan Plateau that makes up most of the southern part of India. Under the Bijapuris, a citadel was constructed, as was a majestic palace for the 'Sabayo' (the name by which Yusuf Adil Khan was known to the Portuguese) which was later used as the Portuguese governor's official residence. Yusuf Adil Khan had also ordered that the city be surrounded with a wall and a moat to thwart any external invasion. To secure his sultanate further, he maintained a large garrison of about 9,000 people there, and to prevent spies from gaining access to the city he appointed a captain to prohibit the movement of anybody without a pass, while magistrates were instructed to stop any strangers from entering and collect their details. Until the arrival of the Portuguese, Goa was the main port of trade for the kingdoms of both Muslim Bijapur and Hindu Vijayanagar, which was one of the important kingdoms in medieval Indian history. For about 200 years the Hindus of Vijayanagar and the Muslims of the Deccan Plateau (divided in due course into the five states of Berar, Bijapur, Ahmednagar, Golkunda and Bidar) were engaged in continual conflict over who controlled Goa.

Goa traded, most importantly, in horses: the best came from Arabia as the ones bred locally were considered to be physically incapable. As a Portuguese contemporary noted, 'the best are the Arabians, next are the Persians and third are those from Cambay [in present day Gujarat]. These latter are worth a little.' As the Muslim Deccan states fought with the Hindu state of Vijayanagar, good war horses were essential and whoever controlled Goa prevented the other from importing them. Naturally Arabian horses were very expensive and the import tax on them – with about a thousand horses passing through every year – was a major source of revenue for Goa.

For the Portuguese, the lucrative horse trade was not the main reason for their interest in the port. In fact, Goa's trade was of little interest. What made it so attractive to the Portuguese was its location, which would allow them to disrupt the spice route that commenced in Malacca and then sailed either to the Malabar coast or to Gujarat and thence to the Persian Gulf or the Red Sea. In addition, Goa had already proved itself to be defensible, thanks largely to Yusuf Adil Khan's efforts. Even though Goa had to import its food from inland, that could be handled. In any case the Portuguese had not come to India to be farmers. The majority had been shore dwellers at home and they would spend most of their time in India on the coast. Given their small numbers, and given the power of the neighbouring kingdoms of Vijayanagar and Bijapur, it is unlikely the Portuguese could have ventured far inland anyway. Largely for that reason, Goa remained, culturally, part of the Indian mainland. Although the city itself would come under Portuguese control, the lands surrounding it – the three islands and the districts of Bardaz to the north and Salcete to the south – reflected the real face of India. It was these two fertile districts upon which Goa depended for its food, and which attracted the attention of the neighbouring Sultanate of Bijapur, which was located eight days' journey away.

Timoji the pirate, as reflected in the *Commentaries of Albuquerque*, continued to insist that Goa was ripe and ready to fall. He knew the city and he assured Albuquerque that the Hindu community there was ready to rise up against the Muslims, for they chafed under their rule. They just needed the Portuguese to come to their aid. Initially Albuquerque was not convinced, for he had set his heart on returning to Hormuz, but to his credit he listened and was gradually won over by Timoji's words. In the middle of February 1510 Albuquerque made his advance and found the pirate's words to be true, as Goa's defences collapsed with little resistance. Albuquerque was gracious in victory, declaring religious tolerance for Hindus and Muslims and a lowering of taxes. His only condition was that the Bijapuri garrison should depart. He also gave strict (and pragmatic) instructions that there should be no plunder and no violence since he knew he had to settle in Goa and wished to cause no antagonism. On 1 March, Albuquerque took possession of the city and rode through its gates accompanied by Lopes and the other *fidalgos*, behind a friar holding a jewelled cross and the banner of the Order of Christ. The city which Albuquerque conquered was relatively small (though it would grow to around 60,000 inhabitants within 50 years – still only one-tenth the size of Madrid). Its population was overwhelmingly Hindu with some Muslim merchants and traders. The number of Portuguese who would settle in the city however was astonishingly small. In 1524 there were only 450 Portuguese householders in Goa.

The ease with which Goa was captured had been deceptive: when the news of its loss reached Yusuf Adil Khan in Bijapur he began gathering his forces. Albuquerque, impressed by the city's strategic location, meanwhile was determined to hold Goa at any cost. Others among the *fidalgos*, however, were less determined, and inevitably fissures began to appear. They warned Albuquerque that the monsoon season was fast approaching; surely it was more prudent now to abandon Goa and head for Cochin? If they failed to leave before the rains arrived and the oceans became unnavigable they could become trapped and would be in danger of being besieged. In the meantime, Yusuf Adil Khan had summoned his general Pulad Khan and ordered him to advance on to Goa. The general, who was more knowledgeable than the Portuguese about the local terrain, spread his forces wide to keep the Portuguese *fidalgos* and their soldiers stretched as thinly as possible. Having done so, he waited for the weather to worsen for he knew that the monsoon would trap the Portuguese in Goa.

Both Pulad Khan and Albuquerque knew that Goa was vulnerable to an enemy occupying the opposite banks of the two rivers, the Mandovi and the Zuari. This meant that, to protect the city, it was imperative to hold the strategic fort at Banastarim which lay around three miles east and adjacent to both waterways, since unless the Portuguese controlled the land on both sides of the rivers, the city could be easily blockaded. Albuquerque sent a general, de Sousa, accompanied by a group of *fidalgos*, to Banastarim, but once they reached it they found it was overrun by Pulad Khan's troops and the Portuguese had no choice but to retreat back to Goa. The situation was now becoming critical as Albuquerque's options dwindled, for now only a narrow canal separated the two armies. Albuquerque may have been determined to hold Goa but Yusuf Adil Khan was equally determined to regain it. However, one morning an extraordinary event took place. The Portuguese saw a man in Islamic dress approaching the water's edge, waving a white flag. To their astonishment, he spoke out in fluent Portuguese, 'My Portuguese lords, let someone come and speak to me to relay a message for the governor.' The man then identified himself as João Machado and begged safe conduct to speak to Albuquerque. So remarkable was the emergence of Machado and so impactful on Lopes' life that I need to pause the battle of Goa for a moment and tell his story.

João Machado was born in Braga in North-west Portugal to a family from the minor nobility. As a young man, he was sent to live with an uncle who was an abbot. He fell in love with the niece of the abbot and, in the words of the 16th-century chronicler Barros, 'the affair ended up with her getting pregnant'. Fearing the wrath of the abbot the two lovers fled and in the ensuing pursuit Machado stole a horse. They were eventually arrested and brought to trial where he was accused of theft, as Barros informs us somewhat unnecessarily, 'on account of the beast, and of fornication because of the girl'. Machado was sentenced to perpetual exile to the *terras perdidas* – the lost lands – in his case the island of São Tomé which lies near the equator off the coast of Africa. His sentence had probably been commuted as deportation was often applied to 'honourable people' as a substitute for other punishments such as public lashings or death. But deportation had a purpose, and the deported men were used for carrying out hazardous missions since, as the historian Castanheda pragmatically put it, 'one does not lose very much if their lives were lost'.

Machado sailed with the second armada in 1500 which was captained by Pedro Álvares Cabral, and he was left on the Island of Mozambique with instructions to gather useful information for future Portuguese fleets. The next time we hear of Machado, just prior to the Portuguese arrival in Goa, he had undergone a remarkable transformation. He had become a Muslim who used the name Cufo (Yusuf), and he had slipped away to India, where he settled for a few years. Adapting totally to the new habits and customs, he quickly learned Arabic, which he seemed intriguingly to have known from his days in Braga, and entered the employment of Malik Ayas (Maiquiaz), admiral of the Sultanate of Gujarat. Following this, Machado travelled further south where he ended up in the service of the famous Yusuf Adil Khan of Bijapur as captain of the 'white people', a military corps that included Turks, Persians, Arabs, Turcomans and Khorasanians (from an area which is largely in modern day Afghanistan and Iran). In addition, the corps included Europeans who were all converts to Islam. It was in Bijapur that Machado had married a Muslim woman by whom he had at least two children (although some sources claim four). In this way, Machado lived in Bijapur, seemingly content, respected and wealthy. In 1510, after nearly a decade there, news reached him of Albuquerque's capture of Goa, and around May of that year, with the monsoon fast approaching, he arrived as part of a military contingent under the command of the Bijapuri Sultanate's great military general Pulad Khan. The Muslim general hoped that he could persuade Albuquerque to abandon Goa, in exchange for a guarantee of the safe evacuation of Portuguese troops to their fleet, which was anchored at the city's harbour, and he needed an emissary to make this proposal to Albuquerque. Naturally he chose Machado. One can only imagine Albuquerque's astonishment when Machado was brought to him – it was only to be expected that he remained suspicious of this strange-looking Portuguese. But Machado spoke openly and confidently. Yusuf Adil Khan had made a truce with the Hindu Vijayanagar kingdom, thus easing his fears of an invasion, and was now free to head to Goa at the head of a large army. In addition, the monsoon was approaching. Albuquerque should leave the island now before it was too late. Leave now while the weather and the Muslims still remained merciful. That day Fernão Lopes was in Albuquerque's camp, and he was present at the encounter. Like the other Portuguese he gazed curiously at Machado and one wonders what he would have made of him, so comfortable did Machado appear in his garb and manners. The two men exchanged no words, after all, why should they? But it would not be the last time they would meet.

By now we know Albuquerque well enough to have guessed how he would respond to Machado's softly veiled threat: 'What the Portuguese win', he bluntly informed Machado, 'they never give up.' But Albuquerque made a further riposte; he declared that not only was he not leaving Goa, he was also not planning to release the Muslim women and their relatives he had seized as captives and whom, he brazenly informed Machado, he would convert to Christianity. Albuquerque's bravado may have been typical of the man but it was a bravado as yet unknown in India, or at least in Bijapur, or to Pulad Khan, for when Machado relayed back Albuquerque's messages, the general was astonished and insulted. Was Albuquerque a brilliant commander or a fool? Time would tell, but the dishonour of not returning Muslim women would not be forgotten.

And so Pulad Khan began finalising his preparations for an assault on Goa. At the same time, in Goa, Albuquerque's words had gone down badly with his *fidalgos*. Why did he cling on so stubbornly to the city? Did he genuinely believe that he could hold out during the monsoon until the next fleet arrived from Lisbon – which would not be before next August at the earliest? The mood among his men was sullen and uncomprehending. To Lopes, Albuquerque's actions would have reminded him of his tyrannical behaviour at Hormuz. It was clear that the Muslim forces would overrun Goa, and with each day the winds of the monsoon gained in strength and the rains sapped morale. Then, on 11 May 1510, with the monsoon wind hammering down, Pulad Khan launched his assault on Goa, taking the Portuguese by surprise and forcing them into desperate street fighting as they were gradually pushed back into the citadel. For twenty days Albuquerque continued to resist until news reached him that Yusuf Adil Khan himself had arrived in Goa and was leading the Muslim forces. The situation was desperate, and Lopes and the other captains now begged Albuquerque to withdraw before calamity befell them all, especially after the Portuguese Muslim João Machado was once again dispatched to Albuquerque, this time with a final warning that unless the governor withdrew at once his boats would be burned and sunk, thereby blocking the harbour and any hope of escape. And so, on the 31st of May, at midnight and in the utmost secrecy, Albuquerque retreated backwards to the quays. Some of the *fidalgos* argued for setting Goa on fire but he refused, claiming that he would soon return to reconquer it. Then as he was about to embark he gave a final and chilling order. He insisted that all the noble Muslim women and children who had been held captive, and whom Pulad Khan had requested be returned, were to be slaughtered. More than anyone he understood how shocking the act of killing the noblewomen was, and he calculated that when Yusuf Adil Khan's generals poured through the gates to prevent his departure they would be frozen at least for a few moments by the horror of seeing their wives and relatives slaughtered, their corpses scattered in the streets, and that in those moments he would be able to set sail.

There was no time to waste. The women and children needed to be killed, and though some undoubtedly were, some of the *fidalgos* refused to carry out the command. One of them was Rui Dias, Lopes' friend on his journey from Lisbon. Dias dressed some women as men and stowed them away on the fleeing ships. Nor was Timoji, the Hindu pirate who had once convinced Albuquerque to seize Goa, able to carry out the governor's orders, and he escorted some women and children to a house which he locked safely to protect them. The fortifications of Goa now undefended by the Portuguese, the Muslim forces flooded into the city and chased the boats into the water, and as the monsoon rain poured down, in the middle of the night, Albuquerque and his bedraggled men departed Goa.

However, as the Portuguese feared and the Muslims already knew, Albuquerque had left it too late, for the monsoon winds now struck the fleet with fury and the torrential rain battered the ships' decks, echoing the cries of grief coming from the city on the shore, as the Muslims discovered their wives and daughters slaughtered. On deck, all able men worked furiously to prevent the ships from twisting in the current, tethering them at bow and stern. Despite their efforts, the Portuguese ships could not reach the open sea. In desperation Albuquerque risked one ship to determine whether it could pass through the sand pits at the river mouth but it was swept into the shoals and lost to the battering of the waves. On board the ships the fury of the *fidalgos* matched that of the monsoon, and the *Commentaries of Albuquerque* reflect this open rupture, for they openly blamed Albuquerque for the dire situation in which they now found themselves – 'out of stubbornness he wanted to die and kill them all'. They now spoke openly, imploring Albuquerque to weigh anchor and try to reach the open sea, but the pilots insisted that they would be unable to navigate past the shoals. Soon desertions began as men dived overboard and swam to shore. For Albuquerque, this was the moment of truth, a crisis unlike any he had faced before and a test of him as a general, as a leader and as a man. In addition, he had suffered a devastating personal loss when his nephew and greatest supporter António de Noronha died as a result of a skirmish with the Muslim forces on the outskirts of Goa. This was his darkest hour and in his despair he locked himself away and prayed fervently on his knees, weeping.

In the meantime, Yusuf Adil Khan, ensconced in his retaken citadel at Goa, was fretting, for throughout his sultanate there were threats that required his urgent attention. The Portuguese may have been driven out of Goa but they were still a force to be reckoned with and they remained in the river. Negotiations for a peace treaty would have to commence. But these negotiations soon hit a stumbling block as Yusuf Adil Khan was insisting on a particular condition that Albuquerque initially could not understand. The Sultan was adamant that the Muslim women who had been smuggled onto the Portuguese ships be returned immediately. Albuquerque believed that they had all been put to the sword and the realisation that some were alive and on his ships was so unacceptable that he flew into a rage. Who, he demanded, was responsible? At first the responses were elusive. Some of the women, he was told, had converted to Christianity, and this claim soothed his fury a bit. Others, he was told, had got 'married' to men in the fleet, and faced with this situation, Albuquerque pragmatically decided to legalise these unions without any formal or religious ceremony. When the Chaplain declared that this was contrary to church law, Albuquerque replied defiantly then the unions would be legalised 'according to the law of Afonso de Albuquerque'. But there were other women who had not converted, mainly the more noble women: the wives and daughters and sisters of the Muslim nobility who were now fighting on the side of the Bijapuris. These women, unlike the others, refused to consort with the common sailors and Albuquerque, we read in his *Commentaries*, now ordered that they be transferred to one of the ships and kept away from the men in a locked cabin under the guard of a eunuch. For the young and hot-blooded Portuguese *fidalgos*, the lure of young and beautiful Muslim women out of their reach was a prize too tempting to resist, and before long the eunuch was reporting to Albuquerque that the men were finding their way into the locked cabin at night. Albuquerque ordered that a watch be set to monitor the comings and goings on the ship. It was soon reported to him that men were observed swimming over to it, where they climbed up onto the rudder and entered via a hatch. When Albuquerque asked how many men, he was told maybe up to three but certainly one; and when he asked who, he was informed that it was a nobleman called Rui

Dias. This enraged Albuquerque, who declared that 'because of the crime of sleeping with Muslim women in such a place at such a time, with such flagrant insolence', there could only be one punishment: Dias was to be sentenced to death by hanging.

According to the accounts of Correia and the *Commentaries*, Rui Dias was playing chess when he was arrested. Once seized, a rope was tied around Dias' neck and he was strung up to be hanged. However, Jorge Fogaça, the captain with whom Dias was playing chess, intervened and cut the rope down, calling out in a loud voice that they were hanging Rui Dias. Rapidly, word spread from ship to ship, and resentment broke out openly among the men. How could Albuquerque give such an order? How could he give the order for a captain and a *fidalgo* to be hanged like a common criminal, without discussing this with them? The fleet seemed on the brink of mutiny, in the midst of which stood Lopes, who knew Dias well, for the two had sailed together from Lisbon with the fleet that had brought them to India. While all this was happening, Correia noted that the Muslims, watching from the bank, cheered and yelled at the discord among the Portuguese.

When news reached Albuquerque that his orders had been thwarted, he climbed into a boat and went to the ship to confront the mutineers. In moments of crisis, even in the eye of a storm, Albuquerque never backed down. Some considered this his greatest strength, others his most potent folly, but he had not backed down in Hormuz, nor in Goa, and he had no intention of backing down now. The men confronted Albuquerque and accused him of wishing to hang Dias by 'arbitrary absolute power, without discussing this with his captains'. They also advanced another argument: if Dias was truly guilty then why hang him like a common criminal when, as a nobleman, he should be beheaded, a punishment befitting his rank? Stoic and impassive in the face of the mutiny, Albuquerque refused to budge and confronting the mutineers face on, he ordered the seizure of Dias and had him hanged from the mast of the ship, leaving his body dangling as a warning, *pour encourager les autres*.

For the time being the immediate crisis was over: the mutineers backed down, even if they carried resentment in their hearts (and in particular in Lopes' heart, for he would not forgive Albuquerque). Luckily for all, fortune finally befriended the Portuguese with a clement change in the weather and winds which finally allowed them to set sail into the open sea. By then Yusuf Adil Khan had lost patience with these troublesome '*farangis*' (foreigners) and had departed Goa. 'May Allah the Merciful be rid of them', he announced as he returned to Bijapur. But though Allah was indeed merciful, he would soon find out that Albuquerque was not.

CHAPTER NINE

'Perfume-drenched
nincompoops'

fonso de Albuquerque is lauded today in Portugal as the 'Caesar of the East'. Though one cannot deny or ignore his violent despotism (a very Caesar-like attribute), nor the vitriolic hatred he had for Muslims, nor yet the brutal and autocratic manner in which he commanded, there lay in Albuquerque the sort of greatness appropriate to a man who was ultimately the architect of the Portuguese Empire in India. It was a greatness which manifested itself in his singular vision coupled with a demonic, indefatigable energy. Above all it was *his* vision and though, in public at least, he claimed to be the servant of the King who possessed the power, he was brusque in his writings to Manuel, for example stating: 'I am fifty years old and I have seen two kings before you and what they did in their time.' For Albuquerque, it was increasingly clear that though there was money to be made in the trade between Goa and Lisbon, Portugal had little to offer India in exchange for its spices. He saw that the real wealth lay in trading within the cities and ports of Asia – as the Muslims had done for centuries.

Albuquerque understood with piercing clarity that the Portuguese Empire could not, despite Almeida's words, be a naval empire. Only possession of territory, based around coastal forts, would make the imperialistic gamble secure. 'Sire', he pleaded with Manuel, 'put your trust in good fortresses.' Elsewhere he urged that 'a good fort once taken will remain so until Judgment Day', and Goa – his obsession – was at the heart of this policy of securing a land empire. His refusal to abandon it had nearly brought him and his men to catastrophe and now, having sailed away, he commenced immediate plans to recapture it. Although an element of revenge motivated him and a refusal to be beaten, there also existed his absolute conviction that Goa was the ideal platform on which to base the Empire. 'Strongly support Goa', he told Manuel, and 'you will thus gain all its territory.' Elsewhere he assured the King that 'there is nowhere on the coasts as good or as secure as Goa, because it is an island. If you lost the whole of India, you could reconquer it from there.' He was of course right, and therein lay his genius. Others failed to understand his vision, and he lacked the patience and humility to explain it. Often he chided the King himself: 'Your Highness should not ignore the things that I say', but as far as Albuquerque was concerned, India was his project and Goa was its key.

Albuquerque's first brush with Goa had taught him two valuable lessons. Firstly, that its capture had been deceptively easy, for he had underestimated the ferocity with which the Bijapuri Sultan would fight to retake it. Secondly, he now understood that to seize and hold Goa he needed allies, and his natural allies were the Hindus who formed the majority population in Goa and resented Muslim rule. Consequently, he now authorised the pirate Timoji to gather these allies, promising them land and property as spoils of war, and before long Albuquerque had the help of 40 Hindu captains whose men were offered further rewards for 'bringing in heads'. For Albuquerque, Hindu mercenaries had the added advantage that they could be obtained at half the cost of Portuguese fighters. Often the Hindus sought no money as long as they were allowed to plunder. Of course there was a great disadvantage on relying on local allies (and Timoji would eventually flout his authority and desert), but for the time being Albuquerque had no choice. While his fleet was being replenished and refitted, he turned his attention to those of his *fidalgos* and soldiers who he now knew viewed him with great suspicion, and who were extremely reluctant to embark on another foray with him. Some of the rebels had been imprisoned following the Dias debacle, and their release was now made conditional on their joining up for the new assault on Goa. As for the *fidalgos*, among whom was Lopes, Albuquerque rebuked and chastised them openly – diplomacy it seems was not his forte. 'Follow me. And those of you who don't', he ordered, should 'leave India and set sail back to Lisbon and give your explanation to the King.' Albuquerque had called their bluff: he knew that for most of those who had sailed with him from Portugal there was no turning back. They had come to India for honour and wealth and although little of either had been so far attained, some had at least been knighted. Now once again Goa lay ahead of them and with it once more the promise of riches and the opportunity to test themselves on the battlefield – to be knighted and potentially become wealthy. He, Afonso de Albuquerque, was their Pole Star. They had to follow him, perhaps reluctantly, but they had no choice. We must not forget that despite his resentment, Lopes was the King's servant and that the venture in India was the King's personal initiative. To speak out against Albuquerque was one thing – many *fidalgos* did that openly – and even to abandon him as had happened in Hormuz could be explained by the fact that Almeida was still the Viceroy. But now that Albuquerque was the governor he was the King's representative and for Lopes to disobey him would mean disobeying the

King himself, and that would mean the end of Lopes' career and aspirations.

By the end of November 1510, Albuquerque had gathered his forces in Cannanore, and he set sail for Goa with 1,600 men. On the 25th of that month, Saint Catherine's Day, with his *fidalgos* crying out loud 'St Catherine! Santiago!', he launched a ferocious and sustained attack on Goa. The garrison left behind there by the Bijapuris was incapable of withstanding the Portuguese attack, and Muslim resistance crumbled. Some of the Bijapuris tried to flee the city across the shallow fords, and many who did so drowned while the others were set upon by the Hindu troops accompanying the Portuguese. 'They put to the sword all the Muslims', Albuquerque noted, 'without sparing the life of a single creature.' Then he sent out the order to ransack the city; his later description of this to Manuel can still chill us 500 years later:

> I have burned the town and killed everyone. For four days without any pause our men have slaughtered ... wherever we have been able to get into we haven't spared the life of a single Muslim. We have herded them into the mosques and set them on fire. I have ordered that neither the [Hindu] peasants nor the Brahmins be killed. We have estimated the number of dead Muslim men and women at six thousand. It was, sire, a very fine deed.

Piero Strozzi, a Florentine merchant who was accompanying the Portuguese, noted grimly that 'no one escaped. Men, women, the pregnant, babes in arms.' So great was the number of the dead, the Portuguese soldiers gleefully acknowledged that even the crocodiles were sated with the corpses, the remainder of which now washed up on the shore. When the battle was finally over and the triumph secured, Albuquerque as he had promised knighted many of those who had fought. Goa had fallen once more to the

Portuguese. What undoubtedly helped Albuquerque, though whether he was aware of this fact is unclear, was that Yusuf Adil Khan had died in Bijapur and had been succeeded by his young son Ismail. Indeed many of the Muslim generals who were meant to be in Goa were attending the funeral in Bijapur.

~~~

The battle for Goa was finally over and for the Portuguese there was no longer an immediate threat. For Lopes as well as for the other soldiers, whose experiences of the city had hitherto been complicated by fierce fighting, there was now an opportunity to look around and to explore their new home. There was no doubt that Goa's grandeur would have overwhelmed a soldier like Fernão Lopes. As he explored the city on foot and on horseback, he would have marvelled at the palace, still known as the 'Sabayo's Palace' after its recent inhabitant, with its perfumed gardens commanding a regal and full view of the river and the quays. As he strolled in the royal stables he could have seen 150 Arabian horses and 100 elephants. It was almost certainly the first time that Lopes would have seen an elephant (they were just starting to make an appearance in Lisbon after he had left Portugal). From distant kingdoms, caravans of bullock carts arrived daily, laden with goods and merchandise, and for the first time in his life Lopes would have chewed on betel leaves and tasted areca nuts which seemed to be everywhere. The whole of Goa was a marketplace where all was bought and sold: horses, spices, dried drugs, sweet gums, as well as a panoply of strange and wondrous items from Sind (in modern day Pakistan) and China, from Bengal and Gujarat. As a young boy, Lopes might have known the fish and vegetable markets of Lisbon but what he now saw in Goa would have taken his breath away. The city bustled daily with goldsmiths, bankers and craftsmen. Jews mixed with Hindus, Christians with Jains and Muslims. Merchants mingled with other merchants: from Persia,

Arabia and Italy, from Abyssinia, Gujarat and the Malabar coast. There were enormous fortunes to be made, fortunes which were beyond the wildest dreams of any Lisbon merchant, as Hindu tradesmen purchased exotic goods through brokers wholesale, and sold them in the blink of an eye for great profit. Silks and satins, damasks and porcelains, and a multitude of other goods – some of which Lopes would have recognised but the majority of which would have left him baffled. Lopes would have marvelled at how quickly numbers were calculated, and if he attempted to decode the hand gestures or the subtle shaking of the heads with which the merchants conducted their trade, he would have been flummoxed simply by the speed with which they were carried out. On almost every street corner there was a market and with every market there were money changers called *xarafos* yelling, cajoling and dealing in what must have appeared to Lopes as a Tower of Babel. He would have walked through the bustle of the slave market where slaves were brought from all parts of the Orient to be sold on in Goa, and would have been bemused to learn that there was even a market for stolen goods, which operated at night but in a well-known location, where goods were sold at very cheap rates. But of all the markets the grandest undoubtedly was the horse market. When the horses were taken out for a ride, beautifully decorated with gold and silver trappings, they were a magnificent sight: the saddles were covered with rich embroidered silk cloth brought from Bengal, China and Persia, while the reins were studded with precious stones with jingling bells of silver.

The numerous Hindu temples were certainly impressive but what would have struck a man like Lopes above all was the dignified demeanour of the Brahmin priests. It seemed that almost the whole of Goa was in their hands, and they were greatly revered throughout the country. Following the retaking of Goa, many Hindus had chosen to remain in the city. To Lopes they would have appeared clever, prudent and learned in their religion, and to the physician Tomé Pires, who on occasion strolled through the city with Lopes, 'A Brahman would not become a Mohammedan [even] if he were made King.' But there were other aspects of Goa which would have alienated and angered a Portuguese like Lopes, none more so than the fact that women were expected to immolate themselves on the pyre of their husbands (the practice known as *sati*) and that those who refused to do so were shamed by their families and forced to become public prostitutes. No matter, India was like a dream, a fantasy, an idyllic paradise full of riches barely imaginable in Portugal, and Lopes would not have been slow to partake fully of them. Brought up against the stern and suffocating background of Portuguese morality, India represented a promise of pleasure which would never have been available to him in Lisbon, with its plagues and its traumas, its forced conversions and its ossified nobility. It offered opportunities of wealth and of lifestyle, and everything was possible; as one *fidalgo* succinctly put it, 'not even Mahomet had it so good'. João de Barros, a contemporary of Lopes, captured this hedonism when he wrote that the land was 'vicious and full of pleasures', and that its inhabitants were given to 'sensuality and all types of sins'. There was an 'infinity' of women in India, he warned, and they offered 'sensual vices'. Certainly the Portuguese gleefully sampled its riches, and were responsible for introducing syphilis to Goa, which became known locally as the 'Portuguese sickness'. To the great alarm of the Church the Portuguese began emulating the Hindu and Muslim habit of taking concubines. They 'were not content with one woman but had four of five in their homes', despite the Church insisting that sexual liaisons with native women corrupted the Portuguese, making them immoral. Above all the Portuguese were transfixed by the *Bailadeira*, which was the Portuguese term referring to the Hindu temple dancers or *devadasi*. The Portuguese misunderstood the ritual dancers who were tied to Hindu temple rituals, mistaking them for prostitutes. They were 'public women who for money do not say no to anyone'. The Church went as far as banning the schools that taught the young girls to dance, arguing that 'there was nothing more to incite sensuality than songs and lascivious and dishonest dances'. In desperation at what they perceived as the moral laxity of the Portuguese, the Church pointed out that even the Muslims – whom the Portuguese viewed as infidels and decadent – had banned these Hindu dancers. They fumed that the dancers were corrupting the Portuguese men and damning their souls. But the Church appealed in vain, for the *fidalgos* were not listening. The allure of India was simply too overwhelming.

Yet beyond the veils of promised wealth and hedonism and for those who searched deeper, as Lopes eventually would, a mystical and ancient India revealed its face. This was the real India, and it was here that Lopes could find himself – or lose himself, but that was still to come. For the time being Lopes had other, more worldly, matters on his mind and in Goa he soon acquired a mistress. That he had left a wife behind in Lisbon was neither here nor there, for in this he was simply following the common practice for the *fidalgos* and wealthy Portuguese. He also purchased a number of slaves from the local slave market for his household and to cater to all his needs. An early 17th-century report indicates that each Portuguese house in Goa had around ten slaves and one assumes that though the number may have been less during Lopes' time, it was not significantly so. At the time of Lopes the houses were spartan with the flooring made of beaten earth stabilised with cow-dung. Goa with its tropical forests provided many different species of wood for the houses, particularly the roofing, door and window frames. Teak was the most expensive wood with coconut a low-cost option for roofing.

We know nothing about Lopes' mistress since this was an age when women were written out of history, but she would almost certainly have been one of the Muslim women abandoned by their husbands and fathers during the conquest of Goa or widowed following the massacre of the Muslims by the Portuguese after the capture of the city. Although many Muslims abandoned the city following its retaking by the Portuguese, a few remained in Goa. She may even, though we will never know for certain, have been related to one of the women whom his friend Dias had helped to escape and who had sought shelter aboard the ships. The fact that she would have been a Muslim was ironically largely down to Albuquerque, who knew that Portugal, small and underpopulated as she was, was unable to provide the manpower to administer the Empire. His aim therefore was to create a class of people who could assist in sustaining and administering Goa and be loyal to the Portuguese. To that aim he encouraged interracial marriages between the Portuguese soldiers and the local inhabitants, and preference was given to Muslim women who were to be converted at the time of marriage. A major cause for the bias was their comparatively fair complexion in comparison to the local Hindu women, as it was surmised that the offspring would be fair. Within two months of capturing Goa, Albuquerque had overseen 200 weddings. He even offered economic incentives for his men to marry, granting them a dowry in cash and land.

So keen was Albuquerque for his men to marry that there were many incidents of confusion. In one ceremony, according to the *Commentaries*, Albuquerque, exercising his powers as governor, married several couples in a private home, but the place was poorly lit and overcrowded and in confusion the men took the wrong wives home and tried to exchange them for the right ones the following day. We have no records as to whether they were successful. Not all the Portuguese agreed with Albuquerque's plans for intermarriage and a more conservative element, led by one of Albuquerque's leading captains, Diogo Mendes de Vasconcelos, and members of the clergy, attempted to undermine the whole mixed marriage project. This led to discontent from among those men who had already married – the *casados* – and eventually a growing discontent and opposition. At one point the sources tell us that the native wives joined a conspiracy to hand Goa over to the Muslims. The story of the wives conspiring to hand over the city of Goa to the Muslims seems at best far-fetched but it does at least demonstrate the fact that a sizeable number of intermarriages must have already taken place.

Lopes would have become accustomed to daily life in Goa, with its slow and languid pace, and he would have participated fully in the local social customs, both Hindu and Muslim. Slowly he would have picked up some Goan proverbs and expressions which undoubtedly would have made him smile. He would have been astonished by the local convention that no Hindu wedding could take place unless the horoscopes of the bride and groom matched – which would have been done by a Hindu priest known as *bhat*. There were so many details to negotiate and endure to arrange a marriage that a common expression was *to get a daughter married you have to wear out several pairs of slippers*. Girls were married very young: *you are twelve, go to the house of your husband*. But there was one expression which would have sharply brought home to Lopes that not all was as tranquil as it may have appeared: *Portuguese justice and a grown-up girl no family would want*.

There is a tendency among the Portuguese, it must be said, to describe the early years of Goa, from its conquest in 1510 until the arrival of the Jesuits in the 1540s, as a golden era. '*Goa Dourada*' is the expression which has entered the language – a period when the Portuguese coexisted with the native Goans peacefully and there was no discontent between the colonial state and its subjects. A contemporary Muslim account however offers a different picture:

> The Portuguese tyrannized and corrupted the Muslims and committed all kinds of ignoble and infamous acts. Their acts of violence were countless ... They hindered the Muslims in

their trade, above all in their pilgrimage [to Mecca]. They robbed them, burnt their cities and mosques, seized their ships and dishonoured the Sacred Book [Quran], desecrated the sacred precincts of the mosques and incited the Muslims to apostasy ... They tortured the Muslims with fire, sold some and enslaved others, and against others practiced deeds of cruelty which indicated a lack of all humanitarian sentiment.

The reality was that golden Goa was neither golden nor even Goa, for until the 18th century the Portuguese, when referring to Goa, were actually only thinking of a small part: essentially the 'island' of Goa in the Mandovi River on which the Portuguese capital, the *Estado da Índia*, was situated. In reality Portuguese policy was one of prejudice and control, one of inquisition and specifically anti-Muslim measures. The Portuguese administration of justice was considered the most corrupt department of Portuguese rule, hence the local curse, '*May he be a victim of Goan justice.*' Another saying in Konkani, the Goan language, compared Portuguese justice with a cobweb that

can only catch mosquitoes: a Gujarati is penalized for squatting to urinate; a Hindu is put in irons for quarrelling with another of his kind or abusing him; but if a favourite of the authorities or a wealthy person breaks open a safe of a Hindu and takes away his goods by force, that is a light matter and permissible.

And golden as it was, Goa was very corrupt. Occasionally, in the midst of bureaucratic rhetoric and in terse sentences, official records tell us all that we need to know. One such account of the revenues of Goa for 1545 concluded, 'This is what Goa yielded last year apart from what was stolen by the officials', while another letter to Lisbon advised, 'for the King's property to increase it should pass through few hands, and the fewer hands of officials it has contact with the greater will be its increase'. For many *fidalgos* India was a get-rich-quick scheme. Many who held command were not only intent on pursuing their own private trade, they were also engaged in plundering the royal treasury almost as freely as they had plundered Muslim ships.

To understand how so many got away with this plundering, one must first understand that from its inception, the Portuguese overseas territories were practically a private possession and enterprise of the King. As early as 1510, Manuel had declared a royal monopoly on commodities like spices, drugs, dyes and indigo, as well as on horses, and he reserved the revenues derived from their sale for himself. The problem, or some would say the opportunity, lay in the fact that royal appointments were made not on any basis of experience, know-how or suitability for the post but purely on personal grounds: the candidate may have served the King or the governor with merit, in which case he would benefit. 'Above all do what appears to further my service', was often the only command that a nobleman received from the King. This meant that as long as the King or governor was satisfied there were no other criteria to be met. There was no acknowledged distinction between private and public funds, nor was the appointee granted a salary worthy of the name, with the bulk of money coming from the taxes which the *fidalgo* levied or the trading routes on which he successfully traded, which meant that he had some exclusivity in specific markets or ports. We do not know if Lopes himself benefitted from any such deal but he must have secured some source of funding or else he would have had to survive on nothing more than the stipend offered by the King. We are fortunate to have an eyewitness account from the 16th century Portuguese historian Diogo do Couto, who through his daily contact as an archivist in Portuguese Asia knew very well what was going on. Couto's assessment was a damning one. He alleged that the whole bureaucracy of the *Estado da Índia* was engaged in systematic thievery of the Portuguese royal treasury in Goa. As far as he was concerned, most of those Goan insiders were 'perfume-drenched nincompoops' who 'would have made the good king Manuel die of shame'. Many of those insiders viewed the posts as property, from which the holder was expected to make a profit. This attitude was expressed by a *fidalgo* who was appointed to a fort in Goa and who claimed openly, 'I am not going to my fort for any other reason than to come back rich.' In some cases extremely rich. For the captains there were many ways of making a fortune. One simple method was by stealing '*soldos velhos*' or old salaries – by simply neglecting to remove long-dead soldiers' names from the garrison muster. Many had not served for 50 years, but unawares, Lisbon dispatched payment which ended up in the commander's pocket. In the rare case that a suspicious Lisbon undertook an inquiry to check the accounts, then the response would be to sadly inform them that those members of the phantom garrison had suddenly and tragically been killed by a daring Muslim raid – may God curse the Muslims!

On many occasions, Lisbon complained that the Portuguese in Goa cared so little that they sold weapons and horses to the enemies. But the truth was that the local Portuguese cared far less about loyalty and honour than they did about profit. There was simply too much money to be made; offices were put up for sale to the highest bidder and posts were chosen accordingly. When the grand-sounding post of the Captaincy of Goa was offered, it was less well sought after than the post of judge of the customs house, where profits were clearly much greater. On paper of course the holders of these posts were protecting the royal monopoly, but in the most cynical manner. Taking advantage of the King's ignorance of what was happening they applied his directives with full force. In Goa for example those who owed money to the Crown were not only thrown into jail but, contrary to royal guarantees for civil offenders, they were also chained and tortured. How much of the extracted money actually ended up in the royal coffers was of course another matter.

What did the native Goans make of Fernão Lopes? For them he would simply have been a *farangi* who remained an infidel. Reports of the time claimed that such men treated their wives (if not any other Muslims) well. He would have bathed rarely and, to the horror of the Muslims, without using water after relieving himself. The colour of his skin was different and so was his hair; his nose was different and so were his eyes. And as for his ears – what kind of man did not pierce his ears? Despite the suffocating heat, he continued to dress absurdly in bell-shaped trousers, lace-trimmed collars and hats, which the locals found terribly amusing. When he ate rice he insisted on a spoon and did not use his right hand like any civilised person would, and as for his childish attempts to drink water from a pot without allowing it to touch his mouth, well, that caused much merriment among the young and old. Why did he not chew betel? And why did he insist on drinking so much wine and *araq*? What strange and absurd customs he had! Goans were very bemused by the Portuguese habit of walking their dogs. Why did they need to walk them? Could the dogs not walk on their own? Admittedly they were skilled warriors, good at using firearms and fiercely brave, facts that could not be denied by those who valued such things. But they were also uncouth and without manners. At best they were exotic, but ultimately they were pirates.

CHAPTER TEN

‘The elixir of mirth and pleasure’

oa now captured, Albuquerque knew that he himself could not remain there for long and he was determined to leave the place with the bulk of his forces as soon as possible, for the partially burned city was unable to supply sufficient provisions for all his men. In addition, in the early weeks of 1511, within four months of his conquest of Goa, Albuquerque received an urgent message from Diogo Mendes de Vasconcelos who informed him that an expedition to capture Malacca was floundering and that Portuguese hostages had been taken. He needed to come to their aid immediately. So in April of that year Albuquerque set sail on a new voyage of conquest with several of his loyal Goan-based Portuguese soldiers, but this time Lopes chose to remain in Goa. It was clear, given the monsoon winds, that he would not return for several months. When the two met again it would be in the most extraordinary circumstances. After Albuquerque departed Goa, Lopes vanishes completely from any historical records. In many ways, this is not surprising for our main source, the *Commentaries of Albuquerque*, focused on the captains and members of the high nobility who surrounded the governor. Lopes was at the edge of this inner circle, important enough to be in the presence of Albuquerque but not significant enough to be mentioned by the chroniclers.

The next time he appears he is in Bijapur and has converted to Islam. Even more astonishingly, he is willing to fight (and indeed to die) for the Sultan of Bijapur against the Portuguese. It is a truly audacious turn of events and for the first time Lopes will take centre stage. Until now he had been playing a minor role to the great Albuquerque, whose force of character dominated every scene. But from this moment the drama of the story shifts, and dramatically so, as Fernão Lopes emerges from the shadows. To attempt to explain this remarkable transformation it is necessary to follow in Lopes' footsteps on the eight-day journey that separated Goa from Bijapur.

It was while in Goa that Lopes would have first heard stories from merchants and travellers, both real and embellished, about Bijapur, the neighbouring sultanate which lay only eight days' walk away. In the words of the 16th-century Persian poet Muhammad Zuhur ibn Zuhuri: 'If they made the elixir of mirth and pleasure, they would make it from the holy dust of Bijapur.'

So far Lopes' only encounter with the Bijapuri Sultanate would have been either in fighting its soldiers or crossing paths with its merchants coming to sell their goods in Goa's numerous markets. For years Goa and Bijapur had traded, and merchants would set out on the eight-day journey which separated them on a daily basis. The arrival of the Portuguese may have disrupted this dynamic, but not for long, and soon trade and bartering began to flow again. But there was much more to Bijapur than trade. Possibly Lopes' Muslim 'wife' may have had connections stretching to Bijapur, and he may have heard stories from her.

Nonetheless he was perfectly positioned to understand that, a mere eight days away, there lay a very different kind of life.

Although today not as well known as the larger Safavid and Mughal Empires, the Islamic Sultanate of Bijapur was, in the words of the art historians George Mitchell and Mark Zebrowski, one of India's 'most mysterious and unknown regions … a place which revels in dream and fantasy'. Positioned between the Mughal Empire to the north and the Hindu Vijayanagar Empire to the south, Bijapur was one of the five sultanates of central India's Deccan Plateau that emerged, beginning in the late 15th century, from the slow breakup of the 200-year-old Bahmani Sultanate. Lopes would have been impressed by the descriptions of Bijapur as being extremely large, well populated and fortified. He would have listened with interest to the picture that emerged of its ruler as a patron of the arts, and tales that its markets were 'filled with rare goods, such as are not seen or heard of in any other town': these were likely Chinese porcelain, Spanish wine, Arabian horses and luxurious jewels such as emeralds. Above all it was Bijapur's wealth which would have fascinated Lopes, for it was well known that the Deccan Plateau was famous for its diamond fields, being the world's primary source of the gems at the time. In addition, iron deposits and rich, black soil perfect for growing cotton helped swell the city's treasury.

The origins of the man who ruled Bijapur when Lopes was in Goa, the *Sabayo* Yusuf Adil Khan, are shrouded in legend. He was, he claimed, the son of Murad II, the Sultan of Turkey. After the Sultan's death, and to eliminate any possible rivals, the Crown Prince ordered that all of Murad's sons be executed. Yusuf's enterprising mother however secretly replaced him with a slave boy and sent him to Persia (alas, history does not recount what happened to the slave boy though one does not hold out much hope). After many romantic adventures, Yusuf reached the court of the Bahmani Sultanate where his personality and intelligence raised him rapidly in the Sultan's favour, resulting in his appointment as the governor of Bijapur. At court, Yusuf had been struck by the opulence and grandeur in which the Sultan lived. He noted how the Sultan was preceded by 100 trumpeters, 100 dancers and 300 spare horses in golden harnesses, and was followed by 100 monkeys and 100 handmaidens, and how the palace in which he resided had seven gates, with 100 guards and 100 scribes at each one; some of them to register those coming in and others, those going out. When the Bahmani kingdom, which held sway over most of the Deccan Plateau, began disintegrating at the end of the 15th century, Yusuf apparently seized the opportunity to declare himself an independent ruler in Bijapur. It is a lovely story but one riddled with at least two troubling inconsistencies. Firstly, the Ottoman sources make no mention of Yusuf (and one can be certain that the sons of Sultans were dutifully recorded), and secondly, Yusuf was a Shi'a, as opposed to the Ottoman Sunnis – in fact he was the first ruler in India to declare Shi'ism the official state religion. A less romantic but probably truer version of his background attests that Yusuf Adil Khan was most likely a slave in the service of Mahmud Gawan, a famous minister in the Bahmani Sultanate. This version claims he was originally from Sava, a town south of Tehran, on the old road from Qazvin to Qom. He would therefore have been known as Yusuf al Savai and this might be the origin of his title *Sabayo* in the Portuguese records. Under the Bahmanis, Yusuf worked his way up until he was appointed to the position of Master of the Horse, putting him in charge of the cavalry, and then to the provincial governorship of Dawlatabad, thereby placing him in a position of great influence and power. He took an active part in the intrigues and civil strife which marked the declining years of the Bahmani kingdom until, as governor of Bijapur, he caused the Friday sermon – the *khutba* – to be read in his own name in 1489. In this version of the story, he is a Persian by birth, and by marrying a Maratha princess, Punji Khatun, he ensured that his successors were a mixture of Maratha and Persian blood. This was significant for many reasons, none more so than for the fact that it symbolised a coming together of Hinduism and Islam.

Whether he was of noble blood or a slave, there could be no denying Yusuf Adil Khan's vision, and, inspired by what he had seen at the Bahmani court, he set about transforming Bijapur from an outpost on the Islamic frontier to a dazzling centre of Islamic culture that drew on Islamic, Hindu and Turkish traditions, blending art, astronomy, mysticism and politics at a vibrant court. Writers, poets, theologians and calligraphers from North India, Iran, Central Asia and East Africa migrated to Bijapur, a city which came to be known as the 'Florence of the Deccan', all seeking patronage at Yusuf's court, which rapidly became a 'window open on an enchanted world'. Under the Adil Shahs, Bijapur was transformed into the jewel of the Deccan Plateau, a centre of art and architecture where a distinctive painting style, representing a fusion of Persian miniatures with the indigenous Hindu tradition, emerged. At Bijapur an extraordinary artistic legacy flowered, one where Hindu architectural elements could be found on Muslim buildings, where you could find Hindu throne legs inscribed in the bases of mosque columns, and square-stepped roof brackets with lotus-bud drops supported the protruding eaves of Muslim tombs. Throughout the circular walled city (with a citadel at its core) palaces, arches, tombs, cisterns, gateways, minarets – each one a gem of architecture, and all carved from the rich local basalt rock, with glazed tiles covering the facades – added to the glorious treasure.

There was beauty in Bijapur but there was also power, none more so than the 55-ton, fourteen-foot (4.3-metre) long cannon called the *Malik-e Maidan*, or 'King of the Battlefield', which sat atop one of the city's outer-wall bastions. Depicted on its muzzle was a lion clenching an elephant in its teeth. Cast 150 miles away in Ahmadnagar and hauled to Bijapur by 400 bullocks and ten elephants, its blast was so loud that men firing it had to jump into a nearby pool of water after lighting the fuse to protect their ears. On occasion the cannon would fire the severed heads of enemies as cannonballs. In the same way that the city attracted poets and artists, it also attracted fighters and mercenaries. We are fortunate to have an eyewitness account that predates the Portuguese capture of Goa in 1510. Ludovico di Varthema, an Italian adventurer, merchant and part-time Muslim convert, visited Bijapur around 1504. He may well have met Yusuf Adil Khan whom he depicts as a Mamluk (freed slave). Interestingly, di Varthema noted that Yusuf was 'particularly fond of white mercenaries in order to increase his power', and that he commanded over 400 Mamluks. 'When this captain can engage any white man, he offers him excellent conditions, and gives him at least fifteen or twenty *pardaos* per month.' But di Varthema then describes an interesting incident: when Yusuf Adil Khan himself wished to assess the fighting skills of the particular mercenary, he 'orders two leather armours to be brought. Each one puts on his, and they come to blows. If he deems him strong, he puts him on his list of élite men, otherwise he reserves him for a service other than combat.'

That di Varthema had chosen to become what one may term a 'part-time' Muslim needs a brief comment. Such a conversion was far from being rare, since many Christian or Jewish merchants who lived and traded in Muslim countries chose to take this route. By and large it was done for practical reasons as it not only helped them assimilate more easily into Muslim society, but it also neatly circumvented the frequent problem of Muslims wishing to trade only with other Muslims. Once the merchants had completed their trading and crossed back to Christendom they simply reverted to their original faith. While in Bijapur, di Varthema noted that most of the soldiers were foreigners. Writing around 1515, Tomé Pires stated that Bijapur

must have about thirty thousand mounted men, besides countless foot soldiers. Those white people [Pires here was referring
to the Turks], whom we call Rumis, used generally to come to
the kingdom and to Goa to earn wages and honour. The King
used to bestow names like so-and-so Malik ... ; and the most
honoured name is Khan.

The foreigners were well paid and the chances of fast social ascent
acted as a powerful attraction for adventurers who were willing
to fight. Portuguese sources mention the presence of as many as
9,000 foreign mercenaries in Goa in 1510 and record that when
Albuquerque conquered Goa, 2,000 'white men' fighting for the
Muslims were killed. The sources also noted that in 1512 when
the governor laid siege to Banastarim, it was defended by 6,000
foreign fighters and 3,000 other soldiers. For di Varthema, the
presence of so many foreigners who chose to convert to Islam
must have come as a surprise but in the 16th century it was very
common. Undoubtedly many of those who flocked to Bijapur were
poor men who sought to improve their material circumstances.
They were impressed by the lack of racial discrimination and an
apparent equality of opportunity which presented itself to them,
since it genuinely appeared that anyone, despite their racial or
societal background, could rise to a position of great prominence
and wealth. And the fact that so many did only encouraged others
to flock to Bijapur. There was no discrimination based on the
social or ethnic origin of the convert: an Ethiopian was viewed
in a similar light as a Khorasani. Some of these converts indeed
rose to great power and the fact that we know so little about these
men is largely due to the fact that they nearly all came from the
lower social ranks and so wrote no testimonies, leaving us, frus-
tratingly, with a blank page in trying to personalise their histories.
The religious diversity which existed in Bijapur was, however, not
an isolated phenomenon, as it also existed in North Africa and in

the Ottoman Empire, which attracted many converts during this period. Converting to Islam or *Turning Turk* as it was commonly known in Europe was an undoubted social reality in the 16th century. The numbers were certainly large: according to the research done by Nabil Matar, who has written extensively on the relations between Islam and England in the Middle Ages, several thousands of Englishmen converted to Islam between 1580 and 1630.

In Bijapur there were Deccanis and Persians, but there were also Uzbeks, Circassians and Tatars. There were Georgians and Turks, and also Ethiopians who had initially been sold as slaves but had gradually found their way into the administration and military services – for many were also highly skilled as warriors. It was in Bijapur that their talent was rewarded, and many rose to become generals, or ministers. And then there were the Portuguese.

≈≈≈

When their former countryman João Machado first appeared on their horizon – dressed in Islamic garb and dispatched by the Sultan of Bijapur with a message to Albuquerque – the Portuguese may not have known who he was. But they did know what he was: he was a *renegadoe* – a renegade. Today the story of the *renegadoes*, those Portuguese who converted to Islam and chose to serve a Muslim ruler, is a largely forgotten one. Partly because it is also the story of the common people – the *gente baixa* – the marginalised and unspoken of in the historical records. These were the men whose actions were, in the words of Diogo do Couto, 'passed over, as if zeal had no merit save in the well born'. They were the ones who had sailed to India every season, who manned the ships and worked the decks: the soldiers, the mariners, the oarsmen. They were the tailors, the innkeepers, the carpenters. Many were simply criminals. If we are unable to quantify the numbers of those who converted, that is not surprising; before they converted they were too insignificant for any attention, and after they did they commenced new lives and vanished. But we do know that so great were the numbers of Portuguese in India in the 16th century who became renegades that Lisbon, alarmed, ordered an inquiry into the reasons. Only a minority had committed crimes, the report concluded, the rest were simply poor and desperate. They deserted, the report continued, 'because they come from Lisbon with that idea. Others desert because they arrive with nothing. Others desert because they were given very little to eat and what they did receive was poorly prepared and rotten.' At first glance it may appear illogical that Portuguese who were brought up in the spirit of the *Reconquista* and sailed to India to fight a crusade against Islam should now flock to fight for the Muslims, but the fact was that the majority of Portuguese soldiers had just cause for desertion. Having landed in India they were largely forgotten by Lisbon and left to their own devices. Certainly the burden they carried was great: they were responsible for clothing and feeding themselves, renting their own houses, buying their own firearms and being ready to leave on a campaign. They were underpaid, paid late or given promises in lieu of salaries. Often they were not paid at all. In most cases they could not practise the trade they had learned because they were expected to serve as soldiers, and the number of those who were exempt (on account of being married – the *casados*) and allowed to work was minimal. In Goa the soldiers were often housed ten to a lodging and they lacked money and occupation, factors which often resulted in restlessness and violence. If they showed any loyalty it was to their *fidalgo*, who was often their only source of food. Indeed a lone soldier had no choice but to live on the charity of a *fidalgo*. Until he married he could not establish himself with a trade or a house. Often he had no choice but to follow a noble, and it was common for a *fidalgo* to have a private 'army' of men numbering from about 50 to 200.

So hard was their life in India that deserters lost very little by leaving the world of Portuguese rule. Given the dire conditions in which they found themselves and given the fact that the soldiers were often posted to remote locations, desertion was frequent, and it was easy. The Portuguese Asian Empire consisted of a series of forts on the littoral of Asia, but inland things were different. Each fort was surrounded by a sea of the native population. The city of Goa may have been a Portuguese political and administrative power but it was geographically part of the Indian mainland. Although the city came under the control of the Portuguese, the other lands which comprised Goa – the three islands and the districts of Bardaz to the north and Salcete to the south – were still entirely rural. It was those districts that reflected the real face of India. Within a few miles a Portuguese could disappear from the sight of his countrymen, entering a world wholly untouched by any European influence. As soon as the Portuguese arrived in India many of them abandoned their posts and rapidly fled to the interior. So serious was the problem that several Viceroys, from the time of Almeida on, advised against placing the soldiers exclusively in the frontier forts since this would 'only hasten their desertion'. Indeed such was the rate of desertion in the frontier forts that Diogo do Couto, writing in 1600, stated that in most forts it would be a miracle to find even half the total number of soldiers listed on the *matricula* – the official list of all personnel in the fort. The King of Portugal was aware of the crisis: 'I have been informed that there are many Portuguese soldiers who serve the Moors and heathens', he wrote, 'some to get better pay and others to escape punishment.' This state of affairs was still very much the case at the end of the 16th century, when the Jesuits wrote that 'Many Christians have left our Holy Faith for the lands of the Moors.' By 1705 the situation had become so serious that shortages in soldier numbers led the Viceroy to propose to the Crown that regiments of local Goans be formed, since 'so many [Portuguese soldiers] flee in all directions'. Knowing little but hardship under their fellow countrymen, many of these *renegadoes* did not have much to lose by deserting, and instead gained immediately and often considerably by doing so. Certainly their knowledge of firearms and weapons made them attractive to the Muslim rulers, for whom they rendered a variety of services, and many of them would eventually assume positions of great authority. As early as 1502, the Portuguese chronicles relate that two Christians had abandoned their posts and passed to the lands of the Raja of Calicut (Kozhikode), where they proved to be excellent artillerymen and bombardiers. We read that in 1507 in Hormuz five men had crossed over to the enemy camp of the Emir, to teach them how to fight in the Portuguese style. Archers and musketeers were those most prized by the enemy side.

Portuguese renegades could be found across India. In Gujarat about 50 renegade gunners were used by Bahadur Shah to fight against Mughal forces in the 1530s. A Portuguese colony of renegades even established itself in the Hindu Kingdom of Vijayanagar. One of the towns in the kingdom, with a population of about 50 to 100 households, was visited in 1567 by a Jesuit priest who noted many Portuguese residents, none of whom had any interest in returning to Portugal. In 1620 it was estimated that there were 5,000 Portuguese working as mercenaries between Bengal and eastern Indonesia and in 1780 the British in Bombay formed a regiment composed exclusively of Portuguese renegades. Renegades were young in age, some very young. Records in the Arquivo Histórico Ultramarino in Lisbon and the Historical Archive of Goa show that many were under twenty, and there are two references to fourteen-year-olds who abandoned the Portuguese and crossed over. Some were scandalously young; even though boys under thirteen were not allowed to serve abroad, the child Bernardo Tavira de Sousa left Portugal for India in the 1680s at the age of nine. Remarkably there were even some Portuguese women who became renegades. Even though the actual number of women who left Portugal to travel to Asia was very small, a report in 1567 raised this issue when it pointed out the problem of women 'going over to the Moors after hiding from their husbands in the asylum of churches'. In his *Travels*, Fernão Mendes Pinto mentions coming across a Portuguese woman in 1545 in (modern day) Laos who informed him she had no intention of returning.

One would imagine that the idea that their Portuguese compatriots would convert to Islam and cross over to fight on the side of the Muslims would have caused shockwaves in Lisbon, but the more one reads contemporary accounts on the renegades, the more one is struck by the absence of any opprobrium or excessive condemnation on behalf of the Portuguese. On the contrary, throughout there are references which hint at a grudging admiration. Diogo do Couto, for example, almost eulogises Sancho Pires, a bombardier who as a Muslim took the name of Firangi Khan (corrupted by the Portuguese into *Fringuican*) and assumed a position of influence in the court of the Nizam Shahs of Ahmednagar:

> This man was so valorous of arm, that he could be counted amongst the most famous that there have been in the world, because arriving alone, and as a murderer in that kingdom, he at once gave such demonstrations of his valour, that the King took charge of him, and made him a captain of the cavalry, in which too he gave such an account of himself, and gave such true evidence of his zeal, that he came to be general of the entire kingdom, and the principal man of those in the King's Council, and he was given so many lands and incomes, that he maintained ten to twelve thousand cavalrymen; and he was so feared by all the captains and Moors, that there was none who did not do him obeisance or did not bow down to him ...
> And if this man had not darkened his deeds with the negation he did of the Faith, dying as Franguican, his deeds would have been marvelled at in the world, and we would have left

a memorial for him that would never end, for his deeds were
such and so many.

Another example was Gonçalo Vaz Coutinho, who was a *fidalgo*
and knight and friend to several viceroys until he was imprisoned for a series of crimes and misdeeds. He fled with other
prisoners from the central prison at Goa in the 1540s and turned
rebel, becoming a mélange of *fidalgo*-pirate. After many adventures, he ended up in the pay of one of the Adil Shah Sultans
in Bijapur, who assigned him extensive territories with a great
revenue, 'where he remained as a perfect Moor with his wife and
children'.

As one may naturally imagine, for Albuquerque the renegades
were a particular source of irritation. That some Portuguese –
mainly commoners – should desert their posts was unfortunate
but understandable. But that they should choose to take up the
Muslim faith was nothing less than abhorrent apostasy. It is clear
that from the moment of his arrival in India he was aware of the
problem, since as early as 1510, during the conquest of Goa, while
sending a messenger to enter into a dialogue with the Sultan of
Bijapur, Albuquerque ordered that the oarsman of the ship's
boat that took the emissary should be one of the local Goans – a
Kanarese – rather than a Portuguese, as he feared that the latter
would desert. Two years later, in 1512, Albuquerque wrote to the
King, informing him that he would be pardoning 'men who have
gone over to the Moors', and a couple of years later he wrote
again, saying that he had 'rounded up several escapees who went
over to serve Hidalcão [Ismail Adil Khan, the Sultan of Bijapur]'.
In 1515 Albuquerque ordered a payment of fourteen *xerafins* to
Jerónimo de Sousa, captain of the galley *São Vincente*, to 'search
for men who went over to the Moors'. He also used Muslim bounty
hunters and in the same year he ordered the factor in Hormuz to
pay 'forty *xerafins* and other goods to Raiz Gaexer, a Moor, for

capturing Diego d'Alvito along the Persian coast, as well as six other Portuguese men who had gone over to the Moors'.

An important point needs to be made at this stage, one which has often been overlooked, but which is critical to gaining a deeper understanding of why the Portuguese chose to cross over to the Muslims. The Muslim rulers may have been eager to recruit the Portuguese and other Europeans who drifted to their courts primarily for their knowledge of firearms, or because they could render a variety of useful services, but though their skills were required, their souls were not. Put simply, the Portuguese who ended up in the service of the Muslims did not need to convert to Islam. There was no obligation to do so, as they could have served, been rewarded as mercenaries, and maintained their faith. The Muslim potentates under whom they served certainly did not request or demand any act of conversion. They could not have cared less as long as they performed their duties, for which they were very well rewarded. In fact there was often an advantage in keeping the Portuguese as Christians so that they could main-tain their contacts and act as intermediaries with the Portuguese Crown without the risk of being ostracised by their co-religionists. Desertion, in other words, was one thing, conversion another.

So why did the Portuguese convert? Many did so because of the degree of social mobility that followed. Once one became a Muslim no one asked about your background and anyone could rise to a position of privilege. It was an egalitarianism which for the Portuguese, accustomed to their suffocatingly stratified hier-archy of nobility and commoners, could have been intoxicating. Christianity simply could not rival Islam in its worldly advantages, and apostasy did not seem to demand much of them. After all, the renegade, having given up his Christian faith, did not seemingly suffer any subsequent divine punishment (in this world at least) but happily prospered as a Muslim. For others it was a matter of the heart – they had married Muslim women. In fact marriages between the Portuguese and Muslim women had been encouraged by Albuquerque himself as we have seen. Often the Portuguese men married into families with no sons, and it became natural that the foreign son-in-law would be virtually adopted into the family of the bride. This custom was common in South India as it prevented the loss of the daughter's dowry and other familial wealth. Soon the men, integrated into their new families, adopted the Islamic manner of dress and customs and became fathers. Many had known hardship in Lisbon and had left it to improve their fortunes. Why would they return?

Although many important reasons have been put forward, one overriding question remains unanswered: why Lopes? Or to ask the question more precisely, why would the *fidalgo* and knight Fernão Lopes abandon his position in society, turn his back on all that he knew and choose to convert to Islam? Unlike the vast majority of the renegades, Lopes did not need to convert for financial reasons, for his life was certainly not one of hardship, nor could he have hoped for better social advancement under the Muslims since he was already well established under the Portuguese. In Goa, he would have owned slaves and was evidently living a life beyond what he could have afforded in Lisbon. Although not of noble birth, he mixed in the inner circles of the powerful and was clearly erudite and educated. After serving a few years in India, he would have looked forward to returning to Portugal where he would have been able to secure a well-remunerated position that would have raised his family's standing in Lisbon society. It was illogical for Lopes to convert – seemingly it served no material or immediate purpose. And yet Lopes not only converted but willingly took up his sword against his fellow Portuguese. It is a mystery which needs to be, in its own time, unravelled slowly and painstakingly.

Lopes' arrival in Bijapur would certainly not have gone unnoticed by the local populace, for though many Portuguese had drifted towards the city, the Muslims found them, on the whole, common, uncouth and uninteresting. Lopes however would have been of interest. His clothing would have appeared distinguished and one imagines that he received a warm welcome and was at once presented with a *khilat*, or robe of honour. Undoubtedly the presence of a man like Machado in the city would have helped Lopes to settle in, and the Bijapuris to recognise his social rank. The presentation of a *khilat*, made of the most elegant silk, was a very important ceremony through which the ruler could bestow honour on his guest and also create a bond of obligation. It was a bond Lopes would have been expected to uphold. He had arrived in Bijapur at a time of political turmoil, for it was an unfortunate habit of the Adil Shah rulers to die young and leave battles for succession behind them. This had been the case with Yusuf Adil Khan, whose death had eased Albuquerque's path in recapturing Goa and who was succeeded by his son, Ismail Adil Khan, who was a minor. Given the new Sultan's youth, a vice-regent was appointed – Kamal Khan (no relation) – who served Ismail Adil Khan as 'protector of the throne'. Kamal was a Sunni as opposed to Yusuf and Ismail, who were followers of Shi'ism. Professor Nayeem in his work on the Adil Shahs of Bijapur writes that, wary of Kamal Khan's ambitions and fearing for her son's life, Ismail's mother Bunji Khatum, aided by Ismail's paternal aunt, Dilshad Aga, plotted to have the vice-regent killed. They found a man to slay Kamal Khan, and promised to richly reward him. According to Nayeem, she told him:

> if you are successful in your attempt you shall enjoy happiness like the other nobles of the court. But if you lose your life you shall rejoice over it for you shall obtain renown for your actions and faithfulness in this world and shall gain reward in the next.

Soon the bloody deed was done, and Ismail assumed the throne in his own right and at once proved himself to be ardently Shi'a. Unlike his father, who had preserved the Sunni call to prayer even though he was a Shi'a in recognition of the fact that the majority of the population were Sunnis, Ismail did not hesitate in changing both the call to prayer and the Friday prayer according to Shi'a rites, and ordering all the soldiers in his army to wear the red *taj* (cap) of twelve notches (*tarak*), symbolising the Twelve Shi'a Imams, on their heads. Whoever did not wear the *taj* was not allowed to come into his presence. Moreover, during his reign it was impossible for anyone to move about the city without the *taj*.

Ismail Adil Shah (who now used the title of Shah, as opposed to that of Khan used by his father) set his sights on the recapture of Goa and the avenging of his father, and for this he needed fighting men. His first act after ascending the throne was to reward those who had been loyal to him, as well as the veterans of his father's rule who had gathered in Bijapur to swear their oath of loyalty. For some reason Ismail Adil Shah had vowed not to enlist any Deccanis or Abyssinians in his service as he viewed them as disloyal, and he subsequently sought to attract as many foreign fighters as he could to Bijapur (of whom the Afghans and Rajputs were the most prized).

It was during this time that the skilled Portuguese soldier Lopes arrived in Bijapur and, given the timely nature of his arrival, he would have received a warm welcome (unlike his father, Ismail Adil Shah did not engage in hand-to-hand fighting to test new soldiers). In Bijapur, swordsmanship was practised by boys from a young age, and soon after his arrival, Lopes would have been asked to demonstrate his skills, and his movements would have been carefully scrutinised – *how well does that farangi fight? How powerful are his cuts, how devious his thrusts?* Swords were carried all the time and they came in many varieties: the *shamsheer*, *saif*, *talwar*, *dhup*, *firangi*, the *kilij*, *khanda* and the *sosun-patta*. When

Lopes had arrived in Bijapur he was carrying a 'firangi sword', so called by the Indians because it was the Portuguese who had brought it to the Deccan Plateau. It was a cut-and-thrust sword with a thin and straight blade used mainly by the Portuguese cavalry. But soon after his arrival Lopes would have been presented with a *shamsheer*, which was truly unlike any sword he would have ever used. No greater symbol of honour and dignity could be given to Lopes than the sword with which he was now presented. Single-edged with a thick, narrow blade, it was curved. with a small grip and made purely for cutting. The sword was ornamented with precious stones and the blade was inscribed with a quranic verse in Arabic, while on the hilt there were invocations imploring help from Allah and seeking His protection. Lopes would also have been given a dagger, a *kindjal*, with its straight, broad and double-edged blade which tapered to a very long sharp point. It had deep grooves on both sides of the blade and the grip was made up of two pieces of ivory or horn. The ubiquity of all these weapons was down to the fact that Bijapur was readying itself to fight against the Portuguese, and to regain Goa from their clutches. We are not certain whether, when Lopes decided to abandon Goa and embark on the eight-day journey, he had already made up his mind to fight against his compatriots, but one assumes that this was clear to him. Why else would the Bijapuris need him? Whether he had made that fateful step the moment he left Goa or whether it had come later mattered little; the fact was that Lopes had now become a mercenary, and the weapons he was presented with reflected this stark fact. The silence of the sources on what must have been going on in his mind certainly allows for some conjecture, but it does not detract from the fact that fighting against the Portuguese would have been the only possible conclusion to his leaving Goa.

As he readied for war, Lopes checked his armour: his helmet was made of chain mail (known as *kulah*), with the nose-guard decorated in gold; his *char-aina* (body armour) comprised four plates – a breast plate, a back plate and two small plates for the sides; and finally he would have donned the *angarkha* – a long robe worn over the armour. As for his horse, its face was protected by a frontlet (*qashqa*), while the *gardani* covered the upper side of the neck. Tied to his horse were a shield and a mace with steel spikes, and a richly ornamented handle with gold inlay.

One of the most common reasons in explaining Portuguese triumph in the Indian Ocean is simply that they possessed fire-arms, and the Indians did not. However, as Lopes discovered in Bijapur, this was not necessarily the case – the Sultan had at his disposal several guns and cannons. As early as 1471, the Bahmani *wazir* (the first minister) Mahmud Gawan, in whose court Yusuf Adil Khan then served, wrote that he had destroyed the fort of Machal by deploying 'roaring thunder [*r'ad*], which having the effect of a thunderbolt, showered [on the fort] like rain'. In 1502, Gaspar Correia recorded that Portuguese naval squadrons were bombarded with cannonballs from the hilltop overlooking the port of Bhatkal, and Albuquerque's own son recalled that when his father took Goa in 1510, Bijapuri defenders greeted the invaders with artillery fire. When the Portuguese conquered Goa in 1510, they found that the Bijapuris had already established a formidable munitions plant in that city. What Lopes would have discovered in Bijapur was quite astounding, for he would have come across factories producing guns of the highest workmanship. The fact was that the Deccan states of India had been purchasing cannons and firearms in return for spices from the Mamluks years before the arrival of Vasco da Gama, and having purchased the weapons they had set about producing them locally. Lopes was not the only Portuguese to notice, for the quality of the guns and cannons had caught the eye of none other than Albuquerque himself. In early December 1513, the governor even sent one of those Bijapuri gunsmiths, probably a prisoner, to Lisbon to work for the Portuguese Crown, presumably to share knowledge with Portuguese military engineers. In the same month, Albuquerque sent a letter to the King praising the abilities of Muslim gunsmiths in Goa who had formerly served the Bijapuri Sultanate, in which he openly acknowledged that these gunsmiths had become 'our masters in artillery and the making of cannons and guns, which they make of iron here in Goa and are better than the German ones'. No greater praise could be offered.

Ismail Shah was determined to regain Goa and he knew that he had to move swiftly before Albuquerque returned to the city. He had been strengthened by the recruitment of many mercenaries who would fight in his army and in particular he was delighted that this Portuguese, Fernão Lopes, had sworn his loyalty. Ismail Shah knew little about Lopes personally, and what he did know most likely came from Machado, but it was clear he could handle himself in the heat of battle and that, ultimately, is what mattered. Consequently, he directed that his commander, Rasul Khan, keep an eye on Lopes, and a bond and friendship would develop between the two men.

It is clear that by the time he set off to fight against his former countrymen in Goa, Fernão Lopes had already converted to Islam. This would have been a simple affair but it nevertheless involved several rituals. He would have been brought in front of a religious judge (*cadi*) and there made a public profession of his faith. Firstly, he was made to take a ritual bath (*ghusl*), following which the *cadi* asked him, in the presence of two witnesses, if he was willing to become a Muslim. Lopes would have replied that he was. Secondly, the *cadi* then held a copy of the Quran above Lopes' head and made the declaration that there was no god save Allah and that Muhammad was His messenger, and Lopes repeated the words. As soon as he had completed the words, a turban was placed on his head and he was made to kiss the Quran. Lopes was then given a Muslim name and though the historical records did not preserve it (all our sources on the life of Lopes are Portuguese), we can hazard an educated guess that it could well have been Abdullah (literally 'slave of God'), which was by far the most common name given to converts, as the name carries the assumption that the convert has assumed a new life, detaching himself from his non-Islamic past. Lopes would then have been given instruction in Islam for one month, during which he was taught the rituals of prayer and given a few Arabic verses to perform. This was very much the standard procedure for any convert arriving in Bijapur. Lopes would have been oblivious to the distinctions between Sunnis and Shi'a, nor did it truly matter to which sect he converted, for the commonalities they shared far outweighed their differences. In any case Lopes was not a theologian, nor was he a man of God. But though he may not have known it, in moving to Bijapur, known at the time as the 'City of Sufis', he had entered into a world of mysticism which would have deeply affected him.

When Yusuf Adil Khan had declared Bijapur a Shi'ite state he had been confronted by many Sunnis who protested, and to whom he replied, quoting the Quran, 'you have your faith and I have mine'. And Yusuf was true to his word: a sense of religious freedom now flourished in the city, which was unlike almost anywhere else in the Muslim world. Largely because of this tolerance, a great number of Sufis had migrated to Bijapur and settled and taught there, and their tombs became shrines which in turn attracted thousands of others. But the spiritual freedom extended beyond the confines of Islam and in the unique and eclectic atmosphere of Bijapur, Sufis interacted with Hindu yogis, creating a dynamic and profound rapprochement between Muslims and Hindus. It was a fusion which was remarkably diverse and erudite. In the words of George Mitchell, a leading art historian, what was produced in Bijapur and in the Muslim states that ranged across the Deccan Plateau was 'the stuff of dreams'. In Bijapur, Islam and Hinduism recognised one another, not in a sentimental syncretic manner, nor even in an ecumenical and diplomatic one, but on the highest and most profound level: both understanding that the Truth was eternal, immutable and One. One of the greatest of the Bijapuri Sultans, Ibrahim Adil Shah who died in 1627, understood this, for he gave himself the Sanskrit title *Jagatguru* (World Teacher) and mused in his writings that his parents were the Hindu gods Ganesh and Saraswati, the goddess of learning. Further, in the book of poems he composed, he offers praise to Saraswati, to Muhammad the Prophet of Islam, and to the Sufi saint of the Deccan Plateau, Gesu Daraz:

> Our tongues differ but our feelings are the same, [he wrote] whether we are Turk or Brahman, the most fortunate person is the one on whom Saraswati smiles. The world seeks knowledge. Be focused on the Word, on the guru, on meditation.

In Bijapur both Sufis and yogis practised rhythmic breath control, and the local use of betel leaf with areca nut and lime paste as a masticant rapidly found its way into Sufi practice. Although it is possible that yoga and Sufism developed some very similar techniques of worship and similar philosophies in isolation, it is more logical to suppose that there was a process of recognition, a result of their long co-existence on the subcontinent. In addition, Sufi poetry was composed in the local vernacular and cascaded down into village life, imbuing itself in the daily lives of Muslims and Hindus. All this does not imply widespread conversion but what it does demonstrate is how deeply and universally Sufism became embedded in Bijapur society, where the majority of the population remained Hindus. This was the Islam of Bijapur: a confident ecumenical Islam interacting with Hinduism, as opposed to the marginalised one that had been driven out of Portugal by the *Reconquista*.

After over a year in Bijapur, Lopes rode out of the city with Ismail Adil Shah's army fanning out in the direction of Goa. The army comprised cavalry and artillery divisions, but Lopes would have been impressed to ride alongside an elephant division, which had sharpened trunks and armoured turrets, their foreheads painted in terrifying masks. The camels and the oxen were used to transport the guns, tents and equipment. A considerable quantity of arms was carried into battle: swords, daggers and maces as well as bows, arrows, heavy guns and cannons. The cavalry was the most important of the divisions and it was made up of Turks, Persians, Abyssinians, Afghanis, Marathas and a few Portuguese, mainly soldiers who had come to India to escape their poverty and had chosen to pursue careers as mercenaries. No common bond held them together for though some had converted to Islam, others had not.

As the Muslim army rode out of Bijapur one wonders, at what moment did Lopes' mind turn to the fact that within days he would be engaged in battle against his Portuguese compatriots? Was there a frisson of doubt or even a flicker of remorse? If so it was well concealed, and one searches in vain for any compunction in his actions. Lopes did not ride alone, as there were other Portuguese *renegadoes* with him, who would doubtless have looked to him as their leader, for they were common men and Lopes, even despite his conversion, was still considered both a *fidalgo* and a knight. Clearly social customs and assumptions, carried from Lisbon, were too ingrained to be dissolved under the Deccan sun. One thing was certain however; Lopes knew as they approached Goa that the dice had long ago been cast and that his fate had been sealed. Ahead lay a battlefield and unless triumph was gained on this field, then he would soon be a dead man. At the same time his mind was set on one thing, which he kept to himself and did not divulge to Rasul Khan, nor to the other Portuguese *renegadoes*. Over the next few days, Fernão Lopes was determined to kill Afonso de Albuquerque.

CHAPTER ELEVEN

Banastarim

One of the main reasons Goa had fallen so swiftly to Albuquerque was the fact that the Bijapuri Sultanate had been in turmoil following the death of Yusuf Adil Khan. This had led to a bloody family struggle for succession which had culminated in the poisoning of Kamal Khan and the accession of Ismail Adil Shah to the Sultanate. Now, with Albuquerque departing Goa, the young Sultan seized the opportunity to besiege the city. An initial force of 3,000 men, under the command of Pulad Khan, who had been the main general under Ismail's father, reached Goa in March 1512. There, they occupied the mainland and, venturing onto the island, established camps at the strategic fort of Banastarim, from where the Muslim forces surrounded the city, holding it under siege. A second contingent of 7,000 shortly followed, commanded by Rasul Khan, at whose side the two Portuguese renegades João Machado and Fernão Lopes rode. News reached Albuquerque, who was in Cochin, of Ismail Adil Shah's advance and the siege of Goa, but the governor remained remarkably sanguine. His men were exhausted after a gruelling campaign in Malacca and in any case the approaching monsoon rendered any hope of an immediate relief of Goa unrealistic.

'With God's help, if there is no treachery', he reassured the King, 'there is no fear of the Muslims attacking your fortress.' But little did Albuquerque know at this stage that there had already been treachery of the most personal kind.

With Albuquerque incapacitated and a relief army unable to reach Goa before October at the earliest, Goa should have been recaptured by the Muslims over the summer months of 1512. The main reason it did not was another internal power struggle in Bijapur – in particular that between Pulad Khan and Ismail Adil Shah. The Sultan, fearing that Pulad Khan had acquired a great deal of power, and fearing that he may break away from under his authority, had sent his relative Rasul Khan at the head of another force to Goa – ostensibly to support Pulad Khan but with the secret order to eliminate him. Rasul Khan was successful in this latter endeavour thanks to an ingenious plan which he partly owed to the renegades who accompanied him. In the absence of Albuquerque, Diogo Mendes de Vasconcelos had taken over as acting captain of Goa. A trap was now set for both Vasconcelos and Pulad Khan. Rasul Khan sent one of the Portuguese renegades, Duarte Tavares, who pretended to be a captive, to Goa with a message for Vasconcelos. Pulad Khan, he informed the acting captain of Goa, was a rebel, and his siege of Goa was strictly against the orders of the Sultan who was appalled by the actions of his recalcitrant general. Rasul Khan had arrived determined to defeat Pulad Khan and to affirm the Sultan's friendship with the Portuguese, and a sign of this friendship was his willingness to release the Portuguese captives in Bijapur. Through his messenger Tavares, Rasul Khan now asked Vasconcelos for help in defeating Pulad Khan, and the ambitious Portuguese captain agreed, only to realise afterwards that with Pulad Khan vanquished he had simply helped rid Rasul Khan of an enemy while weakening himself and his garrison. One imagines Albuquerque shaking his head with fury at Vasconcelos'

naïvety. Rasul Khan now consolidated his strength and tightened his siege.

The momentum was now with Rasul Khan. It was the summer
of 1512 and he knew that with the monsoon season underway no
help could reach the Portuguese until October at the earliest, and
he had to press home his advantage. Albuquerque would return
and that, Lopes warned Rasul Khan, would be another matter.
The Portuguese may not have been the best of soldiers, and in
1570 an Italian in Goa commented that 'this nation was not born
for war nor for order because here one does not find the discipline,
the honest rigour, and the obedience demanded by the military'.
Perhaps, but what one did find deeply embedded in the Portuguese
psyche was stubborn tenacity when confronted by insurmountable
odds.

Day and night the Muslims launched ferocious assaults with
the aim of breaching the city's walls. At first they tried in vain to
ram the entrance doors with wooden stakes, and then resorted to
launching firebombs over the walls, but that year the rains had
come early and the sodden roofs failed to catch fire. And still the
assault continued. A large cannon which had been captured from
the Portuguese was positioned to deter any defenders from access-
ing the top of the wall.

As the summer progressed, the Portuguese situation in Goa
became graver, for both the Muslim siege and the monsoon, which
cut Goa off from any help or supplies from the sea, tightened their
grips. With each passing day the desperation and hunger of the
Portuguese increased. Much of the city's food was already rotten
thanks to the endless humidity, and rice, the only staple food that
was available, ran out. Before long, people were dying in the street
and as Rasul Khan had calculated, deserters began to trickle into
the Muslim camp. The first to desert were the Portuguese soldiers and the *gente baixa*, the 'low' people, who were the first to
run out of both food (which was distributed by the *fidalgos*) and

hope. Moreover, they knew that they possessed skills that would be recognised and welcomed by the Muslims, and so to begin with it was the archers, bombardiers, musketeers and gunsmiths who made their way to the Muslims. But there was another important incentive for them to desert, and that was the presence of the Portuguese renegades fighting on the Muslim side. Some recalled João Machado, so confident and assured in his Islamic dress, and most knew Fernão Lopes very well indeed for, unlike Machado, Lopes had lived and fought by their side and now look, how he had prospered! Albuquerque had warned that as long as there was no treachery then Goa would be safe. But Goa was not safe. In the words of a contemporary historian, the Portuguese soldiers

> fled for the enemy camp, jumping down from the walls, and they were musketeers and archers as they were the ones who were received with the greatest of welcomes, and as soon as they were in the enemy camp, they immediately asked for João de Machado, calling him by his Moorish name.

The number of Portuguese who deserted is not known: some historians mention eighteen while others put the number as high as 70. The escapes began singly but soon men fled in droves. One of the renegades was Pero Bacias who originated from the lesser nobility and had chosen to settle in Goa and marry a Muslim woman. Although the Portuguese were under siege in Goa, the Muslim inhabitants of the city such as Bacias' wife found it relatively easy to leave and enter, and one assumes that they would have had relations living in Bijapur to whom they could escape. Bacias now fled the Portuguese camp and made his way to the Muslim one, where he was met by Machado and Lopes, who were clearly recognised by now as the ringleaders of the renegades. On seeing Bacias, Machado was taken aback and asked, 'What's this? Is it so bad that cavaliers are now beginning to desert?', to which

Bacias replied, 'My lord, hunger and toil with no remedy in sight makes one do these things, and the main thing is the faith in your presence here.' It is a remarkable reply in many ways, for it reflects not only the desperate situation in which the Portuguese found themselves but also how they viewed the renegades: not only with no sense of recrimination but with almost open admiration. Not only were the deserters willing to abandon their faith and convert, but they joined the Muslim ranks knowing that they would have to fight against their former colleagues, and that thought did not seem to deter them. They deserted because they were hungry and they were poor and they had lost any hope of rescue, but they also deserted because those who had gone before them and openly embraced Islam were clearly so much better off. The Muslims knew that, and made a point of parading the renegades in front of them. 'Look', they cajoled the Portuguese soldiers, 'come over and you can be like them.'

For the Portuguese, hope would come in the most unexpected of ways, for João Machado now took the surprising step of defecting back to the Portuguese camp. He had been mulling over that decision for a while and the sources state that he had a fervent hope to return to the religion of his birth. As far as Machado is concerned however we need to read these sources with care, embellished as they are with a certain Portuguese *Schadenfreude*. We are told that before he fled the Muslims Machado, who had a Muslim wife, drowned his two children as he could not bear the idea that they would grow up in the Muslim faith. Another account however tells us that before his departure he had them baptised as Christians before abandoning them which, given their Muslim mother, appears a somewhat contradictory if not careless decision. Whatever happened, Machado was determined to abandon the Muslim camp for the Portuguese, and prior to his departure he attempted to take some of his companions with him. Machado now approached Lopes and tried to convince him to return to Goa where he assured him he would be welcomed back, but according to the chronicler Barros, Lopes rebuffed him bluntly: 'I am now a Muslim, I can no longer live among the Christians.' He had no interest in returning and neither it seems did the other Portuguese renegades who had also committed themselves openly to fighting on the Muslim side. Ultimately, about a dozen men returned with Machado, mainly Portuguese who had been captured and taken as prisoners of war. The rest remained with Rasul Khan. It is striking how fluidly the Portuguese could move from being renegades to recanting and returning to the Catholic fold, and although the Machado incident is a fascinating one, we only know about it because the Portuguese chroniclers could not fail to celebrate the return of a prodigal son. As for the other nameless Portuguese renegades who chose to remain on the Muslim side, a veil of silence is cast over them.

Machado was received in Goa with an outpouring of joy and relief and a thanksgiving procession was organised. According to the chroniclers, 'everything changed with the arrival of João Machado', who, at Albuquerque's request, sailed out to meet him in Cochin where he briefed Albuquerque about the siege and talked 'about the things of the Moor Rasul Khan'. At first this meeting appears rather puzzling since earlier encounters between the two men had been hostile and there is no conclusive evidence of how Machado managed to win Albuquerque's trust so quickly. Some sources claim that he divulged important information to the governor which was verified, thereby winning his trust. But what is significant is how a public recantation of his Islamic faith and a return to the Catholic one re-integrated Machado so seamlessly into Portuguese society. It was during the debriefing with Albuquerque in Cochin that Machado would have informed him about the appearance of Fernão Lopes on the Muslim side. We are not told how Albuquerque reacted but given what we know about him and his avowed hatred for both traitors and Muslims, we can well imagine it. There had of course been many Portuguese who had shifted sides but they were by and large commoners. Lopes was different. Slowly the tide was turning in favour of the Portuguese. In August 1512, at the tail-end of the monsoon, Albuquerque dispatched eight large carracks to Goa, loaded with soldiers to help fortify the city. He himself waited for the arrival of the annual fleet from Lisbon, for the number of men at his disposal was too small to be effective. Later in the month his forces were further strengthened by the timely arrival in Cochin of the 1512 fleet from Lisbon, which immediately afforded Albuquerque the use of 2,000 men ready to fight. Then, on 10 September, with the monsoon dying down, and armed with sixteen ships, Albuquerque departed Cochin for Goa, confident that he could defeat and dislodge the Muslim force. A few months ago Lopes had urged Rasul Khan to seize Goa before the monsoon season ended, but despite the Muslim general's best efforts, Goa had withstood the siege. Now the Portuguese fightback was about to start.

Albuquerque was determined to launch a surprise attack on Banastarim to catch Rasul Khan off guard. Dispatching the rest of the fleet to Goa under the command of one of his most senior commanders, Dom Garcia, so as to land the men to prepare for a march to Banastarim, Albuquerque commanded four ships along the Zuari River to cut the fortress off from the sea. For this manoeuvre to succeed, however, the ships needed to come right up to the fortress alongside the bastions, and this would expose them to artillery fire. Albuquerque knew that the recapture of Banastarim would not be a simple matter. Its strength lay in its location between the two waterways, while its walls, towers and bulwarks had been fortified by Rasul Khan who had positioned a massive mounted cannon, which was nicknamed the 'Camel', on a strategic point overlooking the canal, aimed so as to destroy any approaching vessels. As soon as the Muslims spotted the cautious approach of Albuquerque's ships, they opened such a deluge of gunfire that the Portuguese soldiers took fright. But, as the chronicles put it, 'as soon as they had lost their fear', Albuquerque ordered the captains of the smaller ships to sail onwards a bit. But first he had to destroy the 'Camel'. He ordered that a brass cannon be loaded onto a barge to be navigated by his commander-in-chief and six gunners. Their task was to take advantage of the night, and to anchor as close to the 'Camel' as possible and destroy it. It was a mission of the highest possible danger but it was carried out with great success. As dawn broke the commander-in-chief opened fire on the 'Camel' and managed to blow it up, 'killing', as the sources tell us, 'two renegade gunners, one a Galician, the other a Castilian who had gone over to the Muslims'.

The biggest threat to the ships now destroyed, Albuquerque ordered one of his captains, Aires da Silva, to bring his ship closer to the fort, but he had underestimated the determination and ingenuity of its defenders: a volley of cannonballs was now unleashed, with one striking three barrels of gunpowder that were stored in the bows. Panicking, the sailors immediately leapt into the water, leaving Aires da Silva, who refused to abandon his ship, as the only person on board. Seeing this Albuquerque immediately insisted that he be rowed to the ship, shouting at the men in the sea to return to the vessel and rebuking them for abandoning their captain. It was an act of tremendous courage and fortitude while under fire and one which was typical of the governor who, to his men, appeared to know no fear. A lull now followed which was needed by both sides in order for them to draw breath and gather themselves for what promised to be a bitter siege of attrition. During those days the gunfire was so deafening that for many days that followed, the sources say that the Portuguese men could barely hear a word. One imagines this would have also applied to the defenders of Banastarim, or perhaps in anticipation they had padded their ears.

The initial aim had been to cut off any sea supplies from

King Manuel I of Portugal, 'Manuel the Fortunate' (1469–1521)

Under his rule, Portugal entered an ambitious period of expansion and began its accession to the ranks of the great European powers. Manuel sponsored Fernão Lopes' rise in society, elevating him to the *fidalguia*, paying for his education, and sending him to India as a soldier for the glory of God and Portugal.

The great Portuguese naval commanders Afonso de Albuquerque (1453–1515) [*left*] and Francisco de Almeida (1450–1510) [*below*], both of whom ruled Portuguese India in a viceregal capacity.

Lopes sailed to India with Albuquerque, as part of the fleet commanded by Tristão da Cunha. Albuquerque would take Lopes' defection, conversion to Islam and subsequent renegade behaviour very personally.

From Livro do Estado da India Oriental, par Pedro Barretto de Resede, Portugal, 1636. (Ms. Portugais 1 Fol. 6v) Bibliothèque Nationale, Paris.

Museu Nacional de Arte Antiga – Lisbon

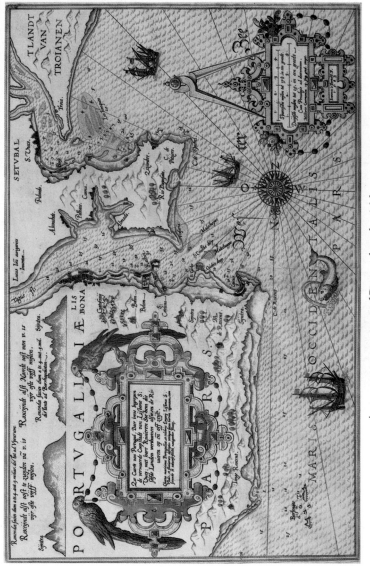

A contemporary map of Portugal in the 16th century.

(The mouth of the Tagus River and Lisbon, by Lucas Janszoon Waghenaer (1533–1606),
taken from Speculum nauticum super navigatione maris occidentalis confectum, 1586. Plate.)

DEA / G. DAGLI ORTI /Lisbon Museu De Marinha

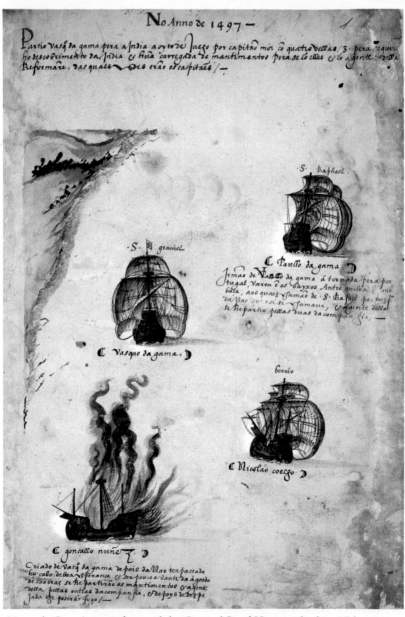

No Anno de 1497 —

Partio Vasco da gama pera a Jndia a oyto de Juego por capitão mor co quatro vellas /3· pera requi
ho descobrimento da Jndia es hũa carregada de mantimentos pera se co elles es co agente della
Reformar, das quaes eram os capitães / —

·S· Raphael·

C Paullo da gama D
Jrmão de Vasco da gama á tornada pera por
tugal, Varou os bayxos Antre quilloa es mo
baca, aos quaes chamam de ·S· Rafael por hes te
da Nao se se chamava, es agente della
se Repartio pellas duas da companhia ·—

·S· grainel·

C Vasquo da gama· D

berrio

C Nicolao coelho D

C goncallo nunez D
Criado de Vasco da gama depois da Nao ter passado
ho cabo de boa esperança es ser pouco a dante da agoada
de São bras se Repartirão os mantimentos es agente
nella pellas outras da companhia, es depois de despe
jada esa poser se fugo / —

Vasco da Gama's caravels round the Cape of Good Hope in the late 15th century
Ships of this type were technologically advanced enough to give Portugal the edge in building
its new naval empire. The flotilla on which Lopes sailed from Lisbon to Goa, and from
Goa to Saint Helena, was made up of both caravels like this and *naus*. (Vasco Da Gama's
expedition in 1497: the caravels rounding the Cape of Good Hope to reach Calcutta.)
Academia das Ciencias – Lisbon

The Battle of Diu

In 1509 Lopes took part in this battle as a member of Francisco de Almeida's fleet, when they won a decisive victory at Chaul (Diu) in India over a combined force of Indian, Arab, Mamluk, Ottoman and Venetian sailors and mercenaries. This dramatic Portuguese victory enabled them to capture key ports around the Indian ocean.

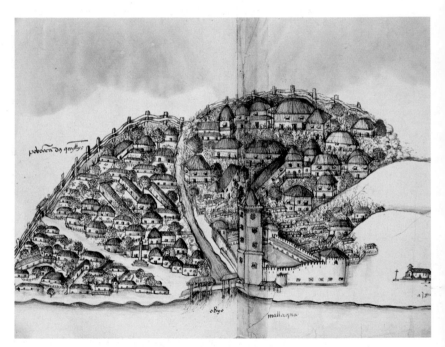

Goa in 1512, as depicted in the contemporary account of
Portuguese India written by Gaspar de Correia.
Arquivo Nacional da Torre do Tombo, Lisbon

Yusuf Adil Khan (later Yusuf Adil Shah) of Bijapur (1450–1511),
on whose side Lopes would fight against the Portuguese.

To the left and right of Yusuf Adil Shah's throne are the next four monarchs of Bijapur.
The British Library Board/ Scala, Florence

16th Century View of Saint Helena Island, engraving from
The Voyage of Jan Huyghen van Linschoten (1598).

reaching the fort at Banastarim and so the Portuguese positioned their ships up the Cambarjua waterway and along the Zuari River. Albuquerque had initially believed that the capture of Banastarim would be a simple matter, but he soon realised that, protected by the two rivers and with its walls, battlements and towers reinforced by Rasul Khan, the fort would put up stiff resistance. He knew that if he attacked from the sea via the waterways that surrounded the fort he would eventually take it, but he also now understood that there would be a heavy price to pay for his soldiers. Rasul Khan in turn had calculated that the Portuguese would approach from the Mandovi River, because it was deep enough for a large Portuguese carrack to pass through. At the same time he had stationed some supply-boats in a small quay alongside the Cambarjua waterway. He knew that when the tide was in, he could escape easily across the Cambarjua if need be. He was determined to fight and to hold Banastarim, but it would not harm him to have an escape route.

Albuquerque next resolved to tear up the palisade the Muslims had constructed around Banastarim so that he could berth his ships and get as close to the walls as possible. It was a very risky operation, to be carried out under cover of night, and one which required tremendous courage. Once again the Muslims were expecting them. They threw down bundles of burning straw from the walls which lit up the sky, allowing them to fire on the Portuguese. Despite urgent pleading for his safety from his captains, Albuquerque chose to lead from the front until he was positioned right under the barrels of the guns. Although his men urged him to seek shelter, he simply replied with his usual assurance that he could not be at ease while they were exposed to such dangers and that he would not leave them. From the walls, a cannon was fired in his direction. At that very moment, during those few seconds before the cannonball struck the ship, Albuquerque took a few lucky steps to the side. The cannonball killed two oarsmen, splattering the governor with their blood and skin. At once a great yell of triumph rang out among the Muslims that Albuquerque – the great Albuquerque – was dead, at which he stood up and, wiping the blood off his clothes, bellowed that Afonso de Albuquerque was not an easy man to kill. Then, casually, he ordered that the cannonball be collected and brought to him. An eyewitness wrote of the battle of Banastarim:

> I do not believe that in all India that there has been an engagement like that one, involving so much artillery and a fortress with so large an enemy garrison ... many times Afonso de Albuquerque rebuked our men for neglecting their personal safety, for our ships were so riddled with gunfire that there was nowhere for them to take cover, except that it was Our Lord's wish that they should be protected from danger.

The initial assault by the Portuguese, despite the fierce resistance and the casualties inflicted, succeeded in its aim of cutting off Banastarim from all possible relief and with that aim achieved, Albuquerque took the opportunity to head back to Goa. Unsurprisingly he made a triumphant entry into the city which welcomed him with open arms. At the city gate he made a speech, following which the garrison's keys were ceremonially handed over to him. His procession then made its way to the church and when at the halfway point priests came to greet him carrying a cross, he dismounted and insisted on marching behind it, bareheaded under the blazing sun, ordering that it be shaded by the canopy originally intended for him. It was a nice touch: poetic and humble. Albuquerque was back in his beloved Goa and he was in his element. Four days after his arrival, Albuquerque was told about a fresh Muslim advance on Goa – this time from Bijapur – and he immediately ordered a two-pronged attack on the approaching forces by land as well as by water. The initial skirmish in front of the city ended as quickly as it had begun. Ismail Adil Shah had sent out a further 200 cavalry and 4,000 infantry to relieve the besieged men at Banastarim but in the face of a ferocious assault there by the Portuguese infantry – composed of crossbowmen, musketeers and pike-men – the Muslim cavalry fled, leaving their infantry unprotected. Albuquerque's force had been strengthened by Hindus who fought on foot and cut down many of the fleeing Muslims. In a frenzied retreat, the Muslim troops now fled towards the fortress at Banastarim in a state of panic, only to discover that the entrance of the fortress was shut. Many of the Muslim infantry were now left outside the fort, and they engaged in a desperate and ferocious rear-guard battle against the Portuguese soldiers and *fidalgos* who fought with fierce abandon. Some of the Muslims fled around the back of the fortress where they sought shelter, others were trapped in the mud and perished, while others attempted in vain to swim the river, only to be intercepted and killed by the Portuguese on the ships. Determined to scale the outer wall the Portuguese made human ladders, but the Muslim response was equally ferocious, and they hurled down buckets of lit gunpowder, boiling oil and tar as well as rocks and stones. Meanwhile deadly accurate artillery fire from the walls saw a number of Portuguese officers killed. Flying stones also hit their mark, and one stone knocked the *fidalgo* Manuel Lacerna off his horse. Lacerna would have almost certainly been killed had not another *fidalgo*, João Decio, heroically come to his rescue. Lacerna, recovered from his blow to the head, immediately commandeered another horse and, with some troops, charged the entrance of the fort, only to be shot and wounded and rescued once again, this time by Dom Garcia de Noronha, who was the great-great grandson of King Ferdinand I of Portugal. And still the Portuguese created human ladders to try to scale the walls and it was the *fidalgos*, the knights and noble-men, who led the way. Rasul Khan responded with arrows, gunfire and bundles of burning hay, yet, according to the *Commentaries of Albuquerque*, 'nothing he could do would force them to withdraw'.

When Pedro Mascarenhas, a *fidalgo*, managed to lead a successful scaling of one of the walls, Albuquerque was so overcome with emotion that he grabbed him and kissed him on the face, and the sources say that this act 'scandalized' many who were present. Albuquerque did not care for he was grateful for the presence of Mascarenhas, who had left the fortress of Cochin where he was captain to come and fight for Albuquerque. These were the *fidalgos* in battle: fighting with unbounded heroism and heedless gallantry, winning booty and glory. It was magnificent but in many ways it belonged to a bygone age. What won battles and secured victories now was discipline, tactics and organisation – all so unromantic and unchivalrous, and yet effective.

So fierce and bloody had been the fighting that Albuquerque, alarmed at the Portuguese losses, ordered his men to fall back from trying to scale the walls. However, before falling back he set fire to a camp that he had built near the fort to prevent the Muslims from using it. With that command the day's battle came to an end. It had been a brutal and bloody day and there had been losses on both sides, with the Muslims taking the brunt of them and suffering nearly 100 fatalities. But Banastarim had withstood the assault and its defenders on the walls had responded bravely, in a lethal and efficient manner.

For the time being both sides took a breath, and twenty days would pass before Albuquerque returned to Banastarim from Goa, this time commanding a force of 4,000 men, 3,000 of whom were Portuguese and the rest Hindus. The troops were split into two battalions with Albuquerque retaining command of one and placing the other under Dom Garcia de Noronha. Once again, the aim was to lay siege to the fort so as to cut off supplies, and to prepare for a final assault. Working at night, they dug a ditch around the fortress as the first step to weaken the walls, and for the next few days both sides exchanged fire, with Portuguese cannon shots becoming embedded in the walls and bulwarks. Having initially focused on the Mandovi River approach to the fort, Albuquerque now turned his attention to the Cambarjua. He was aware that this offered a much greater risk, since, though the Cambarjua was less guarded, the Portuguese ships would be stranded if caught in the low tide. To test the lie of the land Albuquerque sent a caravel up the river, with a smaller keel designed for shallow waters, but he had miscalculated and the caravel hit a sharp submerged rock and began to list and take on water. The Muslims, who were watching from the fort, now let out a great cheer as the vessel rapidly overturned and sank, though all on board were saved. His first attempt thwarted, Albuquerque then dispatched, according to the sources, a boat and a caravel, both armed with munitions, which, despite the gunfire from the fort, were successful in passing through the stakes which the defenders had erected, and getting close to the walls of the fort. But just as rapidly the tide began to turn, and the two vessels had to turn back or risk being stranded. On the Mandovi side however Albuquerque was more successful – the four vessels he had dispatched there successfully cut off the main supplies to the fort.

Albuquerque now planned for the next stage in his campaign – the main assault on the fortress – and his captains were ordered to prepare their artillery and scaling ladders. A ditch now began to be dug around the fortress and stockades were set up. In the meantime, shielded by wooden mantelets, the Portuguese set up artillery around 30 feet from the walls of the fort and relentlessly pounded away at it. So fierce was the noise that the sources tell us that the water lizards, spooked by the sound of the battle, took cover in the vegetation and did not emerge for several days.

With supplies cut off from Banastarim, the pressure on the fortress was finally beginning to tell as ammunition ran low along with food and hope. For weeks Banastarim held out and Rasul Khan hoped for a relief army from the Sultan, but as the days passed and the Portuguese assault refused to abate, he understood that it would only be a matter of time before they breached the walls. Only a few days earlier he had escaped with his life when a cannon shot had struck a tower and showered him with debris, and it was no longer possible to walk freely in the courtyard as Portuguese artillery, mounted on their stockades, were now so close they had a line of sight on the courtyard and could pick off the Muslims. Albuquerque knew that the tide had turned when he realised that the Muslims were firing reused cannon shot the Portuguese had originally fired at them: the Muslim side had run out of ammunition.

Rasul Khan's mind now turned to negotiating a ceasefire to allow his forces to withdraw to Bijapur while he surrendered the fort. He gathered his commanders, among them Lopes, and informed them that they were cut off from all supplies, that much of the outer wall had been destroyed and that they were running out of food and gunpowder. Their safety, he concluded, no longer rested in armed resistance but in negotiating a truce. Many of those present agreed with Rasul Khan but at this point the *Commentaries of Albuquerque* mention that a renegade spoke up (perhaps it was Lopes) arguing that the fight should continue. 'Do not forget', the renegade warned Rasul Khan. 'With the Portuguese their fury will never let up – it's like attacking a lion.' But the Muslim general was not listening and, on 19 November, he ordered that a white flag be raised and an envoy sent to the Portuguese. Initially he had wanted Lopes to be the envoy, but another renegade, Fernandinho, approached the outer wall's edge in view of the Portuguese. 'We are calling a truce!' he shouted, but then he made it clear that there was only one man whom the Muslims were prepared to negotiate with: 'We want João Machado.' Machado, however, was not in the camp and the Portuguese side replied that instead of Machado they would dispatch Bastião Rodrigues who 'understands your language'. Rodrigues was then escorted to the fort where he met Rasul Khan and received the general's conditions, which amounted to a request for a few days' truce to agree upon the terms of a settlement between Albuquerque and Ismail Adil Shah.

When Albuquerque received Rasul Khan's terms, he summoned his men and asked for their opinion, and his captains spoke almost in one voice: there was no need to accept any terms. Rasul Khan was simply stalling for time: the walls were nearly breached and instead of negotiating for peace they should attack the fortress, force their way in and take it by storm. Supported by Dom Garcia, Albuquerque disagreed, arguing that if they stormed the fortress they might well capture it but only at the cost of many lives, for the Muslims were desperate and would certainly fight to the death. Rodrigues had informed him that around 8,000 armed men remained in the fortress, and that finishing them off would involve much bloodshed on both sides. Albuquerque then declared his own terms: if Rasul Khan surrendered the fortress with all the guns, horses and everything else intact he and his men would be given safe passage. But, Albuquerque insisted, he would also need to hand over the renegades, including Fernão Lopes. If Rasul Khan refused these terms then a ferocious assault would be launched with no mercy shown. Rodrigues was dispatched back to Rasul Khan with this message, this time accompanied by João Machado who must have been summoned to return to the camp to act as an intermediary. The two men conveyed Albuquerque's message to Rasul Khan who listened to it in silence. We do not know if Machado and Lopes exchanged words that day. Perhaps they did or perhaps there was nothing left to say. Rasul Khan knew that his situation was desperate and that further resistance was futile, and he replied that he would accept some of the governor's terms, but not all of them, for he would not hand over the renegades, and he would certainly not hand over Lopes. He knew that, though some renegades may be spared, given their lowly status or their abject poverty, it was certain that Lopes would be put to death, and his faith did not allow him to hand him over. When Machado returned to Albuquerque the governor's face turned red and he thundered that 'Nothing in this world will make me allow them to remain with Rasul Khan. This is no more than others in my position would ask for.' Of all the conditions which had to be met, he insisted, the handing over of the renegades was the first, otherwise, he warned, the truce would be void.

Albuquerque's ire and refusal to compromise shook Rasul Khan – his mouth trembled and he was unable to speak. For a long period he remained silent, lost in contemplation. Handing over Lopes would result in a certain death sentence, for Rasul Khan knew by now that Albuquerque never showed mercy. Lopes had converted and embraced Khan's faith, and had fought with courage and bravery by his side. He had shown nobility and honour. But the situation in the fortress was beyond desperate, and the Portuguese were getting increasingly bloodthirsty – soon Albuquerque himself would be unable to hold them back. Khan knew that he had no choice and that Albuquerque had cornered him. He would have to accept the terms. Lopes and the renegades would have to be handed over. But still Rasul Khan did not speak, and the silence lengthened, while the Portuguese envoy waited for the Muslim general to reply, as the daylight began to fade. Rasul Khan remained silent, lost in thought. And Lopes' fate hung in the balance, between Albuquerque's fury and Rasul Khan's silence.

'I will agree to the governor's demands.' Rasul Khan's weary voice was so low it was barely audible. 'And I will release Lopes and the renegades. But I will do so on one condition: and that is that their lives are spared. Beyond that I will not go. I cannot go.' Rasul Khan then slipped a diamond ring he was wearing from his finger and asked that it be passed on to Albuquerque as a sign of his sincerity. The ring was rejected by Albuquerque. According to the *Commentaries* his words were scathing. 'You fool', he scolded the envoy, 'people will say I am acting this way because of it. You take that stone right back! Now! Before I stab you in the chest!' But he also had a message for the Muslim general: 'Inform Rasul Khan that I will spare the lives of the renegades.' Albuquerque's words were carefully chosen and magnanimous in appearance, but magnanimity was not a quality in abundance in his soul. He would spare Lopes' life, but only after he had made it not worth living. In the meantime, while Albuquerque agreed to the terms, dramatic events were taking place in the fortress. By the time Bastião Rodrigues returned carrying Albuquerque's message it was already past midnight and the fortress was in tumult, for Rasul Khan himself had used the escape he had previously planned, and had managed to abandon Banastarim unnoticed, in a skiff with his wives and guards. The boatman, who was Portuguese, was likely bribed to carry his passengers across the river. Rasul Khan was convinced that Albuquerque would not accept his request to save the lives of Lopes and the renegades, and at the same time he knew that he could not hold the fortress any longer. Saving Lopes could mean the massacre of hundreds in the garrison, but to surrender him went against Rasul Khan's faith. Tortured by this dilemma, general Rasul Khan, Adil Shah's greatest commander, became so paralysed with indecision that he decided his only option was to flee under the cover of night. It was in many ways a cowardly act, one of a man who had lost his nerve. His faith had initially prevented him from handing over Lopes (though there were other Portuguese fighting on the Muslim side, there was no doubt that Lopes was the ringleader, and the man whom Albuquerque had demanded be handed over), but in the case of Rasul Khan it does seem that faith had its limits, and in fleeing the fort he must have known that he was abandoning Lopes to certain death.

At first the Muslim captains, unaware, waited for Rasul Khan in the fort. When they could not find him it gradually dawned on them that he had abandoned them, and that unless they acted quickly and in unison a great calamity would befall them. The angry lion Albuquerque needed to be satiated or he would devour them all. Lopes, when he received news of Rasul Khan's escape, would have realised at once that he had to flee the fortress or he would be dead by dawn. He had trusted Rasul Khan, but he had no reason to trust the men who surrounded him, least of all the mercenary Turks and Khorasanians, whom he did not know. It was well known that he was a wanted man, and what better gift could any of those captains, lurking in the shadows, offer Albuquerque than the head of the renegade Fernão Lopes? He had to find a way to escape and he had no time to lose: his life depended on it. But it was too late – he was grabbed by guards sent by Rasul Khan's captains and placed under arrest.

There was no time to waste, for news of Rasul Khan's flight had by now reached the Portuguese soldiers and the scent of blood was in their nostrils. Only with great effort were the Portuguese captains holding back their men who angrily clamoured for blood, looting and fire. Lopes was handed over to Bastião Rodrigues, the Portuguese envoy, and dispatched to Albuquerque with a message that read: 'here is your accursed renegade. Do with him what you want. Now let the rest of us have safe passage!' On the very same night that Rasul Khan fled, Lopes, hands chained behind his back, was escorted out of the fortress to the Portuguese camp. At once he was taken to Albuquerque's tent where he was thrown at the governor's feet. Albuquerque had been waiting impatiently for news of his envoy and was fatigued from lack of sleep. Without addressing any words to Lopes, or even looking at him, he signalled for him to rise. Rasul Khan had not only abandoned the fortress of Banastarim, he had also abandoned his word. Albuquerque, who had vowed not to kill Lopes, now no longer needed to keep his promise and Lopes ran the risk of being hanged by dawn. But Albuquerque was too tired then to decide on his fate and signalled

for Lopes to be led away, in chains and under guard. Not one word
had passed between them.

Soon after sunrise Albuquerque summoned his forces and
marched on the fortress. The entrance gates were thrown open
and Rasul Khan's most senior commander emerged to offer the
fortress' surrender. All morning Albuquerque had been urging his
fidalgos to ensure discipline among their men but when the gates
opened many infantry and cavalrymen, no longer able to contain
themselves, charged inside and began to loot indiscriminately.
Albuquerque was determined that the surrender of Banastarim be
dealt with as peacefully as possible: he could not take the risk of
confronting thousands of Muslims who now had nothing to lose,
and this would elongate the battle. He was eager to secure the fort
so that he could set out on another campaign in the Red Sea. The
sooner the Muslims retreated, the better. Seeing the commotion,
Albuquerque desperately tried to prevent his troops from entering
before the evacuation of the Muslims could take place, but such was
the tide of men rushing into the fort that he found himself forced
back within its walls. Only with great effort was order restored, such
that the evacuation of Banastarim and the transfer of the Muslims
to Bijapur could commence. Strict orders were issued that all
Muslims, their wives and children could depart unharmed (it was
customary for families to travel with the Muslim commanders, even
for battles). All that was allowed to be taken out of Banastarim
were the clothes on people's backs. Everything else, all weapons and
horses, had to be left behind. Even then, the challenge of transfer-
ring the Muslims across the waterways was an enormous one. There
were so many thousands of Persians and Turks and Khorasanians,
as well as the local people, that it took days to get them all across.
But Banastarim had finally fallen, and Rasul Khan had retreated,
leaving behind his splendid horses, which Albuquerque took in the
name of the King. Albuquerque wrote to his monarch that 'India is
now tamed. May our Lord keep it so.'

Albuquerque was not certain, however, that Rasul Khan would not launch a new assault. Accordingly he dispatched a letter in which he offered him the opportunity to ally himself with the Portuguese. He would have known that Ismail Adil Shah would be furious at Rasul Khan's abandoning of the fort, and Albuquerque attempted to exploit this opportunity: 'should you wish to remain in Goa in the service of the King of Portugal instead of Hidalcão [the Portuguese name for Adil Shah], I will grant you some control of lands here in Goa, in the King's name, provided that you swear allegiance.' When Rasul Khan did reply to Albuquerque his tone was defiant, and he demanded the return of the Portuguese renegades (including Lopes, one imagines) even if he did appear more concerned about the return of his 'prized horses'. Perhaps Rasul Khan's abandoning of Banastarim was due less to a loss of nerve, and more a tactical withdrawal which would allow him to launch an attack on Goa. Whatever it was, Albuquerque was not taking any chances. Rasul Khan did eventually launch a raid on Goa, but it appeared to be a half-hearted one during which, we read, a 'few renegades' were killed, and then the general vanishes from our story.

The time of reckoning had come. Albuquerque now turned his attention to Lopes. Although other renegades had also been rounded up, it was Lopes who, in the words of Gaspar Correia, 'was to be punished more severely as he had a greater standing'. The fact that Correia specifically mentions Lopes, even though there were other Portuguese *renegadoes* who had been handed over, is of great interest: it is easy to imagine that he would have been viewed as the ringleader. Lopes was undoubtedly the most senior of the Portuguese renegades present, and he certainly knew Albuquerque. Perhaps Albuquerque was still irked by how he had defied him in Hormuz or at the hanging of Rui Dias. But Rasul Khan's fleeing from Banastarim had removed any obligation from Albuquerque to keep his word: Lopes, he decided, would be hanged. To his surprise, however, the matter turned out to be not so simple. As we read in the accounts of Correia, Barros and Castanheda, the Chief Justice of Portugal (*Ouvidor-Geral*) was due in Goa as part of his circuit visit, which he made from Lisbon. The title of Chief Justice was equivalent to that of a judge of appeal of the King's Tribunal, and was considered the highest legal opinion in the land. To Albuquerque's displeasure, the Chief Justice now informed him that the Portuguese renegades could not be killed since King Manuel, who felt that he could not afford to lose fighting men in the East, had already decreed that their lives should be spared. The Chief Justice went even further, informing Albuquerque that according to the royal decree the renegades should not even be punished. As for the men whom Albuquerque wished to put to death, he, the Chief Justice, was not prepared to take the responsibility for settling their case and in his official capacity he would need to refer to Lisbon. Both men knew that if the case went back to Lisbon then the men would receive a pardon, since it was clear that Manuel would not approve the hanging of renegades. In any case, for a message to reach Lisbon and to receive a reply would mean the men being held in prison for a year or so, their fates hanging over their heads. Nevertheless the Chief Justice would not budge: he would not condone the putting to death of the renegades. Although Albuquerque, in his capacity as governor, was effectively the King's man in India and could have put the men to death with impunity, he perhaps felt he could not overstep this mark and defy the Chief Justice, whose presence undoubtedly saved Lopes' life. It was not the only time that a Chief Justice would have a dramatic impact on his fate.

Lopes and the others would not be put to death, but Albuquerque was determined that they would not be forgiven. An example had to be made, and so Albuquerque drew up and signed a decree in the King's name, outlining the mutilations which Lopes, as the ringleader, would have to suffer. Lopes would not be killed but he would be punished, and in the most public and graphic manner.

With ropes around their necks and their hands tied behind them, the renegades, with Lopes at the front, were taken up to 'a public place frequented by the young and the people of the city' of Goa, where they were stripped to their waists. In front of a baying crowd, and in the presence of Albuquerque, a proclamation was then read out loud in which it was declared that the King of Portugal had commanded that, although the lives of the accused men had been spared, they were nevertheless traitors to the law and their King, and justice had to be done. Some of the renegades knelt while receiving their sentence, others beat their chests. Some hung their heads while others prayed. One or two refused to accept their sentence even though the time for refusal had long passed. As for Lopes, he was stoic, his face impassive, his eyes cast to the ground.

Though the King's name was used, Albuquerque would have known that his method of dealing with his prisoners actually went against Manuel's order that no renegades should be punished. For Albuquerque, who had drawn up the proclamation himself, this kind of mercy was nothing short of foolhardy; punishment was necessary. The proclamation having been read, Lopes was placed in the stocks and jeered at, and his beard was plucked out. Mud mixed with pig dung, specially prepared for this occasion, was rubbed into his face and eyes to such an extent that his face was no longer visible and he was left thus, at the mercy of the flies for the rest of the day. As Lopes lay in the stocks people were encouraged to urinate on him and many rushed to do so, some bringing their children. Others spat on him. At the end of the day he was returned to the prison where he lay shackled with iron chains around his ankles, hands and neck, not so much lest he escape, but so that he may suffer. That night Lopes would have endured a despair he never thought possible as he lay in various types of excrement. But compared to what was to follow, that first night was one of mercy.

On the second day, Lopes and the renegades were once again brought to the public place and stripped to their waists, and the same proclamation was read out loud. The crowd was larger and more boisterous than the day before. And on the second day, amidst the baying and clamouring of the crowd, amidst the flies and mosquitoes, amidst the Hindus and Portuguese, Albuquerque ordered that Lopes' nose be cut off. To punish a *fidalgo* like this was unheard of, for noblemen were never disfigured – a fate which was left to commoners – and even the sturdiest of men blanched as Lopes' screams of agony filled the public square. With blood pouring from his gaping wound, more mud from the pigsties was rubbed into his face. Albuquerque, his face betraying no expression and no emotion, now ordered in a voice loud and strong so that all could hear that Lopes be made to stand so that his right ear could be cut off. When that was done, Albuquerque ordered that his left ear be cut off, which severed an artery, causing blood to pour out. And as on the first day, people urinated and spat on him as he lay whimpering on the ground, a broken man. At the end of the day Lopes was carried (for the pain had caused him to faint) back to the prison, into which he was flung with iron chains around his feet and neck, and shackles around his wrist, though mercifully a cloth was placed on the left side of his face to stem the flow of blood from the severed artery. In this condition Lopes spent the second night.

On the third day, Lopes had lost a lot of blood from his wounds and could hardly walk. He was also delirious with fever, but he was escorted roughly back to the public square where the proclamation was read out loud for the third time, once again in the presence of Albuquerque. This time an even larger crowd was gathered, for word had spread in Goa that Afonso de Albuquerque was taking his vengeance. So large was the gathering that people had to lean forward, their necks craned to see what was happening. On the third day Albuquerque ordered, in a loud voice, that Lopes' right hand be cut off, and his screams once again filled the public square. And when that had been done Albuquerque ordered that Lopes' left thumb be cut off. By now the *fidalgos* were getting restless: to punish an infidel or even a commoner thus may be one thing, but Fernão Lopes was one of them. He had fought bravely under Almeida, and had been knighted. He had played chess and joked and laughed and eaten with them. It would have been nobler to have put him to death. After all, the *fidalgos* mumbled, had Albuquerque not hung Rui Dias for a much lesser transgression? There was no honour in this. Lopes' screams hushed the crowds. Perhaps sensing a restlessness among his *fidalgos*, or perhaps feeling that Lopes had suffered enough, Albuquerque now declared that the punishment was finished and that Fernão Lopes could go free.

He may have been free but Lopes had nowhere to go, and so he was taken back to the prison where his wounds were dressed. By now, however, the intense heat meant that infections had set in, and over the next few days, one by one, several of Lopes' fellow renegades succumbed to their wounds. Theirs were slow and anguished deaths, far from their loved ones. They had known nothing but poverty and hardship throughout their short and brutal lives, and their deaths as the gangrene spread through their limbs were agonising. Lying fitfully in a makeshift bunk, drifting in and out of a coma for days, Lopes' life hung in the balance, as any infection would have killed him. But slowly and among a few moments of lucidity and many of despair, Lopes regained his health, although his mind remained in a state of shock. He was disfigured in body and broken in spirit, forsaken and abandoned. The moments of pain when they came were excruciating, and the slightest touch to the end of his right arm where the nerve endings had not yet healed made him scream out in anguish. With the torture over, Albuquerque had pardoned him. But although he was in theory a free man his pardon held no real meaning. He was barred from the military and was unable to work. He had been publicly humiliated and disfigured and his honour abased. And so he remained in Goa, and as the weeks and months passed he roamed the streets constantly searching for scraps of food. We hear no more of his Muslim wife, and although we do not know for certain perhaps he found lodging with her or with her family. People recognised him of course, but they shunned him, often out of embarrassment or pity. He had been broken in an extremely brutal and graphic manner and had aged considerably. It seems that after the punishments handed to the renegades, Albuquerque had ordered that they be returned to Portugal, but according to Correia, two had chosen to remain. One was a man called Pedreannes who, Correia writes, 'led the life of a good man, helping our clergy, and burying dead men who were men of the country who died abandoned'. The other was Lopes.

On occasion, one can imagine that Lopes thought of João Machado and their conversation, when he had urged him to follow suit and abandon the Muslim side, to recant as he had done and return to the Portuguese fold, and he would have wondered whether he had made the right choice. He had been tested by God and shunned by society, he had been disfigured and abandoned, mocked and abused. People had spat at him and had encouraged their children to urinate on him, but in the depths of his torment and anguish, perhaps he found consolation. Machado may have gained the profit of the world but Lopes, slowly and amidst storms of despair and tears, and nights of impenetrable darkness and abandonment, may well have begun to comprehend, if not with his mind then at least with his soul, that all was not lost, that a seed had been planted and that he had gained something – though he had no idea yet what he had discovered. The evidence of this seed was that at the height of his torture, though the pain had made him scream, he had neither begged for mercy nor recanted his faith, and though Albuquerque had ignored him over the three days, the crowds could not have failed to notice that Lopes had also ignored the governor. As if they were two actors on the same stage but in different plays.

PART III

The Third Journey

'Looking through the eyes of Don Fernando,
Saint Helena you must've been a pretty sight, I know that
loneliness was ever with him, But the freedom that you offered,
Made ev'rything alright.'

'LOOKING THROUGH THE EYES OF DON FERNANDO',
WORDS AND MUSIC BY RALPH PETERS, 1979

CHAPTER TWELVE

Caesar Is Dead

Even the great and indomitable Afonso de Albuquerque had to die. His energy appeared undiminished to the end, he slept little and got up before dawn to attend mass before donning a straw hat and confronting the endless daily challenges. Gaspar Correia noted that 'his four secretaries [of which Correia himself was one] trailed after him, servants of the King, with paper and ink, so that he issued orders and dispatches which he signed there on horseback as he went'. Throughout he remained eagle-eyed: 'So long that I am present all goes well, but the minute my back is turned each man acts according to his nature.' Nine years had passed since his arrival in the Indian Ocean, during which Albuquerque had become a legend. He had worked tirelessly, surviving shipwrecks and intrigues, defeats and disasters, all overcome by his unwavering will to enforce Manuel's vision. He had become known as the 'Lion of the Sea', or simply the 'Caesar of the East', but even that glorious label did not do him justice, for he worked on a scale vaster than that of the Caesars, administering an empire which stretched from the Red Sea to Malacca, a distance of over 3,000 miles. He was assuredly the greatest of the Portuguese empire-builders and one of the towering figures of the 16th century.

He was also a man who made enemies, and who was capable of savagery and violence that shocked the most hardened of *fidalgos*. He was the intended victim of several assassination attempts; on one famous occasion his food was poisoned, but Albuquerque survived. Death, he announced with sangfroid, had to wait, as he did not want to die from poison. But now the darkness was drawing nearer and the 62-year-old Albuquerque understood that his race was nearly run. On 6 December 1515 he wrote his final letter to Manuel. He then instructed that he be dressed in the surcoat of the military order of the Knights of Santiago (of which he was a member) and in which he gave instructions that he was to be buried. With time slipping through his fingers he wrote his will, sealed it and requested that a clergyman be summoned to give him his absolution. He was then carried to a window to take a final look at Goa before taking his last breath. Albuquerque's body was carried by torchlight to the church under the gaze of the Goans, who came to pay their silent respects to their aged Lion of the Sea, whose beard was so long that it reached down to his waist: the great Afonso de Albuquerque was dead. The Goans insisted that he be buried in Goa for they firmly believed that as long as his bones stayed there, Goa would remain Portuguese.

In his shaky handwriting and with death casting a long cold shadow in his cabin room, Albuquerque had scribbled his will. When his son and his executors opened the seal to read its contents they understood that, though he had never spoken of it to anyone, he had never forgotten, for two new bequests had been made. In the first Albuquerque instructed that money be put aside to say 90 masses for the soul of Rui Dias, whose hanging had haunted him in silence. The second request was a simple one: the cannonball that nearly killed him, fired from the walls of Banastarim, was to be covered in silver, and sent to the church of Our Lady of Guadalupe in the Algarve. Not once in the intervening years had Albuquerque mentioned the name of Rui Dias. But, it seems, Albuquerque had not forgotten.

The sources tell us they came in their thousands that day to pay their final respects. And among those who came was Fernão Lopes. We do not know why he had chosen to attend: was it an act of respect, or one of defiance? Perhaps he just wanted to make sure that Albuquerque, the man who had cheated death on so many occasions, had truly taken his last breath. But like the others who noted his presence in silence and left him alone, Lopes took his turn to gaze at the corpse of Afonso de Albuquerque, laid out in the cathedral in Goa which the governor had himself ordered to be constructed following its capture in 1510, and which was dedicated to Saint Catherine. All the sources paint Albuquerque in a favourable light, but Lopes hated him, with a hatred which had taken him to Bijapur and then to open rebellion, and though one can put forward several possible reasons for this hatred (Rui Dias, Hormuz, even personal ambition), one instinctively feels that the relationship between the two men was much more nuanced and complex. We will never know for certain what occurred between them, but in a way the paucity of the sources allows for some conjecture. Albuquerque was the type of leader whom it was easy to hate, but he was also a man who engendered tremendous loyalty from his men. His remarkable bravery at Banastarim, where he refused to abandon his men, would not have gone unnoticed by them, and his openly kissing the face of one of his noblemen may have scandalised some of his *fidalgos* but it clearly demonstrated that he possessed the common touch so necessary for a leader. In Goa he had truly cared for his men, and had personally arranged marriages to help them settle, and there is something genuinely moving about the remorse he felt over Rui Dias, which was touchingly reflected in his will. For this alone, I am not convinced that hatred was a truly convincing explanation for Lopes' actions. There must have been another reason.

What did it now matter if Albuquerque was dead? But in fact it did matter and greatly so: the new governor, who had been in India for three months already, carried with him a royal pardon for the Portuguese renegades, including Fernão Lopes. It was not a coincidence that the pardon immediately followed Albuquerque's death for, alive, he would probably have refused to implement it. But now, Lisbon announced, all had been forgotten and Lopes was free to return to Portugal to be reunited with the wife and son whom he had not seen for ten years. News of the pardon came as a huge relief for Lopes; 'there is nothing left for me here, but in Lisbon I may yet still find comfort with my wife if she will still have me'. Clearly Lopes had no intention of remaining in India. One is tempted to ask why he did not choose once again to embark on the eight-day journey to Bijapur and reside there – the answer is that he would have been of no use to Ismail Adil Shah. He had been initially welcomed there because of his fighting skills and swordsmanship, but what use would Bijapur have for a man who could barely hold a sword in a left hand shorn of its thumb? Certainly, we have no records of any further contact being made between Lopes and Bijapur. But then again, why would there be?

With the decision made to return to Lisbon, Lopes had no time to waste. Albuquerque had died on 16 December, and once the pardon had been given the next departing ships needed to be away before the end of the favourable north-east monsoon winds, which was in March. Although there had been no provision from the garrison for his return to Portugal, as would normally have befitted a *fidalgo*, the sources tell us that the King covered the costs of any renegade who wished to return to Lisbon. Historical records show that there were only two ships of the 1515 Lisbon fleet making the return journey in 1516 on which Lopes could have sailed. The first was the *Sancta Maria da Serra* and the other was the *Sancto António*. We know that the *Sancta Maria da Serra* left India within days of Albuquerque's death, certainly before the end of December, and it is unlikely that Lopes would have been pardoned and able to depart so rapidly. A more accurate supposition points to the *Sancto António*, which set sail in early 1516 and arrived in Lisbon in November of that year.

And so, in the early days of 1516, Fernão Lopes departed Goa heading back to Lisbon. The captain of the *Sancto António*, Simão da Silveira, would have been told the history of his remarkable passenger in case it was necessary to keep an eye on him, and in particular since he was the only renegade who was on board, but given the pitiful and broken state of Lopes it was clear he would cause no threat. Although it would have been expected that he lodged with the other *fidalgos*, there was no question of that happening since the *fidalgos* no longer wished to mix with him, and so Lopes found himself enduring the much harsher life of the sailors and the crew. One imagines that in an age of such strict social hierarchy, where the Portuguese orbit was divided between those who were *fidalgos* and those who were not, this demotion of the way in which Lopes sailed back to Lisbon would have impacted greatly on him and symbolised yet another stripping of his honour. But even to them he was of no use since his handicapped state rendered him useless for any meaningful labour. By and large Lopes kept to himself and if the other sailors knew that a renegade *fidalgo* was in their midst, they neither minded nor cared. They were the dregs of society, the commoners, on whose broken backs Portugal was building its empire. If not by their actions, most of them in any case were renegades in their hearts. These men, more than others, recognised hardship and suffering, and they recognised them in Lopes. But otherwise the mood on the *Sancto António* was a festive one for the men were returning to Portugal and to their loved ones. Crewmen frequently celebrated with jigs and shanties, dice and cards. On occasions when the workload was light and the weather clement, the ship's boys broke out in song. Left largely to his own devices, and despite the disfigurements which would have made him stand out, Lopes was quickly forgotten by the crew and the *fidalgos*. Living in the shadows of both he kept to himself and, unable to work, he strolled the deck in a brooding silence.

Although a decade had passed since Lopes' outward journey, the daily routine of life on board a Portuguese ship had remained largely unaltered, nor had the risks to lives lessened, and the hardships and mortality rates remained horrendous. Between Goa and the Cape of Good Hope, the *Sancto António* docked at six points at which water and provisions could be taken: Malindi, Mombasa, Kilwa, the Island of Mozambique, Quelimane and Sofala. The trajectory was well known, with the ship sailing east of Madagascar before putting in at Malindi and then taking to the open sea where, with the right winds, it would have made good speed. The appearance of albatrosses however would have alarmed the sailors, for it signalled storms ahead, and indeed as the *Sancto António* rounded the Cap Sainte Marie on the southern end of Madagascar the ship was struck by strong headwinds and steep waves. Rapidly the merriment felt by the crew at the prospect of heading home was replaced by their fear of the sea, unspoken so as not to tempt the gods. To add to their woes, the captain imposed rationing of their food as the headwinds beat mercilessly against the ship, slowing its advance so that it appeared as if the *Sancto António* were crawling along the ocean.

By May 1516 the *Sancto António* had rounded the southern tip of Africa and had taken on water and provisions in Mossel Bay, which lies halfway between modern day Cape Town and Port Elizabeth. The next stop for provisions would have been Table Bay, but Captain da Silveira ordered that the ship not halt there but keep to the open sea. There was a chilling reason for this, for it was at Table Bay that Viceroy Almeida had been killed by the ferocious Khoikhoi tribe. As the *Sancto António* sailed past the bay all on deck, including Lopes, lowered their heads in silence and in prayer. For Lopes in particular it would have been a poignant moment: he had fought with Almeida and had been knighted by him. Had Almeida remained in India would his destiny have been different? But for Lopes, the poignancy of the moment was also pregnant with a sharp pain, for though today the bay in which Almeida was killed is known as Table Bay, in his time it carried a different name. In 1503 the Portuguese admiral António de Saldanha had anchored there and replenished his water supply. Unsure if he had rounded the Cape, he decided to climb the mountain adjacent to the bay to see where he was, becoming as he did so the first European known to have climbed Table Mountain. Setting off, he named the bay Aguada de Saldanha (the watering place of Saldanha). About a century later, in 1601, a Dutch seafarer and cartographer called Joris van Spilbergen identified a different bay further north of the Cape as the Aguada de Saldanha, and the bay at the foot of the mountain was renamed Table Bay. But Lopes would have known it as Aguada de Saldanha, and he would have known Saldanha, for the two had met, albeit on opposing sides: at Banastarim, when Saldanha had charged at him and attempted to kill him.

Now, as Lopes pondered his destiny, the captain of the *Sancto António*, with a simple decision, altered it. Having bypassed the bay of Aguada de Saldanha, and with still one-third of the journey ahead of him, Simão da Silveira calculated that he would now need to make an additional stop for water and steered the *Sancto António* along the Benguela Current which flowed northward in the South Atlantic Ocean along the West coast of southern Africa, until he found himself in warmer water. At this point, he picked up the south-east winds that guided the ship steadily towards the deserted island of Saint Helena, where fresh water was available.

~~~

When Fernão Lopes received the royal pardon offering him the choice of remaining in India or returning to Portugal, he jumped at the opportunity to return to Lisbon. The despair of his torture and the abject poverty of his life as an outcast in Goa must have been an endless ordeal, destroying his mind and crushing his soul. As long as Albuquerque was alive there could be little hope of any relief from his tribulations, and though Lisbon was in a conciliatory mood, Albuquerque would have remained in an intransigent one, one imagines, for though he took little interest in Lopes he was not prepared to forgive him. And so Lopes remained patient, convincing himself that he was at least cultivating virtue even though in reality he knew that he was simply cultivating pain. But now Caesar was dead and life, albeit a new chapter of his disfigured and tortured life, could begin again. Lopes would not have hesitated in accepting the choice to return to Lisbon because he knew that, had he remained in India, his loneliness would have driven him mad. Even his belief that his wife might take him back dripped with despair, deluded and confused as it was. The royal pardon had offered Lopes hope and he would have clung on to it with all his failing strength as a drowning man in an ocean clings on to a plank of wood. But as the days passed and the reality of his freedom began to sink in, as the *Sancto António* made its way back to Lisbon, Lopes' mind would have begun to clear and the enormity of this decision would slowly have dawned on him. It had been almost ten years exactly since he had set sail as a young man from Belém, full of hope and a sense of adventure, confident that all was possible and that life offered an endless list of opportunities. But if India had taught him one thing it was that life was little more than a solitary and increasingly suffocating path. His dream of returning to Lisbon was an illusion. What welcome could he expect? By now everyone who had known him in Lisbon was familiar with his story, of his betrayal of the King and of Portugal, and even for those who did not know, etched on his disfigured face was proof of his guilt. How would he make a living? Who would even wish to be associated with him? There were no prospects for him in Portugal and he would have to live off the *misericórdia* charity, which had been set up in 1498 to feed the poor and clothe the naked, until he died a pauper's death. As Lopes walked up and down the deck, it is easy to imagine the questions that would have struck him in waves of despair. What about his wife? It had been ten years since he had last laid eyes on her. He would barely recognise his own son, his flesh and blood. Did he honestly believe that his wife would be waiting for him to return home, as if he had simply stepped out for an hour to buy some figs from the market? It is likely that neither she nor their son would have wanted to have anything to do with him, for his actions and defiance had brought shame and dishonour to the family. He had even deprived them of the honour of claiming he had died in battle. If he were to return, and if in some fanciful manner resume his patriarchal position at home, he knew that any public association with his son would signal the death knell of the young man's career and any possible position at court.

As Lopes pounded the deck of the *Sancto António* a flock of white birds appeared that he would have recognised as fairy terns, which the Portuguese believed were signs of God and called 'angel terns', since they believed it meant that their ship would be guided safely to land. Soon after, on the horizon, Lopes would have spotted the contours of an island beginning to emerge. As the ship navigated its way towards Saint Helena, Lopes' mind might have gone back to his friend João da Nova, who had stood up to Albuquerque in Hormuz and who had been the first to discover this island. He would now have heard the crew talking among each other: the stop at Saint Helena would be a very brief one, a few days at most, enough to gather water, for they were eager to press on to Lisbon and their loved ones. In any case there was nothing *but* fresh water on the island of Saint Helena, for no human soul resided on it, cut off as it was by thousands of miles of ocean. As the crew chatted and the island began to take shape, neither its sheer cliffs, carved by the sea, nor its dense vegetation, nor even the streams, which had incised deep valleys, could conceal its desolate nature. And as Saint Helena drew nearer and nearer, a thought may well have settled in Lopes' mind: here was a godforsaken place for a godforsaken soul.

CHAPTER THIRTEEN

A Portuguese Robinson Crusoe

They were in their thousands now, forming a dazzling mosaic of light and blue, as the sun's rays filtered through their wings. The Portuguese also referred to the terns as 'White Pigeons', and now these birds welcomed the *Sancto António* as it approached Saint Helena and flew in so low that the sailors leapt, trying to catch them to cook and eat. 'What stupid birds!' they said to each other and laughed as some flew into the rigging and fell to the deck. By now the wind was whipping up the sea and at the base of the towering cliffs massive breakers were pounding the rocks, causing a groundswell. Captain Simão da Silveira steered around the south-western point of the island before anchoring in the sheltered north-western side where there were no breakers and where the water lapped gently against the shore. Nowadays called James Bay, it would have been known to the Portuguese as Aguada da Nova. Before long a boatload of soldiers landed on the stony beach, above which rose sloping banks scattered with thickets of gorse covered in bright yellow flowers, and the men were delighted to see a grove of fig trees. On some of the trees, the men noticed, the names and dates of previous Portuguese ships were carved, and some of the sailors were quick to add the name of the *Sancto*

António while others carved vulgar jokes. The trees had, in fact, been planted by the Portuguese around 1505, for there were no indigenous fruit or vegetables growing on the island. Although, according to some historians, the Portuguese built a chapel upon discovering the island, there is no evidence to support this. In fact they never even formally claimed the island as a possession of the Portuguese Crown, nor did they fortify it or establish a permanent settlement there – the reason being simply that they saw no need to do so. As Filippo Pigafetta, who compiled a series of travel narratives in the 16th century, recounted when he asked a Portuguese why Saint Helena was neglected:

> the answer was made unto me that there was no need to do so; for that the island serveth to no purpose for a voyage into the Indies, because there is another way for that passage, and it is also a very hard matter to find it out; but, in returning from thence it lieth full in the way, and is very easily descried; so that it would not quit the cost to bestow money and time in maintaining soldiers therein, without any profit, seeing no other vessels come thither, but those of the Portuguese.

In other words, the uninhabited island was simply a watering stop for Portuguese ships on the way back from the Indies.

When Lopes had first set eyes on Saint Helena the island, surrounded by vast cliffs, had been shrouded in early morning cloud and mist, giving it a forbidding, enchanted feel. In the interior the land, which rose to a sickle-shaped central ridge, was exceptionally steep and rugged, dissected by deep valleys with many cliffs overlooking an endless ocean in every direction. The cliffs were dense with vegetation and in particular a green-blue plant with thick, fleshy, smooth leaves. On the shore the sailors came across seals but when they tried to attack them and club them for their meat, they quickly found they were too large to be intimidated and, rearing up, they emitted a throaty roar which had the men scattering. The captain's orders were that the men were allowed only two days' leave on the island, enough time for the ship to stock up with fresh water from the streams before setting sail. And it was at some point during those two days that Lopes abandoned ship and chose to remain on the island. Whether the decision had been impetuous and panicked or a planned one is not clear, but some time after leaving Goa he must have come to the conclusion that he could not face returning to Portugal. Certainly he would have had several months of sailing to reach this decision. Perhaps he regretted not remaining in India – but the time for regret had passed. And yet one remains puzzled as to why Lopes should have chosen Saint Helena. Although the voyage was nearly complete and Lisbon was getting closer, now no further than a few weeks of sailing away, there were other stops still to be made, most notably Madeira or Cape Verde from where he could easily have slipped away to Africa. Why choose an island which was uninhabited, where he would be totally isolated and alone in a blank expanse of ocean? What must have crossed Lopes' mind to make such a seemingly suicidal decision? Was it a moment of madness, the actions of a panicked man? The truth is that we will never know how clear Lopes' mind was when he took his decision to abandon ship and hide, but if one had to guess then one of the only valid conclusions would be that these were the actions of a man in despair, one who had lost his senses, even his will to live. In many ways they were the actions of a frightened animal.

What Lopes did not know, what perhaps he could not have imagined, was how fond the captain and the crew of the *Sancto António* had become of him. He may largely have kept to himself but perhaps it was his dignified demeanour, or the elegant way he carried his suffering, that caused the captain, when he heard that Lopes had vanished, to at once send out a party to search for him, even though it was clear that given the sheer precipitous cliffs and the thick gorse which covered the land there was little hope of finding him. But the men searched and called out his name, 'Lopes, Fernão Lopes!' Undoubtedly he heard them, but he did not respond. One wonders if he reflected on the consequence of his actions; did his mind race that far ahead? What happens when the ship leaves? For the moment however he remained in a small cave, which he had stumbled on when he had slipped away from the ship.

Like an animal, he was crouched down, barely breathing, his eyes fixed on the ground, his ears pricked to the sound of his name echoing across the island. But he did not respond. He did not move. He would not move.

At the end of the day the men returned to inform the captain that there was no sign of Lopes and that unless he returned by himself there was little hope of him being found on the island. Faced with no other choice, da Silveira ordered that the crew prepare to set sail, for little more could be done. Before the ship departed, however, the captain ordered that provisions be left behind for Lopes, and so a barrel of biscuits, slices of meat and dried fish, rice, a cooking pot and utensils were stacked on the shore, as was some salt. The captain then lit a fire for he knew that Lopes with his handicap would struggle to light one. Then in a gesture of respect for this tortured soul, and one which testified what the crew thought of Lopes, the men left behind clothing to keep him warm. Finally, the captain wrote a letter which he had nailed to a tree. There was little hope of it surviving, but it was addressed to the crew of the next Portuguese ship to dock there, and it stated that the island of Saint Helena was no longer deserted, for there now resided on it a Portuguese knight, and that news should be brought to Lisbon of whether this knight was alive or dead. If he were to be found alive it said, he should be treated with respect and afforded what he needed, for there was nobility in him.

Lopes would likely have watched the ship set sail from the cave, from which he had a clear view of the bay, his eyes fixed on it until it had become a speck on the horizon. The enormity of the ship's departure would have hit Lopes like a wave of terror. He was in the middle of nowhere and, in the very best-case scenario, he would remain there for at least a year since no Portuguese ship would stop at the island before then. Lopes' isolation could have hardly been more absolute. The volcanic island known as Saint Helena lay 1,200 nautical miles from modern day Angola and 1,500 nautical miles from Brazil, as if it were disowned by the two continents. It was so isolated that for its 14 million years of history no human had ever inhabited it. Lopes had effectively fallen off the face of the earth. The food left for him would soon run out and he would starve. What he had done – if it had been intentional – was suicidal, an act of madness. May God have mercy on his pitiful soul.

⸻

Remarkably, Fernão Lopes would remain on the island of Saint Helena, in almost total solitude, for an initial period of fourteen years and then, after a brief sojourn, for another dozen years or so. His isolation from the world and his hermit-like existence – indeed he would become known as the Hermit of Saint Helena – paradoxically made him, for a brief moment, one of the most famous men in Portugal and brought him to the attention of not only the highest in the land but the highest in the whole of Christendom. It is an astonishing story but before we tell it, we must first tackle the Robinson Crusoe elephant on the island. From the moment of its publication in 1719, Daniel Defoe's *Robinson Crusoe* has come to symbolise the archetypal character of the castaway on a deserted island. Traditionally, stories of shipwrecks and castaways can be traced back at least as far as Homer's *Odyssey*, an epic poem of Odysseus' long voyage to Ithaca following the fall of Troy, during which he is shipwrecked and becomes a castaway before eventually finding his way home, with the physical journey reflecting a spiritual one. However, it was not until the 18th century and Defoe that fiction dealing with deserted islands and castaways became an established genre, with *Robinson Crusoe* followed by Jonathan Swift's *Gulliver's Travels*. Certainly by the 19th century, with the publication of *Kidnapped* and *Treasure Island* by Robert Louis Stevenson, *Mysterious Island* by Jules Verne, Johann Wyss's *Swiss Family Robinson* and R. M. Ballantyne's *Coral Island*, the predicament of the castaway had become a favourite topic of the popular adventure stories. And yet in many ways *Robinson Crusoe* remained not only *the* definitive castaway novel, but also *the* prototypical novel about the colonial quest in the 18th century. In fact despite its commercial success, which saw 41 editions of the novel published in the 40 years following its publication, it was not until the 19th century that the story truly captured the public's imagination, when it ran to at least 700 editions and translations as well as imitations, with Defoe's story coming to exemplify Western man's ability to master himself and his environment even when faced with seemingly insurmountable obstacles. One can go as far as arguing that the 19th century saw the canonisation of *Robinson Crusoe* as *the* archetypal modern adventure story.

Robinson Crusoe owed its phenomenal popularity not only to its exotic settings and peoples, but also because it linked colonial expansion to social and individual advancement, and in so doing foreshadowed British imperialism. Finding himself isolated on an island, Crusoe, unlike Conrad's Kurtz or Roberto in Eco's *The Island of the Day Before*, does not succumb to a life of madness, savagery, sloth and brutality. Rather, through the application of the Enlightenment values of tolerance, reason and practical work, he 'reforms' himself and his environment, transforming the island from an untamed wilderness into a cultivated paradise. He establishes a strong moral foundation, a strong Protestant work ethic and a hierarchy in which he assigns to himself the role of master to his goats, cats and later his native servant, Friday. Defoe depicts Crusoe as a solitary spokesman for tolerance, reason and the virtues of work and routine. Drawing upon the Puritan literary tradition, particularly spiritual biographies and pilgrim allegories, Defoe's ideas were also defined by his age – that of Newton and Locke – that placed, in matters of selfhood, religion, morality and politics, a great emphasis on empirical observation and social reality. In that sense, in *Robinson Crusoe*, Defoe attempts to answer the question: 'What happens to an individual when he has to survive in isolation?' from an 18th-century rationalist perspective. Not surprisingly, the philosopher Jean-Jacques Rousseau claimed that Defoe's tale 'affords a complete treatise on natural education' and that it serves as a guide for progressing towards a 'state of reason'. When Crusoe is shipwrecked, he lacks a strong sense of identity but he gradually transforms the island, through fences, hedges, plantations and his various dwellings, into his image and identity as a white, middle-class, Christian, British man. His spiritual awakening is equally imbued by the spirit of the age, which placed significant emphasis on more progressive and morally agreeable forms of colonialism, such as religious conversion and the 'elevation' of colonised people through exposure to Western customs. He saves a native islander from hostile cannibals and names him Friday, and then converts him to Christianity. But the act of naming is also a means of exerting power and authority, a form of branding and affirmation that Friday is *his* possession. The naming also eradicates Friday's history and former life, and his identity thereby becomes intertwined with Crusoe's as a reminder to those who exist outside colonial power structures on the basis of race, ethnicity, class or gender. Henceforth Friday's name serves as a continuous reminder that his new life is a blessing bestowed upon him by his master.

That there existed parallels between Fernão Lopes and the

story of the (let us not forget fictional) character of *Robinson Crusoe* can only be expected, after all, a 'man on deserted island' story can only have so many permutations. It is of little significance whether Defoe based his Crusoe on the life of Fernão Lopes. There can certainly be little doubt that he was aware of the Lopes story while composing his novel, but in reality *Robinson Crusoe* is much more a pastiche of a variety of characters stirred by Defoe's powerful imagination than any one individual. Although the consensus appears to point to Alexander Selkirk, a Scottish sailor who spent more than four years as a castaway on a small tropical island in the Pacific, as the main inspiration for Defoe, I remain unconvinced if for no other reason than the fact that Selkirk was in life so dissolutely different from the saintly Crusoe.

When I write of *Robinson Crusoe*, though, it is not to determine whether or not Defoe based his character on Lopes – that in itself can count for little more than a curious historical footnote – but to clarify how different Crusoe was from Lopes. *Robinson Crusoe* was the affirmation of a new age: a puritanical, empirical, rationalist one, and Defoe was writing, consciously and subconsciously, for that imperial age. Edward Said captures this eloquently when he writes that *Robinson Crusoe* was the prototypical modern realistic novel, and that it is not an accident that the novel is about a European creating a fiefdom for himself on a distant, non-European island. So while we cannot write about Lopes without acknowledging the symbolic value of *Robinson Crusoe* and recognising Defoe's brilliant imaginative writing, we need to set him and Friday aside for the remainder of this story. If we turn away from Defoe's Crusoe, though, it does not mean that the age of Fernão Lopes was not dominated by another 'Robinson Crusoe'; but before I tell that story we need to return to the island of Saint Helena.

≋

The food left behind for Lopes was more than sufficient to last him several months, for the captain, knowing Madeira and Cape Verde were close, could afford to be generous. Anyway, ever since his torture Lopes had survived on only handfuls of food. Fresh water was everywhere, with streams gushing thanks to the almost daily rain. Nor would he have been concerned about the fire going out, as he had learned how to kindle fire in Goa (and he must have been able to continue to do this despite his disability). But now a different, deeper and more visceral fear would have gripped him, the fear that he was totally alone. What madness was this? The sheer scale of the solitude on Saint Helena would have been simply too large to frame or to make any sense of. Lopes' only option would have been to focus on himself and ignore the solitude. This was his only hope for survival.

A disfigured Adam now began to explore his Eden. In the valleys on the shore there was only fog, but if Lopes ascended, the fog would have become a drizzling mist which soon turned to thick rain towards the higher levels of the island. Alongside small brooks grew shrubs over three metres in height that gave off the aroma of walnuts. If Lopes were tempted by them, he might have found the taste to his liking: this was a jellico, a *Sium bracteatum*, related to the celery plant. Near the coast there were edible plants growing, and herbs such as purslane, a dark-green leafy vegetable with stems of yellow flowers that are highly nutritious. In India Lopes is likely to have consulted *vaidyas* – the physicians who used plants and herbs as Ayurvedic medicines – and to have experienced first hand the natural ointments mixed by *panditos* – Hindu doctors who could have helped him to ease the pain of his torture. He would have been unfamiliar with most of the plants and herbs on Saint Helena, since the majority were found only on the island, but one imagines that Lopes must have experimented: eating some raw, and boiling others, a matter of trial and error. It was clear that this was a verdant island. Many of the plants had reached this isolated and remote location when their seeds were carried in by currents from as far away as the Cape, while others would have arrived here in the plumage of, or in the mud on, the feet of birds. There were so many varieties: the *Chenopodium*, which is an edible leafy vegetable, and the *Euphorbia*, a strange hairy herbaceous plant which is still used today to cure eye infections. There was also the *Pelargonium*, which is known to alleviate the common cold, and *Plantago*, which can cure urinary infections.

Birds were everywhere: songbirds, finches, and on occasion a hoopoe or a cuckoo would have made an appearance. Lopes would have recognised these birds, as some of them could be seen in Portugal and some in India. But Saint Helena boasted its own bird that he would never have seen before, which looked like a lark but which was in fact a plover: the wirebird. Not used to having human beings around, they were very tame. On occasion Lopes would surely have caught a sea bird for its tasteless meat, not an onerous task as they made no attempt to fly away, unaware of the danger in which they found themselves.

On the island of Saint Helena, Lopes would quickly have discovered that an astonishing diversity of the local flora was neither poisonous nor thorny. The weather was largely clement with no extreme cold or heat, with a cool south-east wind keeping temperatures down, even though on higher ground it was much cooler than on the shore. Many years later a Boer prisoner on the island summed up the weather thus: there is a rainy season when it rains, he wrote, and a sunny season which looks so much like the rainy one you cannot tell the difference. But the winds decreed that the rain only fell in certain areas, so that on the outer part of the island the land resembled a desert. Lopes would also have noticed a peculiarity in the weather: although in winter the clouds descended and the rains came with such force that they appeared to be washing the island away into the sea, there was never any thunder or lightning.

⸻

Daily the birds go about their silent business. Briefly Lopes feels that they have come to greet him and this feeling fills him with a sense of joy, of companionship; but the birds ignore him, sidestepping him.

Near the rocky shores it would have been possible to catch an eel, some of which grew up to six feet in length. Although they had a nasty bite, once gutted and cooked they were delicious. The shallows also boasted the reclusive but flamboyant angelfish and hundreds of butterfly and goat fish. There were pipe fish, about a foot long and totally see-through but with no taste, and a slimy and grey fish – the soap fish – as inedible as its appearance. On occasion Lopes would have been able to watch the many spotted dolphins which swam and leapt energetically, and which would themselves have been delighted to have finally found an audience with whom to share their joy. Out at sea, majestic humpback whales returned to calve in season, and the island was even visited by the whale sharks, the biggest fish in the ocean.

He thinks back to a day on the Sancto António *when the ship was crossing the Cape, when he had thought about leaping into the sea and ending his suffering. He now wonders whether the current was strong enough to have carried his dead body all the way from the Cape to Saint Helena, and how long his corpse would have taken to float from the Cape to be with him here.*

On cloudless nights the sky above the island laid on a spectacular show. To this day, Saint Helena is officially one of the darkest places on earth, with no human-made light for miles. In fact its remoteness was why the island was specifically chosen by Edmund Halley when he set up an observatory there in 1677, to make the first scientific mapping of the southern sky. In 2012 the International Dark Sky Association assessed that Saint Helena qualified for 'Gold Tier' status – the highest accreditation for the absence of light pollution – thereby making it ideal for astronomy.

The island's position near the equator and its height above sea level would have afforded Lopes a panoramic view of nearly every star in both the northern and southern hemispheres.

The stars would have shone so brightly as he stood transfixed gazing heavenwards that they seemed to be pressing down on him, so close, he could almost pluck them by hand. There were times when the stars were so numerous that they overwhelmed him with such desolation that it felt he was falling off the edge of the world. But there were also times when he felt that he was a king to whom the stars and planets, the moon and the sun had all come to pay silent homage. The moon that shone over the island was bright, and when it was full Lopes could see as clearly as if it were early morning.

Under the island's dark skies Lopes looked up and as he turned around he saw the Milky Way stretching from horizon to horizon in an arc. The heavens above Saint Helena are studded with thousands of stars and nebulae and just a few degrees above the equator the dramatic Magellanic Clouds with their cross-shaped constellation can be seen clearly hanging in the sky. In 1510 Amerigo Vespucci, when he had first spotted the phenomenon, had called it the 'four stars' and soon navigators were using it to sail by.

On certain mornings he would wake up convinced he was back in Goa and the sight of the cave would fleetingly fill his heart with terror at the thought of his isolation. On other occasions he dreamed that he was a young man back in Lisbon: handsome, not disfigured, and he would awaken with a heavy heart as he wiped his face with his right stump. But the worst nights were the ones when he dreamed of his parents and what they had endured.

CHAPTER FOURTEEN

Fragments of an
Ancient World

The island Lopes found himself on rose abruptly out of the sea: a mass of dark rock looming heavenwards from the ocean, separated by valleys that cut deep chasms, as if some enormous power had rent it asunder to form steep ravines. It was an island of ascents and descents, of spurs of hills, of rough crags and streams of clear water. He would surely have discovered the rocky reefs with caves and the different bays of cobbles and sand, each in its own habitat, from the scrub vegetation on the steep inclines to verdant green pasture in the centre, to lush humid cloud forest on the peaks and the blasted, eroded semi-desert in the South and East of the island, which presented nothing but utter isolation. He could have observed how one side of the island received less rain and that in some parts wet mist hung around all day, while only a few steps away there were baking clear skies with little scudding clouds. At the extreme West of the island large fragments of rocks in the oddest shapes lay scattered on the surface. Some were standing upright in rows like the enormous forlorn tombstones of long-forgotten ancient gods.

The temperature was mild, but the reflected heat from the sides of the valley when there was no wind would have reminded Lopes of the heat of India. If the heat became overwhelming, he only had to walk for an hour to find that the temperature had dropped dramatically and that there was a sharp gust of wind rising over the steady breeze to chill his bones.

The shores of the island abounded with sea birds, which deposited their eggs on the cliffs. They also deposited their white droppings so that the cliffs appeared as if they were the sails of the island. Not all the birds headed for the cliffs, and one specific type of sea fowl preferred to make its nest in the woody, central eminences of the island. Lopes would have frequently seen one of these birds flying across the island with a fish in its beak. Sometimes the birds, careless or distracted, dropped the fish and Lopes would watch it fall. He would sometimes have come across flying fish dead on the rocks – a result of their fleeing from porpoises or sharks. Some of these fish were up to two feet in length.

With the four fingers of his left hand and the stump of his right Lopes dug into a ravine which had been formed by centuries of rain, and which in the course of time had opened up a hollow large enough to be turned into a small cave. The soil was soft and damp underground so it was possible for him to scoop it out, and soon earwigs and black beetles were crawling all over his hands. He then enlarged the cave and lined the walls with gorse until it was large enough for him to shelter and sleep in. As he dug he could not fail to note how the sides of the hollow exposed a variety of beautiful layers of coloured earth: tints of white, blue, grey and red, revealing the island's volcanic origin when the sun shone upon them, reflecting colours of breathtaking beauty. Near the deep hollow in which he made his cave, almost shut in by precipices, a small waterfall poured water into a dark pool from which a stream ran. Lopes noted how in dry weather the stream had so little water that one of the sudden puffs of wind which buffeted the island was enough to convert it into a spray, covering the nearby rocks like a thin delicate lace

*veil. At other times when the island was pummelled by heavy rain the
waterfall cascaded like an avalanche down the precipitous sides of the
ravines, carrying everything away with it with such force that it seemed
the whole island would be washed into the ocean. But, he reasoned, if
it were not for the rain and the fresh water streams then no ship would
have stopped at the island.*

In the vast expanses of open ocean winds raged, unhindered by
land for over a thousand miles, and forming unbroken fast-moving
waves (reaching 70–80 knots) called rollers. At first appearing to
move slowly forward, their swells increased, urging other waves
on until they struck the island with tremendous force. A towering
sea, seemingly calm a few minutes earlier, would violently and
viciously unleash all its fury onto the defenceless island, threatening to envelop it. These rollers were frequent enough that Lopes
would have lived through a few of them, and the noise would
have been stunning as the waves crashed against the shore and the
waters swept over the empty plain. One can picture the breathtaking majesty and beauty of the ridge of the wave cresting on its
summit with spray and foam, confronting the wind so that the
top appeared to be carried back against the curl of the swell as a
bending plume. As quickly as the waves struck, though, their fury
was over, and eventually Lopes would come to learn to read the
signs, and would be able to tell when an ocean roller would strike
one or two days before it did: the swell normally accompanied the
flood tides at full moon.

*A hoopoe bird arrived near Lopes' cave. 'Solomon, what are you
doing here with me on this island? Are you not supposed to be deliver-
ing a message to the Queen?' The hoopoe did not reply and startled by
Lopes' voice it flew away and he realised his error, for the bird's name
could not be Solomon. And the next day, or it could have been a few
days later, or a few days before, he apologised to the hoopoe and asked
its name, and this time the bird looked up and replied, 'My name is
Bijapur. I have been here long before you. What are you doing here?*

Do not imagine that the journey is short, and one must have the heart of a lion to follow this unusual road, for it is very long.' But the next day the hoopoe did not come and Lopes never saw Bijapur again.

If the chill of loneliness was particularly raw Lopes could have made his way to the shore and retrieved the captain's letter, with its final sentence: 'there resides on this island a noble knight, Dom Fernão Lopes. Treat him with respect and honour.' But perhaps one day another captain would come across it and would take it with him to Lisbon, and would make the effort there to find Lopes' son and give it to him, and his son would undoubtedly take it to his mother and show it to her.

A few years earlier an enterprising Portuguese, we are not certain who exactly but perhaps one of those who sailed with da Nova when he first discovered Saint Helena, had planted fig trees on the island, and Lopes would have been surprised to observe that the trees bore fruit continually. On every fig tree there were blossoms: green figs and ripe ones all at the same time. The fruit would have been a constant source of sustenance and Lopes would have noted that the soil was fine and fertile.

As he traversed the thick growths of vegetation, Lopes would have disturbed the peace of a multitude of bugs and moths. The land rose out of this vegetation steeply through the invasive ground-level ferns – their woody stalks rising four metres high, their surfaces blanketed in thick water-retaining moss, and their leaves dripping with moisture, giving off a heavy and damp aroma. Interspersed with the fern trees were gumwoods and ancient black cabbage trees, the likes of which he had never seen. As he walked below the ferns, showers of tiny bright yellow woodlice would have rained down on him, and enormous black and white spiderwebs were strung across the narrow path. Under his feet the ground where the water was trapped and retained by a dense carpet of moss was moist and slippery. The otherworldly nature of the surrounding trees and the mist hanging in the air gave a feeling of remoteness, almost one of foreboding, as if Lopes had stepped into a prehistoric land, a fragment of an ancient world.

There were days when nothing happened, and then there were days when nothing happened.

Lopes' family in Lisbon, if they thought of him, would have assumed that he had died either in India or somewhere on the way. Had they mourned him? Had there been a period in black? Were prayers recited for his soul, candles lit in his memory, a soul that those in Lisbon believed was traversing from this world to the eternal bliss of the next, but which in fact was alive and well and refusing to die? And what about India? Lisbon could be forgiven for forgetting him, but Goa? He had made many friends and a few enemies there, both Portuguese and Hindus. Some he had considered good friends – he had drunk and gambled with them and some, very few, had not recoiled in horror when they saw his tortured figure cross their path, or at least they did their very best to conceal it. They had seen him board the ship back to Portugal, but did he ever cross their minds now? In Bijapur he had had many close friends, he had knelt with them towards Mecca and had ridden into battle with them. His own life had been saved by Rasul Khan's insistence that he not be put to death, but if he were to get a message to Rasul Khan, what would the reply be? Would it be anything more than a 'Lopes? Was he not one of the *farangis* who fought for us?' But was being forgotten Lopes' greatest fear, or was it the fear that he was unwanted?

Saint Helena rises several hundred metres above sea level, the mist getting thicker the higher one goes, with the sun often blotted out by heavy cloud. The temperature also rises and the air, heavy with a cloyingly honey-sweet scent, was almost unbearable, making Lopes feel both light-headed and nauseous. As the wind rushed down from the plain above him, he could not help but shout aloud, only to find his voice echoing back at him with such clarity that it was as if someone else was calling him from the far-off caves. Eventually the path began to level off as he reached the ridge that formed one of the central peaks of the island, today known as Diana's Peak, which was shrouded in almost constant cloud but nevertheless afforded him a majestic view. This was the highest point, not just of the island but for 1,000 miles. Lopes, near the sheer drop, would have been transfixed by the spectacular panorama and beauty of what lay ahead of him, gazing at the gentle curve of the surrounding oceanic horizon blending into the sky. Turning west, he could have looked along the central ridge, with its lush green steep slopes. The view from the east was a marked contrast, looking out over desert landscape, volcanic rock and ash layered to form angular jagged rocks. The view was partly clouded by huge plumes of dust, which were swept high into the sky by the stiff Atlantic winds. From here, one could look out over the spectacular natural bay where the *Sancto António* had anchored, with its red and purple rocks, with white lines of guano marking the knife-edged ridges of the volcanic ravines. The sea in the distance was rough and the waves crashed again and again against the breakers, barring any safe anchorage; but even from this height green turtles would have been visible nesting on the black gritty beach, with thousands of seabirds circling languidly, effortlessly above.

He understands that it is not that the island is isolated by more than 1,000 miles of ocean. For in all of its beauty – ranging from the rugged ancient volcanic cliffs to the millions of sea birds, from the crystal clear waters of the ocean to the shoals of butterfly fish, and from the blue azure skies to the nights laden with stars – the island is actually protected by more than 1,000 miles of ocean.

How long had Lopes been on the island? He would have had no idea: how can you count days when every day is exactly the same as the one before, or the one after? In any case, what did it matter since he was probably counting the days till his death? Is that not why he had abandoned the ship? Was it not an act of suicide? But the simple fact was he had not died; in fact his health seems to have got better for what Lopes did not know, though he must have sensed it, was that the constant trade winds which blew across Saint Helena rendered the island a very healthy place. The British were to learn this when in the mid-19th century several soldiers arriving from India in poor shape were, after a few months on the island, restored to full health. It was also reported that a gentleman who arrived from England suffering from the final stages of pulmonic consumption was, after a couple of months on the island, completely restored.

He had named his fleeting hoopoe friend Bijapur and near his cave he had daily come across a fierce-looking rail, which resembled a misshapen chicken with its short rounded wings, large feet and long toes. But this rail had a fierce soul as it constantly moved, always alert, always pecking. It was a stupid bird, which continued daily to peck at a piece of barren ground only a few yards from one that clearly offered richer pickings. An ugly, stubborn bird, Lopes observed, and he named the rail Albuquerque.

The waxing and the waning of the moon, from its crescent sickle shape to its splendid fifteenth day fullness when its light bathed the island, would have helped Lopes to regulate the passing of months, even though he probably had no idea which months they were. There had been a period when the rain had fallen more frequently and there had been a period when it had not, but how long each season had lasted he would not have been able to fathom. Might he, on spotting the crescent moon on the horizon, hovering briefly, shyly, like a fair maiden attending her first public dance, have recalled the Ramadan he had spent in Bijapur? His beard, once trimmed, was now shaggy and unkempt and his fingernails were long and hard. Time had passed but it was like a dream where a lifetime could occur in a few seconds, and a few minutes could feel like a lifetime.

In the beginning there could not have been the Word. There could only have been silence. The Word was with God and the Word was God. And God was alone. And God was silent.

One day, during Lopes' exile on the island, a distant white speck became visible on the horizon, getting bigger until it slowly became a ship. Lopes' ordeal could now be over. He had survived, and now he could return to Lisbon. He could even take the captain's letter with him. As Lopes watched the Portuguese ship make its slow approach towards Saint Helena, guided by thousands of seabirds, might he have recalled his first sighting of Saint Helena and the thought that in this most desolate and isolated of places he could forget his suffering? Given what he had lived through, could he ever have been truly alone on the island? Likely he had never been alone. Afonso Albuquerque, surely, had been with him all the time and so had the corpse of Rui Dias. And the three days that he had been tortured could not possibly have left him, nor the comrades who had, in the moment of truth, stood fighting by his side at Banastarim. And though these events had in reality only occurred once, they cannot have been truly forgotten. Most likely they took place a hundred times a day in Lopes' mind, assailing and tormenting him until his screams echoed across the island and he began drifting in and out of that shadow world that sane men label madness.

Amidst tempests of torment, in moments of lucidity, he could not but be startled by the way the events that were inflicting such brutal torture on his mind paraded themselves. It was during the dark night of his soul with his mind playing tricks on him that his heart remained true: it not only anchored him by asking incisive, penetrating questions but carefully steered him through the dark labyrinth of insanity which was enveloping him. 'How can there be so many variations of the same story? Surely they cannot all be true?' 'Do you not notice how these thoughts assail you but never last more than a few seconds, that they pass like the clouds in the sky?' Above all his heart whispered to him, 'Have you not suffered enough?'

Now, with the ship getting closer and closer, Lopes would have known that if he boarded it he would carry Albuquerque and Dias with him not only to Lisbon, but for the rest of his life. There had surely been moments on the island when in desperate loneliness he had begged God to return him to Lisbon, even if he had to die as a destitute beggar on its streets, but now he understood that his journey was not yet over. On the contrary, it was just beginning. We will never know for certain why Lopes chose to remain on the island. Certainly, it would have required a tremendous act of courage and fortitude. Perhaps he had lost his senses and once again chosen to hide. Perhaps, but that interpretation I believe goes against the grain of his future behaviour and actions, so unless he somehow regained a sanity that he had lost we must assume that his decision to stay was made in sound mind. In my opinion, Lopes chose to remain on the island because in that first year of solitude, a year between ships leaving and arriving on Saint Helena, he must have sensed the inkling of a profound inner transformation, one that would take many years to come to fruition. Later in the book I shall try to touch on this most mysterious and mystical of relations – the one between man and silence – but for the time being, if it is the historian's task to interpret the silences of history, then I believe that Lopes chose to stay on the island because he sensed, on some still undefined level, that it was there that he would make sense of the thread that linked the events of his life and would finally liberate him from his torment.

As he stood at the summit in his ragged clothes with his straggly beard, the thought crossed his mind that he was the first human being since God's creation to have stood in this place of astonishing beauty – he, Fernão Lopes, a mockery of a man, a renegade. And he remained standing at the top of the summit, shaded by birds. He had nowhere else to go. As he looked downwards he noted a number of ridges and ravines converging towards the sea. In the distance the sea rushed between two craggy cliffs whitening the surf with its spray. Almost exactly 300 years later a French Emperor would stand in the same spot, bemoaning his isolated fate.

CHAPTER FIFTEEN

The Shadow of the Past

or Captain Francisco de Távora, dropping anchor at the island of Saint Helena for a few days would doubtless have been a relief, for ever since the rounding of the Cape, his ship the *São Christóvão* had been severely buffeted by the trade winds and his men stricken by illness. At least on uninhabited Saint Helena there would be some calm, and the ship could gather water before embarking for home on the last leg of its journey. It is important to note that the *Sancto António*, carrying news of Lopes, had reached Lisbon in November 1516, by which time the *São Christóvão* had already set sail for India. This meant that neither Távora nor his men would have had any idea at this stage that the island was anything but deserted. It was, therefore, an astonishing turn of events when, after a few days on the island, according to the sources, the captain was told by two of his men that they had stumbled across a cave containing clothes, and definite signs that someone had been living there. Clearly the man was not dead, for they had found ash from a fire which was still warm. But if there was someone alive on the island, why had he not made himself known? Given that the island was a mere 46 miles across it would have been impossible for him not to have been aware of the ship as it approached, nor of the crew's arrival on the island. Perhaps he was not Portuguese and he feared for his life, but that was unlikely, as any soul after such a long period of isolation would not have hesitated for a moment to rush to seek human contact. But who was he? And how did he manage to make his way to this island in the middle of the ocean? It was a baffling mystery.

Perhaps Lopes had been listening, concealed from the crew. With the sea calm and the wind low he could likely hear the discussions clearly. As long as he stayed quiet he would not be discovered. It had been a year since he had heard human voices and it would have taken a few minutes for his ears to adjust to the fact that several conversations were taking place at the same time. Since his punishment he probably could not judge where sounds came from and would have found it disconcerting when he tried. Perhaps he tried to overcome an initial reaction to greet them when he watched the Portuguese sailors come ashore. For one year he had lived a life of total isolation on a scale that others would have found almost impossible to comprehend, but it was also a time when he had forgotten his disfigurements. What would he say to the sailors as they stared at his face? Who would be the first to ask, 'What happened to you?' He would then be assailed with questions and taken back to Lisbon. He did not want the questions. From all available evidence, he did not want Lisbon.

And so Lopes did not reveal himself to the men and he probably watched in silence as they left food and clothing for him on the island. One wonders if that act would have touched him on some level or whether he would simply have looked on impassively. Whichever it may have been, the following morning Lopes would have watched as the *São Christóvão* raised its canvas and began to edge out of the bay. If he had been watching, Lopes would have spotted that something black had fallen off the ship, splashing into the water. It was a cockerel. A huge black cockerel: bedraggled, dazed, but very much alive as it thrashed in the ocean.

The thought of eating its meat must have occurred to Lopes but if it did, he chose not to. It was company, even if admittedly it was not the brightest of companies. From the moment of its rescue, the cock, as tame as a dog, followed Lopes everywhere he went, day and night. At night it roosted on a perch over his head as he slept, and every morning the bird emerged from the cave and gave him his wake-up call. Fernão Lopes had a friend.

When Lopes returned to the cave he found that the Portuguese had left him, in addition to the food, a second letter. But there was something else Lopes noted, and that was that the first letter had been taken by the captain. The letter carrying his name was making its way to Lisbon (and eventually, we assume, to his son. Is it too much to imagine that this would have filled his heart with a burst of joy?). It was as if a part of him was returning home.

When I first stumbled across the mention of Fernão Lopes as a 'Portuguese Muslim', the only inhabitant of Saint Helena, the passing remark intrigued me and determined the path I was going to take in researching and writing this book. What I was to discover was that Lopes may have possessed a spiritual hinterland that added texture and nuance, one that I believe could go a long way towards explaining his actions. Fernão Lopes, in other words, wanted me to write a different story. It was a passing comment, made by an elderly South African who had lived on Saint Helena and with whom I had been in correspondence on matters relating to the island, that first alerted me to the fact that Fernão Lopes may have been originally Jewish. Eagerly I asked how this information had come to light since none of our main sources on Lopes' life made any mention of it: Gaspar Correia did not, nor did Barros nor even the letters or history of Albuquerque which were compiled by his son. In fact I have not been able to find a single public document attesting to the fact that Lopes may have been originally Jewish. The South African gentleman explained that a few years ago he had been researching the life of Lopes, having learned about him when he lived on Saint Helena. In doing so, he had entered into correspondence with the renowned historian of Portugal, Harold Livermore, who had casually remarked that Lopes had been originally Jewish. But, this passing comment aside, I had no other information or any clues to pursue. I asked to see a copy of this letter but the gentleman was unable to locate it, for he had not given it much attention, Lopes not being his main interest. Harold Livermore had passed away and scouring his books revealed nothing. Haunted by the possibility, I could not let the matter rest. I contacted several established Portuguese scholars and historians but not one of them was aware or had come across any source that hinted at this fact. One distinguished professor remarked that it was like trying to find a needle in a haystack (or *une aiguille dans une botte de foin*, as we were forced to converse in French). Another pointed out that in those days registering births was not compulsory. A third pointed me to Lopes' contemporaries, Gaspar Correia, Castanheda and João de Barros, as well as the letters of Afonso de Albuquerque. But I had been through them before. I also learned that it would be highly unlikely that a trace of Jewish origins would emerge from the records since, if not specifically mentioned in a document, it would be impossible to recognise Lopes as a 'New Christian', especially given the full assimilation of the names. A good example of this was the pilot of Cabral's armada in 1500. His name was Gasparanda da Gama and he was Jewish. Gasparanda simply chose to adopt the da Gama name when he converted. His Jewish origins are attested in the sources, but his new name demonstrates how complex it is to untangle the origins of those mentioned in the records, especially when there are no extant Portuguese documents that explain the criteria used in the adoption of the names. We know that Lopes, a Lisbon resident, married and had a young son. We know that, as a minor nobleman, a squire and a *fidalgo*, he rose quickly in society. But there was no mention of whether, as a young boy, Lopes was taken from his parents and baptised, nor would there be, since once baptised a door on the past was firmly shut. Fernão Lopes, it seems, emerged from history fully formed as a minor *fidalgo* in Lisbon with a wife and son.

I headed to Lisbon and, aided by two Portuguese scholars, I scoured the official records searching for any mention that could shed light on Lopes' early life. I knew that the devastating earthquake of 1775 had destroyed most of Lisbon's parish documents and with them any definitive hope of resolving this mystery, but I persisted in the hope of stumbling on at least a passing reference. But instead of 'my' Lopes, other Lopeses emerged from the records, eager to tell their long-forgotten stories. There was a Thomas Lopes who was arrested in 1501 for continuing to write in Hebrew; there was an Afonso Lopes who was imprisoned for stubbornly refusing to marry into an Old Christian family and choosing to marry instead a fellow New Christian (and, one hopes, his love), Isabella Lopes. I came across a Joana Lopes, who was overheard exclaiming in public: 'May God forgive the King who made us Christians!' Then there were more substantial New Christian Lopeses: there was Duarte Lopes, the Portuguese trader to the Congo and Angola who, with Filippo Pigafetta, published one of the earliest maps and descriptions of Central Africa in 1591. Perhaps the most famous of them all, there was Rodrigo Lopes, whose father Afonso was one of the physicians of João III. Afonso had been forcibly baptised and his son, born a Christian, rose to become the physician-in-chief of Queen Elizabeth I of England from 1581 until he was accused of plotting to poison her and was executed. It is believed that he may have inspired the character of Shylock in Shakespeare's *The Merchant of Venice*, which was written within four years of his death. When Shakespeare wrote: 'Thy currish spirit Govern'd a wolf, who, hanged for human slaughter', the audience would have known that he was referring to Lopes (*lupus* – wolf). But as far as Fernão Lopes was concerned the records were silent and I was unable to discover any clue as to why Livermore would have made his comment. But, I also then wondered, in as stratified a society as 16th-century Portugal, could a New Christian actually *be* a *fidalgo*? The answer was yes, since it appears that Manuel had tempered the severity of the forced conversions by conferring nobility on those Jews (now 'New Christians') who had constituted the elite in their society, thereby affording them access to the privileges and honours of court positions. From this I wondered whether, if Lopes was originally Jewish, he had come from a family of good standing, since when we first come across him in the sources he is being appointed a squire. A Pedro Dias, for example, was nominated as a notary in the city of Lamego, and it is said that he had already served in the same role when he was a Jew. We have similar references to a Lourenço Vaz who had previously been called Isaac, and of a Manuel, son of Juda. The more I searched for the possible Jewish roots of Lopes, the more ambiguity my search revealed, until I began to understand that ambiguity was actually part of the story and part of the search. In the words of Benzion Kaganoff, compiler of the *Dictionary of Jewish Names and Their History*: 'The investigation of a Jewish family name is charged with all the suspense of a thrilling detective story.'

Was Lopes originally Jewish? Was he one of the 'lost boys' who were ordered to be taken by Manuel and placed with Catholic families? Although I understood that there could not be a final determining answer and that the answer depended as much on politics, psychology and linguistics as on history, I was left frustrated by the lack of evidence and by Livermore's assured (and passing) comment that Lopes was Jewish. Certainly one could argue that some of his actions as an adult could be more fully understood in the context of his having endured forced conversion as a child, but the temptation there is to read significance into things that simply did not exist. To deconstruct that which was never there in the first place. A final point troubled me. Surely, had Lopes been a New Christian would Portuguese historians not have been certain to make a point of this after his act of betrayal in Goa? How easy it would have been for the Portuguese to have accentuated his Jewish origin to explain away this act. And yet on this point there is simply silence. However, I believe that in this silence there must lie tremendous significance.

The sun is bright and warm. White cirrus clouds cover the sky all along the horizon. He can spot one break in the clouds to the south. The wind is calm and the sea is calm. The brightness of the celestial bodies is reflected in a brilliant blue light, which radiates from the ocean and appears to shine from everywhere. He watches the sea glow so brightly as if a host of candles had been lit under the surface of the water. The light of the stars reflects the light on the ocean. Light upon light. He sits there absorbed by the sheer beauty.

CHAPTER SIXTEEN

'*A soul in dispute*'

Like most Portuguese, Lopes felt great loyalty to King Manuel who had helped him rise in society. It was Manuel who had appointed him as a squire and it would not be too much to say that Lopes owed almost everything to him. The King had sought a unity of religion based on Christian orthodoxy – One Religion, One Church, One King. But what had emerged from the King's efforts was not a unity but a duality, not a single identity but a split one. Manuel's aim may have been to melt all races and religions into the pot of Catholic Portugal but what transpired was that it simply accentuated an otherness at its heart – even after they became Christians (and there was no barrier to their full integration), the *conversos* never lost their sense of otherness. Eventually this tension would play itself out in the form of the Inquisition, which would see thousands of New Christians burned at the stake.

When Lopes had been pardoned in India his first instinctive reaction had been to return to Lisbon, but we know he never arrived there and that somewhere during the sea voyage he had changed his mind. He must have sensed that he would never be accepted back in Portugal and for many reasons: certainly the betrayal of his King, for that is what it was, would not be forgotten, even though he had been pardoned. How could it be when he wore his disfigurement as a badge of dishonour? But one wonders if there was a deeper sense of foreboding which helped make up his mind to abandon ship. If Lopes had been born Jewish then he would have known for certain that, had he remained on the ship and returned to Portugal, those who crossed his path would, in words or in looks, attribute his actions in India to his background. 'You see,' they would have muttered, 'I told you we could never trust those New Christians. They will take the first opportunity to stab you in the back.'

He is lonely, tired, discouraged, dirty. Within a few days he would be dead, he is certain of that. He is getting older. He is old.

Conversion may have seemed a simple matter but when it comes to the sacred there are no simple matters. The more successful the New Christians became in their careers, the quicker they rose in society and the more they would have sensed, openly and darkly, the discrimination against them. For the New Christians it seemed that Portugal, its traditions and faith belonged exclusively to the Old Christians. It was a sacred heritage that could not be shared. It is my contention that if indeed Lopes was Jewish, then this split identity became the essence of his life. The constant shift between the two poles of Jew and Catholic effectively meant that there was no longer a centre, simply an appearance of a centre; no genuine feeling, simply the pretence of one. If this were the case, one could argue that Lopes was a man whose actions – ambitious, nostalgic, angry, determined and confused – revealed a life in deep existential crisis.

The island's beauty is splendid and ever changing, but it imprisons him. He cannot leave. The horizon maintains its distance. It never alters, never gets closer. He is trapped. Trapped from the world he loved.

When Lopes departed Lisbon in da Cunha's fleet in 1506 it

was with a great sense of adventure. He was young and had risen fast in society. He had become a squire and gained an education. The royal court was not unfamiliar to him and he mixed with nobles. He had even secured himself a good marriage. Now India with its promised riches lay ahead and he had no reason to doubt himself or his abilities. In many ways he symbolised the dawning of this glorious new age of Lisbon. For the Portuguese it was not a coincidence that the rounding of the Cape and the conversion of the Jews coincided, for both were signs of divine destiny and prophetic assurance.

Above the island the sky is grey and dark. It is an angry sky and it fills him with a fleeting moment of terror. The sea is choppy and the swells tell him that there is a storm out in the ocean.

And yet one can argue that Lopes' sense of optimism, which in 1506 he carried with him as a young man, barely concealed fissures that ran deep in society. Ahead lay a new world and a bright dawn, one in which he was determined to have his rightful place. Lopes would have known, however, that not all *fidalgos* were alike for no nobleman would publicly acknowledge having New Christian ancestry. Before his departure in 1506, Lopes would almost certainly have heard the rumours, spread across Lisbon, of how the Jews had poisoned the wells which caused the outbreak of the plague, but did the people not note that the plague killed Jews and Christians alike?

The 1506 massacre of the New Christians that took place in Lisbon just a few days after Lopes had departed the city was particularly chilling, because they were singled out individually. Despite Manuel's diktat of One Church and One People, the Christians remained wary and suspicious of the Jews, who in return concealed anger and sorrow on their visages but not in their hearts. If my contention that Lopes was a New Christian is correct then this meant that he increasingly found himself living between two faiths, his soul inhabiting a spiritual shadowland. To an extent therefore Lopes' departure from Lisbon, though guised in the manner of adventure and fortune, was, even if unspoken to himself, that of an exile, one which was as much internal as it was physical. As the 20th-century Dutch philosopher Jakob van Praag so eloquently characterised it, he, like many New Christians, would have been a 'soul in dispute'.

As he gazes out onto the horizon he wishes he could share the beauty with someone. He always thought he was a loner, but now on the island he realises how much people mean to him. He wonders, is there anything sadder than witnessing beauty or sensing joy and not having anyone to share it with? I was a Hidden Treasure, and I wanted to be discovered. He is separated by the horizon from all those whom he loves. From all those whom he may still love.

CHAPTER SEVENTEEN

'The enemies we brought among us'

Throughout the journey back to Lisbon Captain Francisco de Távora's mind had been preoccupied with thoughts of the letter that he had found on Saint Helena, and with its enigmatic resident. Who was this Fernão Lopes? And why would Captain Silveira, a man whom Távora knew well, for both had sailed to India together, have written about him in such respectful terms? It was inconceivable that Lopes could have survived on the island on his own. Távora would have concluded that only three options were possible: either Lopes had died on the island and his men were wrong about the ashes, or he had lost his mind and was surviving as a wild man, or he was simply a fugitive who knew he would be hanged if returned to Lisbon. And yet if Lopes was a common fugitive, how to explain the tone of Silveira's letter? On arriving in Lisbon Távora unloaded the goods from the *São Christóvão*, and sought out Silveira. Little could Távora have realised that Silveira himself was eager to know about Lopes. Once the two men had greeted each other and had a few drinks, Silveira asked Távora whether he had dropped anchor at Saint

Helena on his way to Lisbon, and when Távora mentioned what he had found Silveira began recounting to him the story of Fernão Lopes. Távora listened in silence, entranced by what he heard. He vaguely recalled hearing about the *fidalgo* who had become a renegade but thought that he had died in India, and when Silveira had finished speaking, Távora told him how Lopes had not come out of hiding. He too had then left him food, enough to keep him alive until the next ship stopped at the island. Both men resolved that they would speak about Lopes to all the captains who were setting sail, in case he was still alive, so that they could keep an eye out for him or at the least ensure that food was left behind.

A few hundred miles away, alone in his kingdom, Lopes would have been certain that he had been forgotten. Little could he have imagined that, thanks to the two captains, Silveira and Távora, he would become the most talked-about man in Portugal.

He gives up bathing. He has abandoned all his habits of cleanliness. He realises that he is not the same person who left Goa. He has lost all his vanity. He eats like an animal in a way which would have once horrified him. He tries to analyse his habits and actions: what is happening? Who am I? Am I the same person? Am I still a fidalgo?

India may have been indifferent towards the Portuguese but the Portuguese were not indifferent towards India. When one of Vasco da Gama's men was asked why they had come to India he replied: 'We come in search of Christians and spices.' The messianic fervour which was giving wind to the Portuguese sails clearly demanded souls in return, but whose souls? In January 1557, the Jesuit Gonçalo Silveira wrote a letter to Cardinal Henrique of Avis, the brother of King João III, in which he wrote openly about the 'evils of India' and the best way of ridding the empire of 'the enemies we brought among us'. For Silveira there existed a clear analogy between Jews and Brahmins. One century later, Joseph Martinez de la Puente declared openly that Jews and Brahmins shared a common origin, and these similar roots were expressed in their identical vices: 'varied and corrupted greed, duplicity, fallacies, apostasies, and superstitions'. Although Silveira and de la Puente were writing after the arrival of the Jesuits in India, one can trace the way they associated the elites of Goa with the Jews from the outset. It was an association in which both were viewed with suspicion, and one where the process of converting the Jews within mainland Portugal was mirrored by one to convert the Hindus in Goa. The reference to 'the enemies we brought among us' points to the fact that the Portuguese New Christians remained distrusted even this far away from Portugal. Friar Simão wrote to the King of Portugal that he had come across many New Christians from Portugal in India whom he accused of following 'neither Christianity nor Judaism'.

It is windy and drizzling. He is standing on top of the cliffs, watching the huge waves break against and over the rocks which lie at the base. Again and again the waves crash against the rocks. It is pitiless and he is mesmerised. He hears a strange noise and he sees four whales. Two are very large and two are smaller. The noise he heard was one of them blowing. They are swimming very slowly. As the large ones roll forward it seems as if there is no end to them. Even from the island, a few hundred yards away, he can see them clearly. Suddenly one whale leaps at least ten feet out of the water, causing a huge splash. Then another whale does the same. They are playing like kittens. He finds himself laughing out loud. He wishes his son could see this.

India, not Portugal, transformed Lopes. Not long after he had arrived in Goa I believe he made the first of the many realisations that would ultimately overwhelm him and would help explain his future actions. Lopes knew very little about India, like most Portuguese. After all, a few years earlier Vasco da Gama had confidently assumed that Hindus were Christians. In Goa Lopes had been unwelcome, and he would have been mocked for his European dress, his manner and his customs. He would have been acknowledged simply as 'Portuguese', or more commonly as the *farangi*. Goans – Hindus or Muslims – were neither able to differentiate, nor interested in differentiating the Old from the New Christian. For the Hindus and Muslims Lopes would have been a strange and alien enemy, but in that indifference towards him, he may well have detected something profound.

He dreads the nights when the clouds cover the sky and there are no stars. He feels isolated, as if he is living in a black hole. There is much solace in the stars.

CHAPTER EIGHTEEN

Like a New Layer
of the Kabayi

The two captains, Silveira and Távora, were true to their word and ships setting sail from Belém were now informed that if they were to stop at Saint Helena on the return voyage from India, then the men should keep an eye out for Lopes, and no ship should depart from the island without first leaving behind food and supplies. If any ship found the food untouched then they should assume that Lopes had died, otherwise he should be left alone until he chose to reveal himself. Three years passed and records show that at least four ships stopped at Saint Helena during this period. There was no sign of Lopes but there was no doubt that he was alive since the food and clothes left behind had evidently been taken. Although the crew were not able to see him, this did not mean they were unable to talk about him, and with each ship docking back in Belém the enigmatic story of Fernão Lopes began to spread among the residents of Lisbon and the merchants of the Rua Nova. The sources speak of the story spreading initially among soldiers and sailors, and as it was told and retold it varied from one that described an exiled tortured figure to one that emphasised an isolated, lone hermit. To a large extent Lopes' standing as a *fidalgo*, minor though it may have been, helped spread the story. One imagines that if he had been one of the *gente baixa*, the common people, he would have long been forgotten.

The sky clears and the stars shine with a brightness that takes his breath away. They are so bright that they appear close enough to touch. He feels light, as if he could float up heavenwards and drift into space. All is quiet. Just the stars, the sea and him.

Today we struggle to fathom what lies within our own souls, so how could we even begin to comprehend the spiritual destiny of a man who died 500 years ago? Keeping this in mind and accepting that any attempt at understanding will only ever be conjectural, that any explanation needs to be complex and multi-layered, we need to try to answer the question: why did Lopes convert to Islam? All that we know, all that the historical records reveal, was that one moment he was a Christian and the next he was a Muslim. The *how* and *why* remain stubbornly beyond our reach. But unless and until we attempt to navigate this mystery, we will never be able to gain a clearer understanding of the man.

I believe that when Lopes arrived in India he was caught between two faiths. But he would not have been able to stay in that state for long, since modern constructs such as 'secular', or 'atheist', or even 'citizen', would have been alien and meaningless to him. Today modern man prides the individual over the community, and in so doing finds terms such as 'Christendom' or the Islamic '*umma*' archaic. But Lopes did not live in a modern, secular ecumene for Christians and Muslims, he lived in a world in which daily communal worship was integral to affirming one's identity and in which not participating in that worship meant to a large extent the loss of one's identity, both spiritual and personal. People identified themselves with a particular faith as much as they did with their place of origin. One was a Muslim, a Jew or a

Christian from a specific location, but one also lived in an overarching spiritually constructed region such as Christendom or *Dar al-Islam*. In that sense the region, or community, was of the utmost importance as it was the constant on which communal worship depended and which set the spiritual rhythm of daily life from the day one was born to the day one was buried.

We know that Lopes abandoned Goa and headed for Bijapur, where he tied his future to the Adil Shahs, and we know that he became a Muslim. But we should not assume that these two journeys – the physical one to Bijapur and the spiritual one to Islam – were embarked upon at the same time, nor should we assume that one inevitably followed the other. Of one thing we can be certain: Lopes would not have made the decision to set off on the eight-day journey to Bijapur in haste, nor, unlike others, would the decision have been made out of desperation. But make it he did, and it is necessary to follow Lopes on his two journeys insofar as we can, the physical and the spiritual, in search of clues.

At first he thinks that birds could only fly for so long, that there is a maximum distance they could fly from shore until they had to return to the island. But he watches birds fly towards the horizon, unperturbed, unflappable. He notices how the birds love the sea when it is rough. They seem oblivious to the high swells, to the wind, to the waves. Occasionally they land on the water and rest or dive at the surface, emerging with something to eat. Not once do they look back towards him. He is invisible.

We have touched earlier on Lopes' hatred of Albuquerque. It was one that had been slowly festering, fanned by the governor's brutal actions and his hanging of Rui Dias, and it was one that would explode in open and bloody violence. It was of course not uncommon for Portuguese to fall out – indeed the kingdom's history is a confusing catalogue of hurt honour and pricked pride, often leading to dramatic and bloody ends. By 1512 when Albuquerque reconquered Goa, the relationship between the two men must have broken down completely and as soon as Albuquerque departed the city, Lopes headed for Bijapur, and we can safely assume that hatred and anger accompanied him on the journey there. Ultimately, though, I do not believe they are convincing enough reasons to explain why, once in Bijapur, he chose to embrace Islam. Many Portuguese abandoned their posts and fled inland, where their skills were put to good use and where they enriched themselves. But they did not abandon their faith, nor were they obliged to do so by the Muslim rulers whom they served, who sought their skills and not their souls. As the Italian traveller Ludovico di Varthema noted when he visited Bijapur in the early 1500s, one could find 'all kinds of men, be they Christian, heathens, Jews or Moors, so long as they fight well, nothing else is required of them'. Lopes could have continued to hate and plot against Albuquerque as a Christian from Bijapur, he could even have ridden into battle with the Muslims against his fellow Christians without himself becoming Muslim; after all, quite a few Portuguese *renegadoes* did precisely that. But hatred can only go so far in explaining Lopes' decision and actions. He had a lot to lose by converting: his standing in society, his wife and son awaiting him in Lisbon, his aspirations to a lucrative sinecure once back in Portugal. Above all, he would lose his honour. He was a *fidalgo*, who had been knighted by Almeida, and it was unheard of for a *fidalgo* to convert to Islam. Nor, from the point of view of the Portuguese, could it be accepted: the brutal violence and punishment Albuquerque inflicted on Lopes were largely down to his having betrayed his status as a *fidalgo*.

His whole body is hurting and his breathing is difficult and painful. It rained hard again last night: ceaseless, merciless rain. The sea is wild and rough with swells of twenty feet. It is cloudy and cold. He feels very ill.

To understand Lopes, to attempt to comprehend his Pauline conversion on the road to Bijapur, we need to look deeper than anger and ambition. The best way to approach this is, I believe, to examine his move to Islam as a conversion in three Acts. The first Act I consider to have been a secular conversion, a social one to an extent. To understand this better, I turn to the magisterial three-volume work *The Venture of Islam*, published in 1975, in which Hodgson coined the word 'Islamicate', which he defined as 'the social and cultural complex historically associated with Islam and the Muslims ... even when found among non-Muslims', as opposed to 'Islamic', which meant 'of or pertaining to Islam' in the proper, the religious, sense. It is an important distinction since it allowed someone to fully adopt all aspects of Islamic social and cultural standards – that is to say, to live with Muslims, dress like a Muslim, eat like a Muslim, marry a Muslim – but not *be* a Muslim. Once he arrived in India, Lopes came to appreciate that the whole region bordering the Indian Ocean, including its port cities, was so culturally imbued with an overriding Islamic ethos that the ethnic identity of individuals mattered little. As long as he remained in Goa, surrounded and protected within his Portuguese enclave, he was on safe ground. When he departed Goa and headed to Bijapur he probably had no intention of becoming a Muslim, but during that eight-day journey he had unknowingly crossed an invisible Rubicon and had found himself in the land of Islam, *Dar al-Islam*. Once he settled in Bijapur he would have had to observe the local diet by not touching pork, and, if he had wanted to communicate, he would have had to learn the local language. Lopes would also have needed to change his clothing, choosing to wear a *kabayi*: a long (often white) tunic with a colourful sash tied across the waist and on occasion a *kallayi*, which was a high conical hat of brocaded fabric. Taken individually or even collectively all these actions, from marriage to diet, from language to clothing, did not make Lopes a Muslim, and he would have viewed them simply as his accepting and adopting of cultural forms which had little or nothing to do with the formal tenets and practices of Islam as a religion. In Bijapur, in other words, Lopes would have found himself eating, dressing and living like a Muslim not because he wanted to, but simply because the cultural tide was too strong to resist. Above all it was a social and cultural bond, but crucially it was one defined in religious terms as opposed to, say, tribal or national terms. Today these cultural transformations may appear merely eccentric, but in Lopes' time and in a world where the religious and the secular were inseparable, they were far from superficial for each transformation, like a new layer of the *kabayi* which he would have worn, carried meaning and consequence.

The rain has stopped, it is cold, and the full moon is out and bright. There are a few clouds that glisten in the moonlight. Physically he feels worse than ever. His chest and back and stomach are hurting. He has to push himself to do anything. He must keep going. He longs to be rescued. He wants to see his family again.

The second Act, which I label religious syncretism, is one where it becomes increasingly unbearable for Lopes to be without a religious identity while at the same time it is impossible for him to keep to Christian feasts. Nearly 50 years earlier, the Russian trader and traveller Afanasii Nikitin faced a very similar experience while travelling and living with the Muslims in India. 'I know not when Easter Sunday, the great day of the Resurrection of Christ, occurs, so I try to guess by signs: with the Christians, Easter comes nine or ten days before the Muslim *Bayram*. I have nothing with me – no book', so wrote Nikitin. 'And I have forgotten all that I knew of the Christian faith and all the Christian feasts. Surrounded by other faiths [Nikitin was referring to Hinduism and Islam] I pray to God that He may protect me.' Similarly, once in Bijapur, Lopes would gradually have begun to use Muslim holy days to keep track of time. Throughout, he may well have continued to rationalise that he was not a Muslim and if he prayed and fasted and feasted with the Muslims it was because there were no other Christians with whom to celebrate the major holy days.

Ingrained deeply in him was the belief that not to celebrate the holy days was in a very real sense to lose hold of his faith, and thus Lent would have become Ramadan. Gradually, I imagine that Lopes developed a syncretic form of Christian–Muslim worship, one where the juxtaposition of Christian and Muslim holy dates evolved from the celebrating of Christian holy days on Muslim ones into the celebrating of Muslim holy days in place of Christian feast or fast days. In all this, Islam's rigid adherence to monotheism and its devotion to the One God would have been of great solace, and Lopes could have found enormous comfort in it. Unable to shed his Christian faith but as an isolated soul, unable to resist his desire to join in communal prayer, he would have lived in a syncretic setting between the two faiths, consoling himself that he was not abandoning his faith, only celebrating God in a new way. Ultimately this would have led to what may be termed a reluctant conversion, as he came to accept that the God of Islam was the same God as that of his Catholic faith. To an extent it was a spiritually exhausting and confusing struggle, as is again reflected in the words of Nikitin, who underwent the same process that we can imagine Lopes did: 'As for the true faith, God alone knows it, and the true faith is to believe in one God and to invoke His Name in purity … The rest God alone knows.'

The wind is dying but the sea remains rough. The moon is so bright that the foam in the wake sparkles like millions of diamonds. There is no one out there. Just him, on a tiny island in the middle of a huge ocean. He prays a lot. Prayer keeps him going. He is in continual prayer, waiting for God.

So we come to the third and final Act: the conversion of Lopes to Islam. Paradoxically, what one would expect to have been the highlight or turning point of the spiritual journey would have been undertaken almost imperceptibly: in the absence of any rite comparable to baptism, conversion to the Islamic faith in the Middle Ages differed from conversion to other religions. When traditional Muslim sources describe the procedure of becoming a Muslim, the verb, *aslama*, meaning 'he submitted [to God]' is used, but there is never any elaboration to indicate the real content of the act. And so we read on numerous occasions that so and so *aslama*: that is, that so and so became a Muslim simply by uttering the confession of faith, the *shahada*, that there is no god save Allah and that Muhammad is His Messenger. The simplicity was remarkable – the conversion consisted primarily of speaking eight words. Afterwards, the person became a Muslim, although even then there is some debate as to the precise nature of this utterance, whether it must be made with the heart or by the lips only. Although the *shahada* is universally recognised by Muslims as being one of the five pillars of Islam (the other four being prayer, fasting, alms giving and performing the pilgrimage if one is able to), these pillars are neither incumbent upon nor conditional to becoming a Muslim. All that sufficed was to utter the *shahada*. In other words, uttering the *shahada* and not performing any of the other pillars still made you a Muslim.

It is my contention that Lopes became a Muslim because in that faith he found what he had once lost. If, as I argue, Lopes was born and raised in childhood as a Jew then he would have instinctively found many similarities between Islam and Judaism that he would have been familiar with. In general, Jews found it much easier to convert to Islam than to Christianity, as, while Christianity's Trinity was equated by certain Jews with idolatry, Islam was seen as a monotheistic religion. For Lopes both Islam and Judaism were based on God-given books – the Torah and the Quran. Both these divine texts were interpreted by an oral tradition – the Talmud and Hadith. Both placed a fundamental emphasis on the law and ritual observance – the *halachah* and the *shari'a*. In fact, the two religions are so close in their structure that the 10th-century rabbinic leader Saadia Gaon used to refer to Jewish law as *Shari'a*, and the Andalusian scholar Abu

Umar b. Sa'di, visiting Baghdad towards the end of the 10th century, related that he attended study sessions with both Muslims
and Jews. Had he been Jewish, Lopes would have immediately
been struck by the fact that in both religions there was a fixed
number of set prayer times each day and that the faithful were
required to engage in formal prayers. As a Muslim, Lopes would
now be expected to perform the five daily prayers (like the three
daily prayers that perhaps he may once have performed as a Jew,
with a fourth on the Sabbath). There were other similarities
between Judaism and Islam: not eating pork, which in any case
was unknown in Goa since neither Hindus nor Muslims cooked
with it, or the way that the day began and ended at sunset, rather
than at midnight or at dawn. As for those inclined to avoid the
literalism of scriptural religion, Sufism and the Kabbalah offered
mystical and esoteric paths for knowing God through the soul and
not by the mind. In fact, Sufism was very attractive for many Jews
who lived in Muslim lands, most notably the son of the famous
Maimonides who was known as a Sufi, and who like many Jews
studied Sufi manuals very closely.

*As a young squire he had been taught the art of comportment: never
to cross one's arms when standing, and to always ensure that one's toes
point out. It is these small things that make a nobleman. So he had
been told, over and over. He now wondered, should he cross his arms
on the island?*

One moment Lopes was not a Muslim and the next moment
he was. There is no doubt that his adoption of Islamic social and
cultural traditions and a sense of community gently aided the
conversion process, as did the many rituals in Islam which, if I
am right, reminded him of Judaism, but in themselves both are
insufficient as reasons to explain his conversion. What I believe
ultimately drew Lopes to the Islamic faith were two factors. Firstly,
it was Islam's trenchant adherence towards monotheism, one
which he would have recognised whether he was Christian or Jew,

and in which he would have found great solace and comfort. This recognition would have allowed him to participate in a syncretic manner in the Muslim communal worship, stressing the first part of the *shahada* that there was no god save Allah, while leaving the second part, the affirmation that Muhammad was His messenger, unspoken. But it was also this recognition that would gradually have convinced him that the monotheism, the Unity of God, also had to be universal, since he would have recognised the same truth as a Jew, a Christian and a Muslim. Secondly, Islam offered him both a method and a way for his soul to get close to God. I have already mentioned the rituals, the prayer and fasting, the Quran and the sayings of the Prophet Muhammad, the communal worship and the alms giving. In all these Lopes would have found a tremendous sense of solace and kinship. But Islam also offered him a Way, which is worth exploring here, for as I mentioned earlier, the Islam which Lopes came across in Bijapur manifested itself in the most profound mystical terms.

One of the most striking aspects of Bijapur, still visible today, is that tombs of saints are everywhere and in every kind of building. Lopes would have been struck by the number of tombs and mausoleums (*maqamat*) dedicated to Muslim saints, to which a continuous flow of supplicants came day and night, often in the guise of *shaykhs* and their disciples. Men and women would stand huddled near the mausoleum where they would recite the opening verses of the Quran, the *fatiha*, and then make their supplications, speaking openly and confidently as if the saint was alive and listening intently. Around the tombs, markets flourished selling almost everything under the sun, from live animals to household goods. Everywhere there was the music of cymbals and drums.

It was the time for evening prayer and the mosque was packed. The rituals of prayer were still relatively new to him and though Lopes understood little of the prayer itself, which was in Arabic, he made the obligatory prostrations cautiously, fearful that he might make an error.

But once the salaam alaikum, salaam alaikum was over, the shaykh who had led the prayer began reciting, in a low tone, prayers upon the Prophet that were interspersed with quranic passages. Gradually his voice picked up a fast rhythm. After about fifteen minutes the shaykh began repeating out loud and with great force, 'La ilah ila Allah,' and all those in the mosque followed suit, raising and lowering their tones as they breathed in and out. At first Lopes remained silent but then he found himself joining in with the declaration that there was no god save Allah. Then at a sign, all those present rose to their feet and formed a circle. In the middle of the circle a young man sat in silence. Once everyone was seated on the ground, the shaykh once again started the utterance of 'La ilah ila Allah,' this time moving his body from right to left and all those participating now following him. Just behind him, though he dared not look, Lopes could hear the gentle beating of a drum maintaining the rhythm. For a few minutes the men, still seated, moved their bodies in unison as 'La ilah ila Allah' echoed across the mosque. Lopes shut his eyes as the hypnotic words and movement cast a spell over him. 'La ilah ila Allah, La ilah ila Allah, La ilah ila Allah.' Suddenly, it seemed he heard the most beautiful singing out of nowhere, and he opened his eyes to see the young man now standing, singing in harmony, praises upon the Prophet, for though he could not understand, the word 'Muhammad' repeated itself. As the men sang, the singer slowly rocked from side to side, his eyes closed. Lopes noticed that no one else was looking at the singer as all in the circle had their eyes closed as their 'La ilah ila Allah' formed a harmonious background to the singing. After a while the man began picking up the speed of his singing, and as he did so the bodily movements of those in the circle became faster and more exaggerated, as if an invisible thread connected the harmony between the tempo of the singing and of the movements of the men around the circle. The mood had now changed completely; the singer's voice heightened and became more intense, the pitch of the 'La ilah ila Allah' becoming higher and higher and the movement in the circle becoming fragmented. Some men abandoned themselves in the flow of the movement and one or two broke down in tears. Then suddenly the shaykh raised his hand and the singing and movement stopped and there was only silence as those carried away by the emotion of the ritual began to regain their senses. For a long time Lopes sat in silence, so still that had a bird entered the mosque it could have perched on his head. What he had experienced had moved him to the depth of his soul, though if asked he would not have been able to explain how or why. What he had sensed was that a veil had been lifted briefly and he had been offered a glimpse of a beauty that he knew would haunt him for the rest of his days.

The temptation to define Lopes as a Muslim from the moment of his conversion needs to be resisted. His desire for communal worship and the gentle draw of an Islamicate culture may have drawn him into the religion but Lopes would not, even after his conversion, necessarily have defined himself as a Muslim. If anything his identity would have been cast more in ethnic than religious terms, so together with the '*Turuska*', '*Parasika*', '*Telugu*', '*Uzbek*', '*Abyssinian*' and others who composed the foreign elements of Ismail Adil Shah's army, Lopes would have been labelled '*Portogali*', or probably the generic word for Europeans, '*farangi*'. For those around him, Lopes' particular religious affiliation appears to have been of little interest. What did interest them were the story and details of his military career and his mastery of military skills. If Lopes belonged to any entity by which he could define himself, then it was to an elite military-political class. This class was not divided into separate 'Hindu' and 'Muslim' segments but constituted a single transcultural social group, one that transcended and cut across the boundaries. Certainly it would have been common for members of this elite to possess competence in several languages, although it is intriguing to ask how Lopes would have made himself understood, for initially he neither spoke Dakhni nor Persian.

He recalled how he had first set eyes on Saint Helena. It had emerged through the mist and the fog, a huge rock that appeared to be growing from the sea. As they approached, he noticed how beautiful the island was, with cliffs rising straight out of the sea. He had glimpsed dense greenery and vegetation inland. This is his world. It has not changed for thousands of years. Sky and water, from horizon to horizon.

CHAPTER NINETEEN

No Harm Will Come to You

He finds that he can survive on one meal a day, and though he initially loses weight, his body gradually accustoms itself to this rigid diet. There is no variation in the food. He reflects on how, in Lisbon and in Goa, he had turned to food to relieve the monotony of his loneliness.

In Islam, Lopes found comfort, solace and tranquillity: in its rituals, in its sense of community, and in its strict adherence to the one God and the love of the Prophet Muhammad. He discovered a sense of belonging among the band of brothers who gathered together in Bijapur and who ate together, fought together and knelt in prayer together. For perhaps the first time in his life I believe that Lopes would not have felt like an outsider, and his creeping sense of otherness would have eased. He was now part of a community with a mutual goal, a mutual desire and a mutual courage. Proof of this adherence to his new faith became clear in the heat of battle: when João Machado offered him the chance to recant and to re-join the Portuguese forces, Lopes had been adamant in his refusal: 'I am a Muslim and I shall die as a Muslim.' They were powerful words – sincere, honourable and true – and even during the punishment which had been inflicted upon him he had never recanted. Spoken to Machado, they were also pointed, for Machado, like Lopes, had become a Muslim but had then chosen to return to the Christian fold.

On the island of Saint Helena, however, alone, Lopes would have felt his Islam slipping away, and would have slowly sensed that as a new convert the roots he had planted in the faith of Muhammad were simply not deep enough. He needed the community, the communal worship to sustain him. He may well have tried to pray as a Muslim on the island but he most likely rapidly forgot the Arabic verses he had memorised. He would have felt himself slipping towards a dark abyss. Given that we have no records of his thoughts it is very hard to construct what Lopes would have been going through during this stage, but it may well have appeared to him that God had offered him a glimpse of a beauty so serene that it had acted as a balm for his anger and loss, but that in His wisdom He had chosen to take it away, leaving him bereft.

Islam was of course not unfamiliar to Lopes even though it was not until he reached India that he discovered it in depth. In Lisbon he would have crossed paths with Muslims on a daily basis but in all probability he would have paid little attention to them. In many ways the age in which Lopes grew up was one of amnesia about the Islamic faith, although it was as much a part of the Portuguese legacy and heritage as the Jewish and Catholic ones. One only had to go back five centuries or so to realise that the language, food and dress of Portugal had all been inspired by Islamic culture. Educated classes of Iberian Christians and Jews had dressed, eaten and moved like Arabs and were so versed in Arabic poetry, manners and customs that they were even given a label – the Mozarabs. But now there was no trace of them. There had been a time when Portugal had boasted a plethora of regional and communal differences that sprang from centuries of local histories and traditions. It was an age when a rich artistic culture existed, in which influences passed fluidly back and forth, an age when a carpet made for a synagogue could be modelled on the Muslim prayer rug with a border inscription in Arabic, or Maimonides' (Musa ibn Maimun's) 'Guide to the Perplexed' could be translated from the Arabic into Hebrew with a manuscript illustrated in the Italian Gothic style. Under Muslim rule, Jews and Christians were given important roles in the running of the state. They remained subdued and heavily taxed, but they were also protected by the Caliph and were free to follow their religion and live according to their laws. Historians have often over-emphasised the 'Golden Age' of tolerance in al-Andalus during this period, for there also existed much oppression and intolerance, but as the modern philosopher and author Yirmiyahu Yovel argues, though tolerance among the faiths may not have been a moral command it was certainly a utilitarian precept. If ever there was a golden age for the Jews in Europe, it was under Muslim rule. Especially when one considers the horrors that were to follow.

There had never been a *Reconquista* of Portugal, for there had been no 'Portugal', Portuguese people or language prior to the Arab occupation – in many ways it was a conquest rather than a re-conquest. At its heart was the imposition of Catholic orthodoxy as the uniting force and law of the Kingdom of Portugal. Henceforth there was to be One God and One Religion, and those who did not adhere to this orthodoxy were to be expelled or converted. Orthodoxy, governed by religious law, sustained the established order and promoted and imposed the Old Christian identity upon the varied and complex political body. Portugal became a place whose subjects were not only confined to the Catholic identity but could be subjected to punishments for deviations from this identity. It was an age when a Muslim woman in Portugal, with her distinctive rites and dress, a white mantle that reached down to her feet and covered half her face, was viewed as a serious obstacle to integration into this new orthodoxy.

It would be astonishing if Lopes' mind, on the island, had not turned again and again to the three brutal days of torture which had followed the siege of Banastarim, and slowly understood why it was that he had to be punished and tortured by Albuquerque (even though the King had pardoned him), and why it had had to be done in such a public manner. Gradually he would have come to the conclusion that what had taken place in Goa went much deeper. In some unspoken way, Lopes had come to symbolise all that the Catholic orthodoxy feared, representing an apocalyptic reminder of the enemy within. It was as if in his Muslim presence (and possibly also his Jewish one), which threatened to destroy all things Catholic, Lopes had come to symbolise all that Portugal had once been or could have been, or even should have been, and all that it now dreaded the most. And so he needed to be tortured in order to subjugate the body and the soul, and to reconcile it to a state of perpetual penitence towards this new orthodoxy. Whether or not Lopes understood his ordeal in these terms, there is no doubt that torture was an instrument for the annihilation of human dignity. It was also a disciplining device, not only for the criminal, but for the good of everyone, which is why it needed to be public since the stage on which heretics were tortured was for establishing religious orthodoxy as much as it was for instilling fear and awe. Lopes was a man ensnared by contradictory times, but if he somehow unknowingly and unwittingly symbolised the Portuguese nightmare, then Albuquerque represented an orthodoxy which refused to accept that the Jewish or Muslim identity was as much a part of the Portuguese psyche as the Catholic one. In reality, Afonso Albuquerque and Fernão Lopes were two faces of the same Portuguese coin.

The way Lopes was finally 'captured' by the Portuguese after many years of isolation is one of the most enigmatic chapters of this remarkable story. We know that he remained on the island for another few years, probably four or five, hiding from the ships that arrived there. In fact the sources relating how he was eventually discovered by the Portuguese are confusing and contradictory, but all tell of a truly dramatic series of events. Our main source is Gaspar Correia, who writes that Lopes actually was on the island for much longer: 'he remained for ten years on the island, never seeing anyone because he hid himself'. But then Correia makes an astonishing statement: 'on this island there remained a boy who had already fled there, who was with him many years. This boy was the one who made him known to a ship which put in there.' It is hard to know what to make of this account as, with a couple of sentences, Correia appears to have transported us into Robinson Crusoe territory, with the introduction of a new character, a Friday. Another source, Barros, goes as far as to claim that a black slave had been with Lopes all the time, which would also imply that he had hidden himself over the years. This statement, however, is contradicted by that of Castanheda, who is certain that Lopes 'disembarked on his own'. We can be reasonably confident that Barros was mistaken since he writes that for several years Lopes was alone on the island, but that does not clarify the question of how this 'boy' suddenly appears in the story. Who was he and how did he get onto the island?

According to Correia the slave boy found himself on the island and eventually revealed Lopes' hiding place to the Portuguese, but as to when he actually arrived on Saint Helena, Correia is unclear. And yet, if examined closely, there exists a fundamental contradiction in Correia's account. On the one hand he writes that Lopes 'remained for ten years on the island, never seeing anyone because he hid himself'. Now since we know that Lopes arrived at Saint Helena in 1516 that would mean that it was 1526 before this mysterious 'boy' made an appearance on the island, but then Correia claims that the boy was 'with him many years', which we must assume to be no less than three years at a minimum, probably more. There are problems with Correia's account.

Firstly, if Lopes remained on the island for ten years without seeing anyone, and then the 'boy' was with him for many years, we are looking at a date around 1530 at least before he was 'captured' by the Portuguese. But we know for certain that in 1530 he was back in Lisbon, and that by that date the island had already been transformed by Lopes, something that would in itself have required several years. One is also tempted to ask, in what unlikely circumstances would a boy have been abandoned or marooned on such an isolated island at all? Correia insists that it was a 'boy' who revealed Lopes' whereabouts to the Portuguese, but I think that the claim of a boy on the island was an error on Correia's behalf, since apart from Barros the other sources are adamant that Lopes was alone on the island. The fact that the source for this is Correia is however significant, as will be revealed later.

It was while the *Santa Catarina do Monte Sinai* was in Saint Helena that one of the ship's cabin boys either spotted Lopes hiding or more likely stumbled by accident on his cave. Most likely it appears that this was the boy whom Correia incorrectly assumed to have been on the island previously. Nevertheless the story of the elusive Fernão Lopes was well known in Portugal and it may well be that the boy was determined to find him. There may even have been a reward on offer, or more likely a sailor's wager to alleviate the boredom. Correia relates that, on spotting Lopes, the boy hurried back to tell the others where he was hiding. According to Correia and Barros, the men lost no time in rushing to the cave, where they surprised Lopes, surrounding him so that he could not escape. On seeing the men, Lopes became panic-stricken and began wailing out loud. Convinced that he would be dragged back to Lisbon he began to resist, kicking out at the men. No words came out of his mouth, just a croaking plea. To the men, Lopes must have presented an astonishing sight: his straggly beard was down to his chest, his skin burned by the sun, the fingernails on his one hand were long and curled. As for the clothes, if one could label them that, they were torn and ragged. Lopes was wearing trousers tied around the waist by a rope and on his upper body a shirt with one sleeve missing. But what drew the men's attention was neither the beard nor the fingernails, it was the nose-less face which was now staring at them. Who was this man? Was he really a Portuguese? Why was he so disfigured? For a while the men kept their distance and did not approach Lopes, who remained crouched down, his eyes fixed on them.

We read in the sources that Pero Gomes Teixeira, the Chief Justice of Portuguese India, was returning to Lisbon when the ship on which he was a passenger, the *Santa Catarina do Monte Sinai*, made its stop at Saint Helena. Teixeira was a biblical scholar who had in his possession a precious Ethiopian manuscript on parchment, which he believed was a Coptic prayer book. He had spent time searching for Prester John, the mythical Christian King of Ethiopia, and was now returning to Lisbon to brief the new King of Portugal, João III, the son of Manuel, who had died in 1521. Upon hearing the commotion and having been informed that the mysterious Fernão Lopes had been located, he made his way to where the men were gathered. Over the years he had heard talk of a wild Portuguese who lived on the island of Saint Helena and whom no one had seen for years. There were many opinions about who he was: some claimed he was a madman who lived on all fours and howled at the moon, others insisted that he was a thwarted lover who had abandoned both society and reason. Maybe a few whispered that he was the bastard son of the King who had been secretly sent into exile. The sources do not mention what exactly took place between Teixeira and Lopes on the island and we can only imagine their conversations, but there is no doubt that a connection occurred that impacted on both men.

I imagine that Teixeira would have ordered the men to stand back and give Lopes space. Unlike the men, who would have remained dumbfounded by what they were witnessing, he maintained a calm composure, so as to neither excite his men nor alarm Lopes: 'This is Fernão Lopes, please give him some space and respect.' Teixeira would have introduced himself, but maybe he sensed Lopes flinch on hearing that he was the Chief Justice of Portugal and overseas. 'Do not worry, no harm will come to you. I give you my word.'

For a while the two men remained silent during which time water in cups was brought. Teixeira could feel Lopes' eyes fixed on him but he chose to look down. After a while Teixeira signalled with a wave of his hand for the men to leave. Initially one or two hesitated, fearing that the Chief Justice could be in danger, but a second wave of the hand sent them on their way. Sensing that with the men departed the tension had eased, he offered Lopes more water. 'You do not need to speak. But please be assured that you are safe. I repeat: no harm will come to you. I give you my word from one nobleman to another.' There was no visible reaction to the words spoken but Teixeira noted that Lopes made no move to flee. As he glanced up he would have noticed the nose-less face and the stump where his right hand once was and wondered what cruel fate had befallen that poor man. Lopes appeared harmless and he had a detached manner as if Teixeira was not present. He had neither spoken nor moved since the first few panicked moments, but was he sound of mind? Surely the isolation of the island would have driven the sanest of men to madness? Teixeira knew that he had to choose his words carefully if he was going to get anywhere. He now informed Lopes that he would be leaving, and he apologised for his men startling him; after all: this was his island.

The next day Lopes was there. Teixeira had not been certain whether he would appear but had brought some biscuits with him. Soon the two men were once again seated on the ground. Any tension from the day before had long dissipated and though Lopes still did not speak, Teixeira sensed that he was deriving comfort from just sitting near another human being. And so he too chose not to speak, and the two men sat in companionable silence. After a long moment Teixeira stood up and silently took his leave. There was no need for words, since he knew that Lopes would be waiting for him the next day. But still Teixeira wondered if Lopes was sound of mind.

On the third day as he took his place on the ground near him, Teixeira noticed that Lopes was holding something in his left hand which he now extended towards him. They were a couple of figs. And it was on this day that Fernão Lopes, after another long moment of silence, haltingly at first and then in a torrent of words, began to tell Teixeira his story. At first Teixeira struggled to comprehend Lopes' words for they were jumbled and rushed, his throat croaky and harsh. And he made no sense for he would launch into a story as if Teixeira was already familiar with the personalities involved and the events described. Names poured out of Lopes' mouth, some Teixeira had heard of but many which he did not recognise. But he was too wise a man to interrupt and he allowed the torrent of words and emotions to flood over him. Several time Lopes stopped talking and instead began to weep, wiping his eyes with his right stump, and even then Teixeira remained silent, leaning in sympathy towards his companion but making sure that his eyes were fixed to the ground. After the first understandable wave of emotion, Lopes' words became more measured and balanced. Teixeira could not but be struck by his dignity. When he had first arrived on the scene he had imagined the wild man of Saint Helena as a poor demented half-human, half-animal: a man who had lost his mind and his soul. But as he sat in silence on the ground, he found himself increasingly transfixed and he listened carefully as Lopes spoke of Goa and of the stars at night, of a Rui Dias whom he did not recognise, and of God with whom he was familiar.

After an hour or so, having patiently allowed Lopes to unburden himself, he finally spoke and asked Lopes if he wished to return to Lisbon, and Lopes replied that he had no desire to leave the island for all that he needed was to be found there. Then Teixeira leaned towards Lopes and spoke firmly: 'I shall not force you aboard. If you do not wish to return to Lisbon then I will respect your wish. I will go so far as to *leave a special signed letter with my own personal seal here, addressed to all captains, that you shall never be forced to leave the island, but that if you should ever change your mind you should be welcomed on board. I will do all this, Dom Fernão, but only on one condition.' As he spoke Teixeira was looking at Lopes who appeared to be lost in thought. But when Teixeira paused, Lopes looked up enquiringly. 'My condition is this,' Teixeira continued, 'you promise forthwith not to hide when the ships call but to show yourself to all crew and to speak freely, for no harm will come to you. My word is my bond.' And for the first time in many years, Fernão Lopes smiled.*

The *Santa Catarina do Monte Sinai* was not destined to leave for a few days and, closely guarded by Teixeira, Lopes now agreed to accompany him to the shore and to mix with the crew, even though strict instructions were given that he should not be approached and that he should be left in peace. There was in reality little chance of that order being taken seriously as the men would have swarmed all over Lopes asking a multitude of questions: 'But how did you not starve?' 'Are you insane?' 'How could you live so long without a woman?', and soon he was clothed in new garments and his beard was trimmed. But when his hair was cut, a silence fell on the men when they noted that his ears had been cut off. By now the men had all heard about his life in Goa and later as a renegade, and though they wished to ask many more questions Teixeira's strict instructions hushed them. For the next few days, Lopes and Teixeira explored the island and conversed about all manners of things, but above all about prayer and God. The more he got to know him, the more fascinated Teixeira became by Lopes. It was clear that he was in the company of someone whose intelligence and lucidity were as sharp as ever. His manner of expression appeared somewhat laborious, that fact could not be denied, but Teixeira attributed this to the solitude in which Lopes had found himself. Lopes also appeared totally disinterested in what was happening in Lisbon for he neither asked questions, nor did he show any signs of curiosity. When on one occasion he had enquired of Lopes if he knew who the King was, he was greeted by a puzzled expression and decided not to pursue the matter.

The time had come for the *Santa Catarina do Monte Sinai* to sail. The men were instructed to say their farewells to Lopes. Some shook his hand while others hugged him. Tears were surely wept on that day. Food and clothes were left for him and, as promised, Teixeira wrote and signed his letter to which he affixed his personal seal and which was left in a safe place. Finally Teixeira himself bade Lopes farewell and asked him if there was any message he wished him to pass on, or if he desired anything, and again Lopes appeared lost in thought, though by now Teixeira understood that this was simply his way of pondering the question, so he waited patiently.

Lopes asked for seeds. Possibly he told Teixeira of how Saint Helena was such a fertile land. If Teixeira was surprised by Lopes' demand, he did not show it, and replied that as it happened he had many things on board which Lopes would find useful. And with that, instructions were given to some men to row to the ship and return with the goods on the list which Teixeira scribbled out. Two hours later the men returned carrying bags of seeds and seedlings. But they also carried with them pigs and goats and chickens. Then Teixeira and the men left the island and rowed to the ship and soon its sails filled and it glided out of the bay, leaving Fernão Lopes with pigs, goats and chickens. Alas, we do not know what happened to his cockerel.

PART IV

The Fourth Journey

'Il faut cultiver notre jardin'
VOLTAIRE, *CANDIDE*

'See the tree, how big it's grown
But friend it hasn't been too long,
It wasn't there'
BOBBY GOLDSBORO, 'HONEY', 1973

CHAPTER TWENTY

Mangoes and Mulberry Trees

ernão Lopes was right: the island of Saint Helena was fertile. The assurance that he had received that he would not be returned to Lisbon galvanised him, and now, armed with the sacks of seeds, Lopes was a man transformed. One can easily imagine that the experience of human companionship after the years of isolation may initially have overwhelmed him. He had grown so accustomed to silence that the sound of words would have agitated and probably irritated him. He had accustomed himself to his spartan life and had hidden when ships had arrived on the island. But once the dam of silence had been breached the words had flooded out. To be able to talk and to be listened to, to have someone else help bear the weight of loneliness. Words mattered, but what mattered more, what Lopes missed most, was the warmth of sharing.

Over the years of isolation on the island, Lopes had come to the realisation that fruit would grow there. However, one of the mysteries of the life of Lopes was how he managed to plant and cultivate the seeds. He may have known something about farming from his days in Portugal, but that seems unlikely, as squires did not concern themselves with the land. Nor do we know how he managed to work literally single-handedly. We know that fig trees had been planted by a Portuguese when the island had first been discovered and that this act of planting impacted on Lopes. When he had first arrived on the island he had largely been kept alive by the selfless acts of charity of the passing crews who left him food and clothes even though they did not know him. Initially, such was the state of his mind that he may well have been oblivious, but gradually one can assume that he became deeply moved by their random acts of kindness. Now as he felt himself gaining strength in both body and mind, he became determined to repay this kindness and, since he possessed nothing, he would endeavour to plant, and to feed all those who passed by the island of Saint Helena. Lopes' life had witnessed a multitude of remarkable transformations and now, seemingly out of nowhere, there is another dramatic shift. From hiding from passing ships and refusing to reveal himself, Lopes, almost overnight, the sources reveal, now openly fraternised with them and asked the crew to help him with the planting.

Starting near the fig trees, which one assumes were on the most fertile part of the island, Lopes would have – probably clumsily but gently – begun planting, and to his surprise nature took its course. He could not fail but notice how rich the soil was, for seeds that fell from the trees sprang up from among the grass as soon as rain fell. The soil underneath was so fertile that heaps of broken rocks and stones were, within twelve months, covered with a great variety of shrubs and trees. The island was not a barren rock. The apple trees were the first of the fruits that he planted to appear, and not once but twice a year, for when the summer fruit was ripe the winter crop on the same tree began to blossom. They yielded exceedingly large fruit, and others followed rapidly and abundantly. Mulberries and mangoes, the trees of which were evergreen on Saint Helena, with glossy and dense foliage and large pink panicles at the ends of the branches, were quick to take root

but, though he had expected them to do so, for some reason neither the cherry nor the pear trees followed suit. Banana trees grew
but did not thrive, but other fruits fared much better: pomegran-
ates and palm trees, orange and lemon trees with their deliciously
aromatic blossoms. Surprisingly, the most abundant of the fruits
was the peach tree, which grew best where the soil was deep and
sandy. Having planted a peach pit, within a few months Lopes
noticed it sprouting and a new peach seedling growing. The trees
bore so many peaches that they fell to the ground and were eaten
by the hogs the crews had left behind. It was almost as if the peach
was indigenous to the island.

The years passed and the island of Saint Helena became
increasingly familiar to the Portuguese. Where there had been
a time when only one or two ships a year would stop there on
the return journey from India, now, during the 1520s, on average
seven or eight stopped there.

The Portuguese were astonished by how transformed the island
was over the space of a few years, and the crew delighted in the
fresh fruit that was now so abundant. Now Lopes rushed to the
shore to welcome the men, greeting them warmly before eagerly
enquiring what seeds they were carrying on board. Lopes would
request the captains spare him some men to help plough more
land or to crop the trees and, though the men would have been
tired and reluctant to work, they found it impossible to turn him
down for they were grateful for his efforts and bewildered by how
much this one-handed man had achieved as he scurried back and
forth, giving instructions as to where the seeds should be planted.
In return for what he had done for them, the men built a small
habitable shelter for Lopes so that he no longer needed to dwell
in a cave, and they provided him with food, cooking utensils and
clothing. Some no doubt tried to convince him to return with
them to Lisbon: 'There is wine!' they cajoled him. 'There are
women! There is wine and women!' But Lopes remained deaf to

their entreaties: he was adamant that he would remain on Saint Helena. And the more he spoke to the passing men, the wider the story of this strange man of Saint Helena circulated around Lisbon as the men related their stories on their return. Gradually, Lopes was becoming one of the most talked-about men in Lisbon. The fact that this occurred almost imperceptibly does not make it any less remarkable. There had been a time, a few years earlier, when the name of Lopes was mentioned in Portugal, it would have been linked to that of a renegade who had turned against the King. This had undoubtedly been one factor in how, having boarded a ship in Goa to return to Lisbon, he had changed his mind and sought shelter on the island. But during the 1520s the story of Lopes began to make a subtle but dramatic shift. It was as if, with every seed that he planted on Saint Helena, a new Lopes was emerging in Lisbon. Whether he himself was aware of this appears unlikely, for it is certain that during this period he was determined never to leave the island.

So the ships docked and departed from Saint Helena, and Lopes remained on the island and the years passed, while the seeds germinated and the trees blossomed. When the men left the island they did not forget him, and in Lisbon they spoke of the fruit they had eaten on this deserted rock, ruled over by a nobleman by the name of Fernão Lopes. When they spoke of Lopes, as they did frequently to their friends, one particular word came up often. On the island, they stressed, lived a hermit. There is no doubt that Lopes left a deep impression on those who met him. Between the planting and the cropping, the visitors to the island would gather around him, curious to learn about his life. It is likely that most of their questions concerned his disfigurement, and his time in India.

The years passed and Lopes continued to plant. On occasion he was asked by the visiting captains whether he ever desired to return to Lisbon and his reply, according to the sources, was always the same: he had all that he wanted on the island. The captains also noted that he never showed any curiosity about what was happening in Portugal, or in India, or in the world. Instead he spoke only about the island and of how the valleys near the sea were wholly barren and barely showed any traces of vegetation, and that in his opinion this was due to the high saline levels in the ground. And yet he explained patiently to the men who gathered around him that in the valleys near the sea, palm trees as splendid and gorgeous as those of India thrived and spread in abundance, producing fine dates. It was also in the valleys where he had decided to plant capsicum seeds, which produced red peppers of the finest quality, cropping two or three times a year. And there, too, turnips and radishes flourished. Had the men tasted them?

Such is the nature of men that Lopes continued to be asked about his disfigurement and what had brought it on, and so he told and retold the story, though for him it must have been as if he were telling the story of an ancient Greek hero in Troy, since the events which he related appeared now so remote from the man he was now.

For those interested, Lopes would insist on proudly escorting them to a great plain which lay about 2,000 feet above sea level and sloped gently towards the south-east. He estimated the land there to cover at least 2,000 acres and it was the most fertile on the island. This was the 'Great Wood', which the British governor of Saint Helena writing in 1711 described as 'that glorious plain – the finest I ever saw in my life, anywhere'. As he escorted the men across the plain, Lopes pointed out that the land was free of any stones larger than the size of a walnut. He also pointed to a soft sort of iron stone which crumbled easily but mixed smoothly with the soil. He explained to the men who were his guests on the island that this rendered it more fertile, though why that was the case he had no idea. On this plain, he declared, he would plant lemon and orange trees which over a few years would produce fruit in the hundreds, as food or even a cure for those who visited the island.

Might Lopes have known that once, a few million years ago, Saint Helena was convulsed by volcanic fire? Given the smoky black colour of the rocks and the vast beds of stone cemented together with lava, that much at least must have been obvious. In some of the beds of basalt he would have come across rocks which were excavated like hollow trunks of decayed trees, with only a thin exterior plate of stone, giving a fragile appearance of a curved and wavy beauty. To the observant eye, it is obvious that this could only have happened if the rock had previously been softened by intense heat. Lopes must have known that the island was ancient. It had once suffered a tremendous volcanic eruption that had visibly affected its composition, and which meant that for thousands of years it could not sustain any plants or animals. The hills were black and ragged with no visible trace of any tree or shrub or vegetation of any kind, giving the island a forlorn and wretched air. The harshness of the black basaltic rock was tempered partly by horizontal layers of red clay giving off a beautiful effect of uniform lines of black and red crisscrossing the island. Occasionally the red was complemented by other colours: yellow, blue, purple and indigo shades of clay. The cliffs, rocks and precipices, so strangely fashioned and blended together in distended cloud-like shapes, would have given Lopes the feeling that he had been transported to an ancient world, or even another planet, where every object was unlike anything he had seen before.

In Lisbon in the meantime, Teixeira had not forgotten Lopes and the few days they had spent together, and as the years passed he would, with increasing frequency, hear the name of Fernão Lopes – the hermit of Saint Helena – being spoken of in the streets and courts of Lisbon.

Above all the visiting sailors spoke about how there were now trees and fruit where once there had been none. They spoke about the ducks and hens and chickens that now roamed the island,

and of the fresh meat they could eat, for which they were grateful. There were even cows and dogs and cats. And there were sheep, and there were goats: goats everywhere. Over the years, the men spoke about the rabbits and particularly the birds that had been introduced to the island: the peacocks, pheasants and pigeons, as well as the guinea hens. They remarked on how partridges in particular appeared to thrive among the bare rocky hills even though there was nothing there for them to eat. There had been nothing, the men stressed, and now there was plenty, and it was all thanks to this Fernão Lopes.

If one wants to plant then one needs fertiliser to enrich the soil, and the island was fortunate that the dung of the sea birds was found in considerable quantity everywhere, for it made excellent manure. Lopes himself may have discovered this by experiment: by mixing soil with the manure of sea birds he would have made the soil, drizzled with only two weeks of rain, highly fertile, and within two months exuberant grass and plants would have covered it. And these days, the men who stopped at the island were tasked to traverse it, collecting as much dung as they could.

Did Lopes ever mention Portugal, Teixeira asked the men who returned from the island. Did he ever mention India? But the answer was that he never showed any interest or curiosity about what was happening in Lisbon and only ever spoke about himself when the men pleaded for him to do so. Even when he was told that King Manuel – may God bless his soul – had died, his face had betrayed no expression. It was as if he had never heard the name before. Perhaps, one of the men surmised, Lopes had been on the island for so long that he did not know King Manuel. But Teixeira knew otherwise, for over the years he had gathered as much information about him as he could. Fernão Lopes knew King Manuel and he knew him well.

On the island he sowed a few grains of barley in a row. In less than two weeks young plants appeared and within two months of sowing, the leaves had grown two feet tall. One month later the ears appeared. Lopes counted around a hundred grains in one ear. Within four months of sowing, the barley was approaching ripeness and the birds were greedily devouring it. The island was coming alive.

Did the men pray together on the island? Teixeira enquired, and the men replied that naturally they prayed together; then, recalling that they were addressing the Chief Justice, they insisted that they were good Catholics. But when he then asked them whether Lopes prayed with them, they were not so certain in their reply, and their answers varied. But a few of the men, perhaps the more perceptive ones, repeated what Lopes had told them about how he spoke to God, and as the men told their story Teixeira leaned in, listening intently. Lopes, the men claimed, mentioned that he spoke to God, and when asked what he had spoken about, he replied that it varied. After all, friends do not expect to have the same conversation every time they speak to each other and neither does God. Is that not why Jesus warned us not to use vain repetition when we talk with God? One of the men had enquired of Lopes: Do you kneel when you speak to God? And he had replied that when one is talking to a friend sometimes you are seated and sometimes you are standing. Did the tax collector not stand when he addressed God? Did David not sit when he addressed his Lord? Lopes then spoke about the need to get to know God, and that it was very simple, for He reveals Himself to us through His Name. At first Lopes explained that like any conversation with a new friend there were moments when he did not know what to say, and at times it felt stilted and awkward. But we need to learn to talk to God in the same way that a child talks to a loving father for that is what He is. The men called Lopes the 'Hermit of Saint Helena', and as Teixeira listened to them he reflected carefully about what he had been told, and when he had reflected he came to the only conclusion that he could. Fernão Lopes' life was in great danger.

Two threads have so far remained unwoven into the story. The first relates to a legend which was both familiar and deeply embedded in the Portuguese psyche of the period. It revolved around the events following the defeat of the last of the Visigoth kings, Rodrigo, in the face of the Muslim armies at Guadalete in 711. Although, according to Arab sources such as Ibn al-Qutiya and Ibn al-Athir, Rodrigo died by drowning in a river, the legend narrates a different tale. After the defeat, Rodrigo together with the Archbishop of Porto and six bishops, followed by their congregation, fled westwards and established themselves on an unknown island somewhere in the Atlantic where they founded seven cities. From this island, known as Antilla, a corruption of Atlantis, or the island of seven cities, Portuguese imagination believed that the 'lost' or 'hidden' king would sally forth, save and restore former greatness to Portugal, defeat the Muslims, convert the world to Christianity, and establish a New Jerusalem. What may have started life as a legend soon solidified into fact and conviction. In the map of 1513 compiled by the famous Ottoman cartographer Piri Reis, one finds the island of Antilla off the coast of the New World, an uninhabited island on which, we are informed, many parrots of different colours lived. Other stories were added to the legend of the lost king on an island, the most alluring one being that the island, visible from a distance, vanished when approached. But it was the image of an uninhabited island which left the deepest imprint in the psyche of the Portuguese and partly explains why the story of Fernão Lopes and his deserted island resonated, even if subconsciously, so powerfully in Lisbon.

During Lopes' lifetime, both in Portugal and throughout Europe, islands held special significance, and there were frenzied conjectures as to the location of Paradise on earth. Christopher Columbus searched the New World for the physical manifestation of Eden, while Gerónimo de Mendieta, and Amerigo Vespucci, although more sceptical than Columbus, agreed that the terrestrial paradise was to be found in the vicinity of the Caribbean. Medieval Church theologians had speculated that Eden was in Palestine, the Holy Land and Mesopotamia. Saint

Thomas Aquinas, for one, asserted that the Garden of Paradise was an actual region of the earth, still undiscovered, shut off from the habitable world by mountains, or seas which could not be crossed. In 1526, while Lopes was on Saint Helena, an expedition was launched in search of the 'island of Saint Brendan', named after a monk who in the 6th century had founded a monastery in Ireland and had supposedly visited this earthly paradise. The world's oldest surviving globe, produced by the German Martin Behaim in 1492, even shows Saint Brendan's island somewhere between the mainland of Europe and the islands of Asia. If today such conjectures and beliefs may appear quaint or quixotic, are they really so different from modern man's fascination with discovering life on other planets? What is striking is how often the image of Eden as a garden was linked to that of a lost or mythical island, for both were enclosed spaces, self-sufficient, isolated, impregnable. They were both also distant and disconnected from the disappointments of daily life. It is on an island that man most clearly resembles God, and on an island that the Edenic image is closest translated into reality. But there is a remoteness to Saint Helena, the symbolic religious significance of which was that in the island's uninhabited seclusion, the Portuguese saw a replication of the biblical paradigm of the wilderness experience. For them the story of Lopes as it filtered back to Lisbon was resplendent with biblical symbolism. In his tattered garb, Lopes would have resembled a John the Baptist, and in the restlessness of his early years he was an Adam.

As for the second thread, we need to take a step back and relate the story of a 12th-century Muslim Andalusian savant and physician by the name of Abu Bakr ibn Tufayl, and a novel he wrote. *Hayy bin Yaqẓan* commences when a baby, Hayy, is deposited on a deserted island (there are different versions as to how he got there). On the island a gazelle becomes Hayy's foster mother and constant nurse, 'caring for him, raising him, and protecting him from harm'. In this environment, with no humans around, Hayy grows up learning to communicate with animals, much as Kipling's Mowgli and Edgar Rice Burroughs' Tarzan would do. When Hayy is seven, the gazelle dies. With no protector, he must now fend for himself, and Hayy uses his hands to make tools and weapons. Later he learns to hunt and then domesticate animals and grow plants, and whereas all other creatures run from fire, Hayy utilises it to cook his food. He also becomes aware of the rhythms of day and night and associates them with the movements of the sun and the moon, and from that he develops a knowledge of mathematics and astronomy. Ultimately Hayy's contemplative journey leads him to the realisation of the necessity of a God who is 'the Cause of all things'.

Hayy ibn Yaqzan became a major literary event and by the time Defoe sat down to write *Robinson Crusoe* in the 18th century, Ibn Tufayl's story was already a best-seller, widely read by many of the Enlightenment-era thinkers, poets and writers such as Bacon, Milton, Locke, Spinoza, Voltaire and Rousseau. Not surprisingly, literary cognoscenti identified Crusoe with Hayy. Alexander Pope, writing to his friend Lord Bathurst in September 1719 – five months after Defoe published *Robinson Crusoe* – jokingly compared Bathurst's isolation at his estate in Gloucestershire to that of 'Alexander Selkirk, or the *Self-taught Philosopher*', the latter referring to the title of an English translation of *Hayy ibn Yaqzan*. Educated readers admired how Ibn Tufayl made Hayy learn to survive without human help or intervention and to toil patiently to cultivate his land and transform a wilderness into a garden. For them, *Hayy ibn Yaqzan* was not a mere adventure tale but an allegorical examination of a rational, empirical approach to understanding the universe, the natural progression of the mind towards discovering the truth, and the story of how *Hayy ibn Yaqzan* actually reached Europe and Portugal is a fascinating one.

Fluent in Latin, Castilian and Provençal French, reading both

Hebrew and Arabic, the Jewish scholar Moses Narboni began studying Maimonides at age thirteen, following which he pursued medicine and wrote biblical and philosophical commentaries. In 1348 he moved from his birthplace in Perpignan to Barcelona, where he commenced working on a commentary on *Hayy ibn Yaqzan* in order to examine 'the regime of solitude' as a means of 'communion with God'. One of the readers was an Italian Jewish humanist from Constantinople named Yohanan Alemanno, who in the late 15th century found himself in Florence, searching for employment and patronage with one of the wealthy Florentine families. In the meantime, Alemanno earned some money teaching, and one of his students was the prodigy Pico della Mirandola. Apart from Marsilo Ficino, Mirandola was the greatest philosopher of the Renaissance. By the age of ten, Mirandola began studying canon law, which was followed by a classical, scholastic education: Latin, Greek, Plato and Aristotle, after which he learned Arabic and Hebrew. He was a brilliant and flamboyant intellectual, daring and provocative. He was also a deep and profound philosopher and a seeker of the truth, no matter where it lay.

> I have read in the records of the Arabians, reverend Fathers, that Abdala the Saracen, when questioned as to what stage of the world, as it were, could be seen most worthy of wonder, replied: There is nothing to be seen more wonderful than man.

Mystical by nature, Mirandola was drawn to the Kabbalah as he attempted to connect the world's traditions of wisdom. His teacher Alemanno introduced him to the tale of Hayy ibn Yaqzan, and the Italian rapidly fell under its spell, drawn to how Hayy's realisation of his isolation ends in a meditative self-actualisation elaborated in a mystical tone. In 1493 Mirandola translated the book from Hebrew into Latin, and copies soon spread across Europe. In England, the philosopher and statesman Thomas More looked to

Mirandola's fascination with Hayy as he developed his own theories on mankind's relationship to God, which he set on an island named Utopia. At a time when Ferdinand and Isabella in Spain and Manuel in Portugal were expelling the Muslims and forcibly converting the Jews, Pico della Mirandola's translation of *Hayy ibn Yaqzan*, with its gentle and mystical message about the human mind and the way it can provide man with proof of the existence of God and His attributes, was making its way across Europe, leaving in its Latin wake the haunting and sensitive image of a solitary man on a deserted island.

Now something remarkable began taking place. With the Jews being expelled or forced into converting to Catholicism, there was a sudden outpouring of Hebrew translations of *Hayy ibn Yaqzan* throughout Europe. Under Manuel, denuded of their sacred texts and unable to perform their rituals, many of the Jews turned inwards towards silent prayer, placing their spiritual values and religious identity in their own private world. To a large extent, they chose to live in their own exile. Many rediscovered the story written by Ibn Tufayl, and what drew the Jewish and New Christian thinkers to it was partly that it was a story of natural science, mysticism and metaphysics, but mostly that it was a story where man is defined not through a biblical perspective but through a philosophical one.

The Church was greatly alarmed by all of this. *Hayy ibn Yaqzan* offered a mystical alternative for those seeking salvation at a time when the Church not only mistrusted mystical experiences but also closely policed them. Visions and mystical utterances, the Church argued, may well be the manifestations of divine blessings but they might also be the works of demons. Since there was no test that could be applied to differentiate between them, the Church reserved the right to be suspicious. While New Christians read the story of Hayy ibn Yaqzan with great interest (as reflected in the numerous translations which appeared during this period) as an allegory of a mystical and philosophical approach to the Divine, as far as the Church was concerned, Truth unmediated by a priest remained both ambiguous and dangerous. While this debate was being waged – one which would ultimately manifest itself in the Inquisition – stories began to appear in Lisbon about a Portuguese mystic who lived on a deserted island. In other words, a real-life Hayy suddenly arose from nowhere.

As each Portuguese ship returning from India docked in Belém, the men aboard spoke about a strange mystic who lived alone on an island, and in the febrile atmosphere of Lisbon many people rapidly became familiar with the name of Fernão Lopes. Among those of the New Christians familiar with the story of Hayy ibn Yaqzan, the appearance of a mystic on an island was intellectually intriguing. But the Church, wary of the emergence of self-proclaimed prophets and messiahs, saw matters in a different light, and Lopes' popularity was a concern. Who exactly was he, did he have followers? More importantly, the Church asked, what exactly was this Fernão Lopes doing on a deserted island and what did he want? It was certainly a dangerous time to be a mystic in Portugal. An apocalyptic mood could be felt throughout the land, what one might term an outbreak of eschatological fever.

This was an age of self-proclaimed prophets and messiahs, which greatly alarmed the Church. Within a year or two of Manuel's proclamation of the conversion of the Jews, the first of the prophets, Inés of Herrera, appeared. Although more of a prophet than a messiah, Inés claimed that the Prophet Elijah had come to her in a dream and assured her that the New Christians would be taken to a place of no want. The fact that it was Elijah was significant, since in Jewish tradition he never died and was taken directly to Heaven, only to return as a harbinger of the arrival of the true Messiah. Soon after, Inés revealed that a messiah would indeed soon appear to end the Diaspora and inaugurate the glory of a restored kingdom. Inés' words spread like wildfire, with many of her New Christian followers holding on to the hope of the immediacy of redemption with fervour. For her beliefs, Inés of Herrera was burned. Then there was Luis Dias, who became known among his contemporaries and numerous followers in southern Portugal as the Messiah of Setúbal. Charismatic, Dias quickly attracted followers among the New Christians who believed that he was in direct communication with God. As the movement spread across the land the authorities quickly stepped in and the Messiah of Setúbal was also burned, alive. Yet another was Bandarra, who was best known for a series of *Trovas* or prophetic verses written sometime between the 1520s and 1540. He too was tried but was more fortunate as he escaped the same fiery fate. But the most famous, and potentially most dangerous, of the self-proclaimed messiahs and prophets during these most troubled of times was undoubtedly the enigmatic figure of David Reubeni.

CHAPTER TWENTY-ONE

What Does He Want?

In 1521 King Manuel of Portugal died and was succeeded by his son João III. Deeply pious and orthodox in outlook, João was described as a man with a 'deep-seated hatred of the Hebrew race' which he shared with his wife Catherine of Austria. As a prince, João had been educated according to the Renaissance standards of early 16th-century Europe and he grew up in a time of peace between the distinct Iberian kingdoms as a consequence of his father's foreign policy, which had been cemented by a series of intermarriages including the one between João and Catherine, granddaughter of Ferdinand and Isabella. Power, however, changed João from the Erasmian Christian prince described by Barros to a suspicious, introspective man who saw treachery everywhere and was described by a 19th-century Portuguese historian as a 'malignant fanatic'. Perhaps one can trace this transformation to his cruel fortune, for it was his sad fate to sire nine legitimate children to inherit him, and then painfully watch each one die.

The new King's nature was a slow and deliberate one. He pondered every word and thought to the extent that on several royal occasions it provoked embarrassment. Similarly, to the frustration of courtiers and ambassadors, João rarely made decisions quickly. Often it was simply because he kept ambassadors waiting as he travelled around his kingdom, but largely it was because he found it onerous to do so, choosing instead to prevaricate. It was certainly not due to a lack of counsellors, among whom were nobles, royal family members and high officers of the Crown. It was the King's practice to take into his confidence two or three private members of his highly informal royal council, and among his favourites were António de Ataíde, Count of Castanheira, and his own brother the *infante* Luís, as well as Francisco de Portugal, the Count of Vimioso. However, his closest companion, and the person on whom he most relied, was his wife, Queen Catherine of Austria. Born in Torquemada, Spain, in 1507, Catherine of Austria was the youngest daughter of Philip the Fair and Juana la Loca, making her a descendant of the royal Houses of Burgundy, Castile, Leon, Portugal and Austria. She was born after her father's death but unlike her brothers and sisters, Catherine remained with her mother in Tordesillas in a secluded asylum. One imagines it must have been a traumatic childhood since her insane mother, out of fear of kidnapping, kept her in a windowless bedroom. Until her betrothal to João she led a life isolated from the Spanish court. However, she would soon prove her worth to him, evolving into an astute advisor to her husband. João would let her frequent royal council meetings, and he often sought her advice on important matters. As the Castilian ambassador noted, 'the King relies entirely upon the Queen, there is nothing great or small that does not pass through her hands'. She was well versed in Greek and Latin, and her library included many of the humanist works (although alas we do not know if it contained a copy of *Hayy ibn Yaqzan*, one imagines that Catherine would have been familiar with the story). There is no doubt that she possessed a certain flair: on one occasion Catherine gave a banquet for women of a wedding party where she sensationally served water from four rivers of the Empire: the Ganges, the Indus, the Sal near Goa, and a river in the Moluccas. When an uncle of the bride attempted to reciprocate, and held a banquet (this time for the men) where only Indian chefs were cooking, the result was less positive, as many fell ill with vomiting and upset stomachs.

It was not long before the story of the hermit Fernão Lopes reached the court, for by now most in Lisbon were aware of it. At first the King paid it little attention, dismissing it as little more than a story that sailors embellished to pass the time. But as the months and years passed the story did not fade away.

Catherine was curious by nature, and she loved collecting things. She now summoned Teixeira and enquired of him who this Lopes was of whom everyone was speaking: after all, had he not met him once? Teixeira replied that indeed he had, and though the meeting had been brief, lasting no more than a few days, and had taken place eight or ten years ago, he recalled the events clearly, for Lopes had made an impact on him. When Catherine asked him what kind of impact, Teixeira told her his strange story. As he spoke, the Queen listened, on occasion perhaps interjecting with a question about Lopes' background: He fought in India? He turned against His Majesty King Manuel? How long has he been alone on the island? Is he a New Christian? Are you sure he is not just a madman? Teixeira would have been able to tell her that he had fought in India, that he had turned against His Majesty King Manuel for which he had been punished and pardoned, that he had been about fourteen years on the island and that Her Majesty could be assured that Lopes was perfectly lucid and sane. A few days later Teixeira was summoned to the court again; this time it was the King who asked to hear the story of Lopes. When Teixeira had finished recounting it, the King would have asked himself one question: 'What does he want?'

The King's mind was elsewhere, for currently residing at his court and having arrived from seemingly nowhere was the enigmatic figure of David Reubeni, whose background is cloaked in mystery. A dark-skinned Jew who was always clad in white and spoke only Hebrew and Arabic, he claimed to be a prince from a distant kingdom, and his name was David. He belonged to the ancient Hebrew tribe of Reuben and was a brother of a powerful Jewish King. His proposal for the King, a jumble of messianic rhetoric, was to suggest a partnership with Christian kingdoms and his brother's 'troops' to take Jerusalem and the Holy Land from the Turks. David Reubeni had first travelled to Rome, where he had audaciously asked to see Pope Clement VII. His story was fantastic and barely credible, but the Pope listened patiently and wrote him a letter of recommendation to João III of Portugal, relieved to be ridding himself of this potentially dangerous messiah. In Lisbon, Reubeni was received with proper regal pomp and lodged in luxury. His arrival caused a sensation, tempered by a mixture of praise and suspicion. Here was a Jew openly proclaiming his faith in a land where Judaism did not exist. For many New Christians, Reubeni's arrival was greeted by an almost messianic fervour. A young man at King João's court named Diogo Pires became inspired by Reubeni, had himself circumcised, renamed himself Shlomo or Solomon Molcho and claimed to be the Jewish Messiah. João was perplexed. Why had the Pope sent him Reubeni? Was he genuine, or a dangerous lunatic? Unable to decide yet, in his slow and laborious manner he retained him at his court. And now everyone in Lisbon was talking about this Lopes, a hermit who lived on a deserted island. These were strange days indeed.

In the meantime, what was to be done with Fernão Lopes, and what did he want? João's nature was to see conspiracies everywhere. Had Lopes after all not rebelled against João's father the King? Could he still be working in secret against Portuguese interests? Saint Helena was an important stop for the ships – what if Lopes was a French agent? What if he was plotting to hand the island to the French? Perhaps he was a mystic, but João was suspicious of mystics. He distrusted the fact that mysticism, like philosophy, pushed the limit of the knowledge of what was known and what was unknown, that it transcended language. Above all João distrusted the way that mystics chose to express themselves with silence, and Lopes' silence troubled João, for he had yet to meet a man who did not want something.

Gaspar Correia wrote: 'And so the king ordered that he should be asked to come to the kingdom of his own free will.'

So it came to pass that the King ordered that Fernão Lopes, the hermit of Saint Helena, be brought back to Lisbon, for he and his wife Catherine desired to speak to him. Why exactly the King wished to take Lopes away from his island we do not know, for the whims of royalty are often impetuous. It was probably no more than curiosity, tinged with some of João's paranoia. Catherine was known throughout Europe as a great collector of curiosities and perhaps she simply saw Lopes as another distraction to amuse her. No matter, the King's orders were to be carried out, and a ship was dispatched on the two-month journey to fetch Lopes. Lopes was of course unaware of all this, nor did he have any idea how famous his name had become in Lisbon and how grateful the crews of the ships were for the fruit and vegetables he had so assiduously planted for them. Unknown to him a new chapter was opening in his life.

Saint Helena was Lopes' life. How might he have reacted when told he was to be escorted back to Lisbon; after all, who then would gather the fruit on the island? Patiently the captain (historical sources do not record his name) listened to Lopes' increasingly frantic entreaties and explained that the matter was settled: the King's orders had to be carried out, and Lopes had no choice.

But Lopes remained adamant he could not leave. Would he be allowed to return once he had seen the King, and in any case why would the King want to see him? He reminded the captain that he had been pardoned, but there was no reassurance given, nor was there any promise that Lopes would be allowed to return. Once again, the captain

informed him that there was no choice in the matter, before firmly stat-
ing that when the ship next set sail Lopes would be on it, even if he had
to be tied and trussed like an animal.

We can imagine that Lopes left the island bewildered, scared
and confused. He would have had no idea what was in store or
even why the King wished to see him. Was it to punish him again
for Banastarim? As the ship set sail, I picture him standing still
on the deck, his eyes fixed on the island. The men instinctively
leaving him alone, sensing that, despite the shouting of the crew,
the barking of orders and the manning of ropes, for the hermit
this was a moment of silence, one of communion. For Lopes, it
would have been the first time in fourteen years that he had left
the island and he would now have gazed at Saint Helena in its full
extent, in all its brilliant green splendour and black volcanic hues.
To his left, he could have spotted his beloved dolphins bobbing
and weaving alongside the ship as if they had come to say farewell.
And above his head, darkening the sky, as had taken place so
many years ago, sea birds would have swirled effortlessly. Did it, for
a moment, appear to have all been a dream? Did he try to imagine
the Fernão Lopes who had first approached the island, a young,
confused and angry man, one shorn of all hope? Had he been
asked how long he had been on the island, he would have said
two or three years but it must have seemed like a few lifetimes.
Soon he would be back in Lisbon, a city which he had not seen
in 24 years. There were so many variations of the man who went
by the name of Fernão Lopes, each a saga in its own suffering. He
had buried them on the island, one by one, ghost by ghost, but
now the memories must have begun to flood back. If Lopes, on
Saint Helena, had convinced himself that he had understood his
life in its totality, he now would have realised that he understood
little. As the ship made its way to Lisbon, Lopes would have had
no idea what lay ahead.

CHAPTER TWENTY-TWO

The Streets of Lisbon

aspar Correia informs us that Lopes 'disembarked secretly in the house of the captain of the ship and went from there at night to talk to the King and to the Queen and they gave him hermitages and houses of friars in which he might stay.'

For the Jews and New Christians David Reubeni's words spread like wildfire, even though Reubeni was careful to behave in the most circumspect of manners. He knew that he was walking a tightrope since, though for the moment at least he had the support of the Portuguese King, any careless word or gesture that could encourage New Christians to revert to Judaism would signal his death. For the young Diogo Pires, who now assumed the name of Solomon Molcho, however, the appearance of Reubeni was like a thunderbolt. Born around 1501, Molcho had acquired a good education and had risen fast in society, reaching the position of secretary in the high court. For many years he had been troubled by dreams and visions but the encounter with Reubeni acted as a catalyst on the young man. After a period of fasting and vivid dreams Molcho proclaimed two visions which had come to him. The first was that a devastating flood would break over Rome, the seat of the Papacy, and the second was that an earthquake would strike Portugal. For many Jews, Molcho's words could only lead to calamity, for their incendiary nature could not fail to arouse the anger of the King. It was during this time, with a frenzied air of messianic mystical prognostications, rumour and tumult abroad in Lisbon, that Lopes returned to the city.

In the quarter of a century Lopes had been away, the population of Lisbon had doubled. The noise that greeted him must have deafened him: the clatter of hooves and wheels on the cobbled streets, the sound and fury of sawing and clanging in the shipyards, the waterfront of the *Ribeira das Naus*, the incessant talking and yelling of men. On his arrival in Lisbon Lopes had initially been lodged near the palace, but it was clear from the start that he was overwhelmed by the noise of the city, and by the number of people who were curious about him and would not leave him alone, and the King gave instructions to move him to a friary. There Lopes was largely left alone, and he found great joy in the vegetable garden and orchard, which was also densely planted with many fragrant flowers. He would have been quick to notice that imported trees and ornamental flowers were popular in the garden and that there were wonders planted there brought from the New World, such as tobacco, chili and sunflowers. By and large the friars left him alone as he waited to hear instructions from the King. At the monastery, Lopes would have noticed that apart from the friars, there were others who inhabited the monastery, including several members of the lower nobility who had once served the King but had now fallen on hard times and had no means of subsistence. Perhaps this is where he would have ended up, had he not jumped ship.

He knew that Lisbon must have changed but he could never have imagined that the transformation would be so dramatic. When he had departed the banks of the Tagus for India the city was barely emerging from the Atlantic obscurity geography had imposed upon it. The Lisbon that Lopes now gazed on, after so many years, had grown and flourished as the centre of a mercantile power outstripping Venice and other Mediterranean trading cities. During his absence, the city had emerged as the nerve centre of a global overseas enterprise, from where ships set sail for the Portuguese Empire and where cargoes from Africa, India and China were unloaded. In 1506 when he had departed Portugal, Belém was barely Belém. Then, it had been known as Restelo, and was no more than a waterfront village on the western outskirts of Lisbon where ships could anchor while the crew came ashore. There a small chapel dedicated to Our Lady Star of the Sea had been built. The name naturally alluded to the protector of those who set off on the high seas but also to the story of the Three Wise Men, whom a star guided to Bethlehem, Belém in Portuguese, the name by which the village became better known. It was in the chapel of Our Lady Star of the Sea where Vasco da Gama prayed on the eve of his historic departure and it was there that Lopes had kept vigil before his own. But now Lopes would have been stunned by the changes and transformations: Manuel had decreed that a glorious new monastery be built there, for which the foundation stone had been laid on 6 January 1502. The date was symbolic – the feast of the Epiphany, the day the coming of the Three Kings is commemorated – as Manuel was determined to build a new Bethlehem in Restelo as part of the unfolding of his messianic vision.

Lopes would have been struck by the number of black men and women who walked the streets of Lisbon. In the words of a contemporary, 'There were so many black slaves that Portuguese cities appeared like games of chess with as many blacks as whites', and it was claimed, perhaps with some exaggeration, that there did not exist a household in Lisbon that did not have a female 'Moor' slave. In Lisbon, Lopes could have observed a black African row a boat while another played the tambourine for a white couple clinched in an amorous embrace, and he could have watched black women carrying containers on their heads – some jars of water, some pots of excrement. Whether from the carriage in which he rode or on the few occasions he walked the streets, he would have come across groups of black women working as street vendors selling rice, couscous, chickpeas, beans, prunes and seafood. And as Lopes quietly observed the black Africans rowing a boat or carrying excrement or selling their wares, he would have been quick to understand that, as the latest arrivals in Lisbon, they were given the worst jobs, even though some, as house slaves, were dressed in fine livery. What he would not initially have known was that even though most Africans were baptised upon their arrival in Lisbon, when they died they were not buried in Christian graveyards but their corpses were dumped in a communal slave pit in unconsecrated ground.

He may have vaguely recalled that the King's palace had been nearing completion when he departed Lisbon but now the Paço da Ribeira stood in all its magnificence on the banks of the Tagus, which was filled with sailing ships and vessels. From the royal palace, which had been designed so that the governmental buildings were distributed around two courtyards, the King could oversee the unloading of goods and animals, the source of Portugal's wealth, and admire the commodities, spices and luxuries arriving in Lisbon from all the corners of the earth. On the lower floors of the palace and strategically built underneath the King's royal headquarters were the customs houses of Africa and India, whose offices lined the courtyard's inner walls. Housed in great secrecy and under guard in storerooms were the keys to this great treasure, the world maps (*mappae mundi*), the books of sailing instructions (*roteiros*) and the nautical charts. It was there that cartographers and cosmographers worked, mapping the contours of foreign lands in great detail. Here was the seat of power. Here lived the King of Portugal, the merchant King.

Much had changed, or was it Lopes who had changed? On the faces of most Portuguese he would have noticed a sadness, and there was in the air of the city a mood of sobriety, almost of gloom, accentuated by the sight of men dressed in heavy, dark, woollen garments (*baeta*) and dark felt hats adorned with ribbons, for the wearing of silk was frowned upon and would soon be banned. It had always been thus, but after the colour of India the gloomy dress of the Portuguese would have given the citizens the semblance of men at an unending funeral. On occasion, Lopes may have been astonished to observe a Portuguese lady dressed in an embroidered Indian cloak, but he should not have been, for during the years he had been away so many Portuguese had travelled to India to seek their fortune in trade that almost every Lisboeta had an acquaintance or a family member who had once been in Asia.

If Lopes had sought out the mosque, he would have found that it no longer stood where his memory would have insisted it should: Manuel had decreed that the building be torn down.

On 8 October 1530 Rome was inundated by floods turning the city into a lake: Molcho's first prophecy had come true.

Lisbon had indeed changed. When Lopes had first departed for India, Asiatic goods were luxuries to be marvelled at, but now it seemed they were everywhere, often bought and sold second hand in the auctions held daily in Rossio Square where the rich and poor meandered to haggle in search of bargains. There were bracelets which Lopes would have recognised at once as coming from Bijapur. There were pelican-shaped earrings and rosaries made of rock crystals. One could purchase a tortoiseshell casket with gold mounts set in sapphire and rubies if one desired, or gaming boards, portable writing desks and large chests, all covered with mother-of-pearl. It was not just goods from Asia that flooded into Lisbon, for African intricacies from what is now Sierra Leone, from the Kingdom of Kongo (Congo) and from Benin were found in the market stalls: leather, wood, feathers and of course ivory, from which many beautiful objects were carved, the most sought after of which were the small spoons. Merchants in Lisbon also sold great quantities of Ming porcelain, and Far Eastern lacquers became all the rage. Apothecaries on the Rua Nova made brisk business, and Lopes would have recognised many of the medicines that he knew from India, such as camphor. Rhinoceros horns, ground into a powder and mixed with wine, were used as remedies against plague, epilepsy and melancholy, as well as poison; they were even believed to possess supernatural power.

There were actual rhinoceroses in Lisbon, imported by the wealthy, the bored and the curious, and in the menageries of Lisbon one came across West African monkeys, bought as pets or trophies, the domesticated American turkey and ubiquitous parrots. And then there were the elephants, the great passion of the Lisboetas. In 1514 the Flemish pilgrim Jan Taccoen witnessed two bulls and one female, which he described as 'big, ugly and grey with large wide ears, having a gentle disposition', drinking at a Lisbon fountain, filling their trunks with water and spraying people around them. Lisbon, Lopes observed, had indeed changed.

On the streets of Lisbon he searched for himself, and for the young boy he had once been. He hoped that if he could somehow find the same cobbled streets where he had played, or the ornately arched doorway under which he had crouched when it rained, or even the tree he had used to climb in the long summer afternoons, if he could somehow find these places and stand in the same spot, the exact same spot, then perhaps he could reach out and connect with the young boy and finally close the circle. There were of course many streets in Lisbon which he recognised but they were of little interest to him, for those streets belonged to the young man who was so full of himself. He wanted to go further back, to peer through the thickening clouds of his mind and to reconnect with the young boy. But even as he searched he already sensed that too much time had passed, that the chasm which separated him from himself was too wide. The streets and doorways and trees were still there but they no longer looked the same: they were smaller, noisier. They smelled differently, no longer of his childhood but of another age. Everything had changed. The clouds had thickened. The circle was broken. He rarely left the monastery for the noise of the crowds disturbed him. He was often recognised – his disfigurement after all was his greeting card – and when he was recognised he was stopped by strangers eager to speak to him. Most asked him to describe his ordeal, insisting on the details; some asked him if he was among those who had tried to kill Albuquerque, and a few wondered if he knew how to save their souls. For that reason he preferred to remain in the garden of the monastery, but now, perhaps upon impulse, he headed towards Rua Nova and it did not take him long to find what he was looking for. As a young man he had often stood staring at the house of the wealthy Florentine merchant Bartolomeo Marchionni, a man who was rumoured to have been so wealthy that he was not able to count his money. For the young Lopes, Marchionni represented everything he had ever hoped to be: wealthy, influential (he was well known as a close confidant of the King), living on the Rua Nova. He tried to recall where exactly he used to stand when looking at the house, and he now took up the same position, an old man in the place of a young dreamer. Marchionni, he was told, had long since died and had bequeathed the house to his niece, an Elena Corbinelli. He was tempted to knock on the door and to inform Elena Corbinelli, niece of the Florentine merchant Bartolomeo Murchionni, that he, Fernão Lopes, had returned to Lisbon. Instead he turned around and headed back to the garden in the monastery.

According to Correia the meeting with the King and Queen was scheduled for the middle of the night and in their private chambers. But before being escorted to the palace he would need to be made fit for a royal audience. His nails would have been trimmed, as well as his white hair and beard: Lopes was now 50 years old.

The sources are all silent about what took place during the meeting. Perhaps records did exist which were destroyed in the devastating earthquake that struck Lisbon in 1755, and there is always the possibility that the archives of Portugal will unearth new documents. But until then we are left with a devastating silence. In itself (and assuming no records have been lost or destroyed) that silence is significant for being so uncommon. Normally meetings are attended by royal secretaries and hangers-on, but all that we are told in the sources is that the King and Queen met Lopes in their private chambers, following which the story continues (according to Correia) in a most dramatic fashion. So how does one interpret this silence? For one thing, we can assume that since the meeting did take place then Lopes would have been judged to be sound of mind: the royal couple would not have met with a man who had lost his senses. That Lopes was lucid has so far been supported by his actions, but the meeting certainly confirms this. The only other fact that we can hold on to is that once the meeting was over, he did not return to the island but instead remained in Lisbon, since the King, it now seems, made the most extraordinary of decisions concerning the fate of Fernão Lopes.

We now come to the most enigmatic event in the remarkable life of Fernão Lopes, as astonishing as it is perplexing. Having finished the audience with the King, Gaspar Correia relates that Lopes returned to the friary where he was lodged and where the friars had been given strict instructions to leave him in peace. He had been hoping that he would soon return to Saint Helena, but as the days passed, and then weeks, there was no sign from the palace and Lopes remained in Lisbon. Finally, when João's orders did come, it was not for Lopes to leave for the island but instead he was ordered to be escorted to Rome to meet Pope Clement VII. No reason is given for João's decision: perhaps he was moved by Lopes' words or perhaps he was persuaded by Catherine, sensing Lopes' nature more astutely. Did something profound occur during the private meeting which made the King reach this decision?

After all, one does not simply send another person to meet the Pope for no reason, but the King's orders were that Lopes would travel to Rome for a Papal audience. We are not told what Lopes' reaction was and within days he was on the move, boarding a ship which took him to Naples and then on to Rome. There, Lopes was summoned to the Vatican for an audience with the Pope, who gave him absolution as he knelt and confessed his apostasy.

It is important at this stage to quote Correia in full, brief though the reference is. Writing about Lopes, Correia says:

> He did not wish to accept anything, but had the King's leave and went to Rome, and made his confession to the Pope who rejoiced to see him, and he had letters for the King that he should command him to be sent back to the island.

It is a truly remarkable story, a meeting between a disfigured, possibly still Muslim, Portuguese hermit who had just a few months earlier been living in total isolation, and the most powerful man in Christendom. Within weeks and in a bewildering series of events, Lopes had met the King of Portugal and the Pope, both of whom had listened to his story and given him their blessings. An astonishing event by all accounts, except that I was far from sure that it ever took place. The first time I read Correia's account about Lopes' meeting with the Pope, I was swept away by the sheer scale of the drama of the story, which was almost epic. The King of Portugal is so moved by the wise words of Lopes that he decides to dispatch him to the Pope, who then with a dramatic flourish absolves him before sending him on his way. What is of particular interest is that it was the Pope who requests the King to allow Lopes to return to the island. But the more I read the narrative, the more troubled I became by what was being described. Put simply, it just did not ring true; like a wrong note in a piece of music, it stood out for its discordance.

The problem with the narrative as it is presented to us by Correia is that when one examines the remarkable life of solitude and the transcendental silence which so transformed Lopes, the words apostasy and absolution simply do not fit in. Are we supposed to believe that on Saint Helena, after a period of fourteen years of isolation, the idea of a Papal absolution held any significance for Lopes? One can perhaps argue that he felt that an element was missing in his life and that he leapt at the chance of Papal absolution. After all, such absolutions were not afforded to just anyone. In addition, Correia's account does not explain why Lopes should have wished to confess his 'apostasy'. It is my personal belief that as a young man Lopes had been forcibly converted to Catholicism, and for a few years he had lived, like many New Christians, in a shadowland between two faiths. In India, we know that he had become a Muslim and he appeared to have found what he was looking for in that faith. In his own words, he had told João Machado that he would die as a Muslim. He had chosen not to revert to the Catholic faith after Banastarim, nor when he was being punished by Albuquerque, nor when he had lived in destitute poverty. And yet we are supposed to believe that on the island of Saint Helena he was suddenly seized by an urge to be absolved? If Lopes had one wish upon setting foot in Lisbon again after so many years, it was to return to Saint Helena.

Nevertheless, the sources tell us that Lopes met the Pope. While priests in Lisbon or Rome were authorised to accept the confessions of penitents, certain transgressions were classified as 'reserved cases' and for these no ordinary priest or even bishop had the authority to grant absolution. Lopes, it seems, was one such case. However, having decided to trace this story back to its source, both in Lisbon and in the Vatican, I was astonished by what I found, or to be more precise, what I did not find. I found no trace of Lopes' meeting with the Pope. I looked at the records of the Portuguese ambassador to the Vatican in 1530 and 1531, the years during which the meeting supposedly took place, and in particular the period around Easter 1530 when we know that Pope Clement VII was in Rome. As the King's representative in Rome, the ambassador would surely have recorded such a visit, especially since it had followed directives from the King. And yet there was no mention of any visit or any meeting. I then turned to the Vatican archives themselves, so meticulous in recording the Papal meetings, assuming I would find what I was searching for. But even there I could not find a single document which noted this meeting. There is no mention of the Pope ever meeting Lopes. It was a mystery. Perhaps the meeting had taken place in secret, but surely there would have been some record somewhere? The only conclusion I could reach was that Correia had made the story up. Lopes had never set foot in Rome.

The question we need to ask is why? If Lopes never met the Pope, why would Correia choose to concoct such a story? Before attempting to answer this question, it is worth making some initial remarks. In 1512 Correia voyaged to India and remained in the East for the next 35 years. This meant that, as far as Lopes' sojourn in Europe goes, Correia was a few thousand miles away from the events he was writing about. It is also important to note that *Lendas da India*, Correia's oeuvre, was not printed until 1859, that is to say nearly 300 years after his death, more than enough time for someone perhaps to have inserted, at a later stage, the story of Lopes meeting the Pope. Correia knew Lopes. He was in India at the same time, and he was an eyewitness to the battle at Banastarim and the events that followed. But what is also very significant is that Correia was Albuquerque's secretary and fiercely loyal to him. We do not know if he shared the governor's views but if one assumes so, then it is only natural that he would have viewed Lopes' betrayal in the dimmest of lights. Once Lopes left India the two men would have lost touch, but Correia had not forgotten him, and basing his research on secondary accounts, he wrote about Lopes' stay on Saint Helena. Correia also wrote about Lopes' return to Lisbon and his meeting with the King, and other sources confirm that this meeting did occur. Is it possible that Correia added a few lines from his imagination about Lopes confessing and being absolved by the Pope? Perhaps he wished to tie up a loose end and give Lopes what he considered a fitting Christian finale, or perhaps he still felt a loyalty to Albuquerque and could not let Lopes 'get away' without a public confession. We simply do not know, but at this point in my research I remained certain that the meeting between the Pope and Lopes never took place. After all, why would a Portuguese King who had so avow-edly defied the Pope and insisted on launching an inquisition have any interest in sending him a hermit from a deserted island?

The problem is that to discount Correia's narration of the Pope story means that one has to turn a critical eye on the whole of the Lopes story. If, in other words, Correia made up this story why would he not have made up others? To that purpose I decided to re-read the story of Fernão Lopes as told in the orig-inal sources with a more critical eye, and as I did so, to focus on the parts of the story related largely or solely by Correia and not confirmed by other sources. I mentioned earlier Correia's story of the slave boy who had 'discovered' Lopes and how, despite the evidence, Correia had written that the boy had been on the island for several years. That was one example, as was the story of the Papal meeting, but I also came across one further story which I now looked at in a different light, and for that we need to return to the story of the cockerel on the island. The story itself is so charming that one wishes it were true; but what if Correia had inserted it there for a reason other than its touching quality? Certainly, if he was offering a clue then the choice of a cock was a loaded one, for the Portuguese of the day would have been familiar with its symbolism. A cockerel played a part in the Passion of Jesus, for when Peter assured Jesus that he would never deny him, Christ replied that 'Assuredly, I say to you that today, even before the cock crows twice, you will deny me three times.' And so it came to pass that Peter denied Christ, and having done so he repented and his redemption was accepted. Thus the cock reminds the believers that Christ welcomes all those who denied him. And the cock is also mentioned when Christ said, 'Watch therefore for you do not know when the master of the house is coming – in the evening, at midnight, at the crowing of the cock, or in the morning ...' The Portuguese considered the cockerel an animal of significance, one to be emulated; as it watched for the morning, so Christians watch for the break of dawn when Christ will return to judge those who lived and died. Denial and redemption – one wonders if Correia wove in the story of the cock as a hidden clue to Lopes' denial of Christ (as a Muslim) and his eventual redemption at the hands of the Pope. Perhaps, or perhaps there really was a cockerel after all.

And in many ways that should have been that. The lack of any documentary evidence of a meeting between the Pope and Lopes gradually led me to the conclusion that for one reason or another Correia had inserted this story into his chronicles. However, having reached this conclusion, things took a dramatic and intriguing turn when I came across a second contemporary source, from none other than one of Portugal's greatest historians, that clearly stated that Lopes met Pope Clement VII. In the late 1530s João de Barros was commissioned to write a historical account of the first half-century of Portugal's Asian Empire which he modelled on Livy's *History of Rome* and it was in the *Décadas da Ásia* that I discovered the following paragraph:

> After many years had passed serving his penance, he came back to this kingdom [Portugal]. From here he was sent to Rome to ask for reconciliation and for the complete absolution of his sins. Having received this, he returned to this

island [Saint Helena] where he was still serving his penance when this account was written.

The content was similar to what Correia had written, with the exception that Correia had added that the Pope had written a letter to the King of Portugal requesting that Lopes be allowed to return to Saint Helena. This is Correia's version:

> He did not wish to accept anything, but had the King's leave and went to Rome, and made his confession to the Pope who rejoiced to see him, and he had letters for the King that he should command him to be sent back to the island.

To dismiss Correia is possible, but Barros is another matter. His *Décadas da Ásia* is a remarkable piece of scholarship, in many ways ahead of its time. Scholarly and thorough in his approach, Barros collected Asian historical and geographical books and manuscripts, and he even bought educated slaves to translate them. He cites Arabic and Persian chronicles and geographical works as well as Hindu chronicles through which we learn a great deal about the Kingdom of Vijayanagar. He even cites Chinese geographical works and argues that the Chinese achievements were superior to those of the Greeks and Romans of antiquity. He was also the first writer to describe the lives and customs of the Thai people.

The fact that, in the midst of all these histories and dynasties, Barros chose to mention the story of Lopes indicates that it must have been very well known in his age. Barros presents Lopes' stay on Saint Helena as an act of penance, making it clear that this was the context in which the narrative needed to be understood (although he provides no evidence that this was the case). However, it is Barros' next comment which is intriguing: '*From here he was sent to Rome to ask for reconciliation and for the complete absolution of his sins.*' What is of interest is that the sentence is framed in the form of a command. There is no indication that Lopes himself asked to go to Rome. Looking at Barros' choice of words, it seems that Lopes had no choice in the matter. What is equally fascinating is that we are not told the reason for his penance, nor what the sins were for which he needed complete absolution. It may have been assumed, but it is never actually spelled out. Was it for his rebellion against the King? That, in itself, would not have required a Papal intervention, so one has to assume that the sin was in his having become a Muslim. Barros then goes on to say, '*he returned to this island [Saint Helena] where he was still serving his penance when this account was written*'. What is fascinating is that when Barros was writing this, probably in the last years of the 1530s, Lopes was alive and living on the island. But Barros then insists that having returned to the island Lopes continued serving his penance, even though he had received complete absolution! One is struck by the passive manner in which Lopes has been written into Barros' account, as if he were a pawn in a game of chess. It may be tempting to read too much into the very few lines in which this story is related, but equally one cannot pass over it in silence.

Barros' recounting does not touch on the point that Correia makes, that the Pope '*had letters for the King that he should command him to be sent back to the island*'. Once again, the framing raises questions. It is intriguing to wonder why it was the Pope who should send a letter to the King, requesting that Lopes be sent back to the island. Surely the King did not need any Papal request to do this. It was the King who had commanded that Lopes remain in Lisbon and be sent to Rome, so why does Correia add this line? Why, in other words, would the Pope choose to write a letter requesting that Lopes be allowed to return to his island? There may be little significance in Correia's comment, but it is important to keep one point in mind: it was during this period that the King decreed that New Christians be forbidden to leave Portugal, under the threat of death and confiscation of property. This, as previously noted, was the first step which would ultimately lead to the Inquisition, but it would have meant that if, as I argue, Lopes was a New Christian, then the royal decree would have forbidden him from returning to Saint Helena. Hence the need for the Papal letter which would have acted as a dispensation. In the face of the cryptic sentences we are reduced to conjecture, but could it be possible that Lopes, knowing he would not be allowed to leave Portugal, had requested the Papal letter as a means of return?

Between the hours of 4am and 5am of 26 January 1531, with Lopes back in Lisbon preparing for his voyage to Saint Helena, a strong earthquake struck the city. The waters of the Tagus flooded downtown Lisbon, and several dwellings along the estuary. Ships were deposited above the waterline. The city suffered great damage with around one-third of its buildings destroyed. Many homes were devastated, with most of the damage concentrated downtown. Meanwhile the cathedral as well as the monastery at Belém suffered structural damage, though neither collapsed. Around 1,000 souls died that day.

A Portuguese contemporary chronicler noted that 'in this kingdom of Portugal there was much work, because there was plague and earthquakes, the earth shaking and houses and buildings falling down where many people died'. Resende, one of the King's chroniclers, wrote a poem describing the fateful day:

> Morning of Tuesday
> There was such a large
> Earthquake in Portugal
> No one ever saw alike
> The water grew with no wind
> Ships touched the ground
> Their keels reaching the bottom
> Like the others were lost
> All things alive

But Resende was in fact describing something more than an earth-quake. Another chronicler, Couto, described the agitation of the sea close to Lisbon:

> in the sea the tempest was so great that it destroyed and broke all ships staying in Lisbon harbour, some say that the Tagus river opened by its middle splitting its waters into a pathway and showing the sand bed.

The description among contemporary eyewitness accounts of a 'flux and reflux', and of how the water rundown was so large that significant areas of the river bed were exposed, strongly suggest that the earthquake generated a tsunami inside the Tagus' inner estuary.

Gil Vicente, the most important Portuguese writer of that time, at once wrote to the King urging him to declare the earthquake as a natural phenomenon and to stop local priests from reading signs in the devastation. Did Vicente have Solomon Molcho in mind? For the Portuguese, the two visions, so dramatically and, many believed, insanely announced, had come true. But Molcho had made a third declaration, one that was far more dramatic than the first two and that was that the Messiah would appear in the year 1540. While many now pondered this point, others asked themselves, how would the King respond? And what was to be done about the man who went by the name of Solomon Molcho?

It was during this time that João seized the moment to write to the Pope for permission to start an inquisition in Portugal, and he followed it one year later with a decree which forbade any New Christian from leaving the country under threat of death and confiscation of property. These two developments heralded a dark age which was about to descend upon Portugal. João may have wanted an inquisition, but Pope Clement VII was less enthu-siastic. He was unconvinced by the argument put forward by the

King of Portugal and sensed that an inquisition would be used by João partly to strengthen the state's control over ecclesiastical jurisdiction, so as to allow him to interfere in religious issues. Wealthy New Christians were also not slow in lobbying the Pope to halt any inquisition, with a simple argument. João, they said, desired an inquisition to ameliorate his finances since confiscation would serve as a form of taxation and directly benefit his treasury. New Christians, they stressed, were faithful Christians, and the King of Portugal was just after their money. Yes, there had been an outpouring of so-called prophets in Portugal but as Mestre Jorge Leão, a prominent physician who acted as spokesman for the New Christians, defiantly argued, how could the New Christians of Portugal be punished for the actions of madmen: 'sixty-thousand souls to be condemned [or live under threat of condemnation] because of some heretics who should be punished as men of good sense turned barmy? For none but lunatics can fall for such drivel'. In addition, the Pope was surrounded by many who were infused by the spirit and thoughts of humanism, and the demand of the Portuguese King for an inquisition struck them, following the Spanish Inquisition, as yet another example of Iberian barbarity. Clement VII was aware that beneath the masks of piety there lay a naked struggle for power between the King and the Church. In that sense João's stance on inquisition was interpreted by the Vatican as being analogous to that of other troublesome monarchs of Christendom, who in order to seize the Church's wealth were prepared to enter into open conflict with the Pope. And Clement VII certainly knew about troublesome kings, for his hands were full with the divorce case of King Henry VIII of England and his wife Catherine of Aragon, a divorce the Pope was determined not to grant. For the time being the Pope was swayed by the arguments of the New Christians and over the next few years he issued a series of conflicting bulls which would see him and his successors renew, revise and annul their actions.

The pendulum swung one way and the other, and at one stage Clement VII went as far as declaring that the original conversion of the Jews was void, as it had been done by force.

Eventually the pressure to grant the Inquisition that was placed on the Pope by the tirelessly obstinate João and by Portuguese public opinion won the day, especially when the Habsburg Emperor Charles V intervened on his son-in-law's behalf. The Pope could not turn a deaf ear to Charles' entreaty, for not only was he the most powerful monarch of the time, but perhaps more tellingly his own troops were stationed in Italy. And, lest the Pope forget, Charles' generals had once sacked Rome itself. João now staked his all and did not stop short of a thinly veiled threat, insinuating in a letter to the Pope that he would follow the example of King Henry VIII of England and formally break away from the Church of Rome. Thus, in 1536, the Inquisition in Portugal was irrevocably established. Its aim, officially at least, was to fight Lutheran and Muslim heresies as well as Jewish ones, but there were no Lutherans or Muslims to speak of in Portugal.

This is not the book in which to detail the twists and turns that followed until the Inquisition finally came into force, but when it did it was harsher and even more inhuman than the Spanish one. It reigned supreme over all other courts, civil and (as the Pope had feared) ecclesiastical, and it answered to the King alone. Over 20,000 Portuguese were condemned and incarcerated with hundreds or perhaps thousands dying in prison. At least 1,379 people were burned alive. So brutal was the Inquisition that, unable to intervene, Pope Paul III took the radical step of ordering it 'suspended', but to no avail since no one in Portugal was listening. The Portuguese Inquisition was known for its theatrics. It was a public event which aimed to deter those who were watching: to scapegoat, to display power and to entertain. It was a spectacle, both deliberate and stylised. Those accused heard their sentence, which could take up to half an hour, while kneeling in front of the altar. Some of those receiving sentences were stoic, while others knelt, beat their chests, prayed, cried or hung their heads. Frequently they protested, but to no avail. The aim of the Inquisition was to root out heresy among Christians. This meant that its greatest and most terrible irony was that it had no jurisdiction over or even interest in Jews per se. The Inquisition could only investigate people who had been baptised as Catholics. But since in Portugal the entire population had been baptised, what this effectively and obscenely meant was that everyone was under scrutiny. Thus, if a New Christian was found to be practising, or had practised, Judaism, this did not mean he was a Jew. What it did mean was that he or she was a *Judaizante* (Judaiser): a Catholic performing Jewish rituals. From 1536 onwards, priests called upon their parishioners, under threat of excommunication, to denounce anyone they believed to participate in such activities, grotesquely transforming the population into accomplices and terrorising the Portuguese people for the next 250 years.

The Inquisition did not cause anti-Jewish fervour. But it did institutionalise the hatred and create a bureaucracy to perpetuate it. Any cultural difference, however small, became the marker of a distinct ethnicity. Even the way a mother combed her daughter's hair might be reported to the Inquisition as suspicious behaviour. Everything was scrutinised: if a New Christian did not attend mass that was noted, and if they did, he or she could be accused of not behaving with sufficient decorum or piety. There was something primal about the Inquisition which went far deeper than religion or even economic or financial gain. At its most profound level the Inquisition was existential, for its aim was to define who was Portuguese and who was not. That is why religion was only one aspect of it, with the focus also being on ethnic, cultural and racial differences. What was being created, thanks to the Inquisition, was a Portuguese sense of self: a Portuguese identity, one forged by a monolithic Catholic religious orthodoxy and a monarchy that sharply contrasted with the relative tolerance of previous monarchs. The Inquisition also defined clearly who was *not* Portuguese, including not just Jews, Muslims and Lutherans, but also homosexuals, bigamists and nonconformists. If torture was needed to affirm, indeed stamp, this new identity and to establish its hegemony in the Portuguese psyche then so it had to be, for God's Will had to be done. In sharp contrast to the 20th-century poet Pessoa's lament and elegy, the Inquisition affirmed through its theatrical terror that henceforth the Portuguese had to live within the narrow bounds of one Portugal, one nation, and above all one religion. To be horrified by the iniquity of the Inquisition is only natural, but to classify it as simply medieval would be wrong, for in many ways in its methods and bureaucratic nature of its terror, in its secret espionage, in its informants and its seemingly detached judiciary apparatus, the Inquisition was a precursor of the totalitarianism of modern dictatorships.

Rome had flooded and Lisbon had shaken, but Solomon Molcho did not live till 1540 to see if his third vision, of the arrival of the Messiah, would come true, for by then João and Charles V, the Holy Roman Emperor, had both tired of the young man and had had him burned at the stake. Nor was the strange and enigmatic David Reubeni spared, for he too was burned alive.

By that time, Lopes was back on Saint Helena where he would remain for the rest of his life. As far as we know, Lopes and Reubeni had never crossed paths, except in the King's mind, but this was an age and a Lisbon where opportunists like Reubeni could emerge from nowhere, make outlandishly tinted messianic claims, and be entertained seriously before being burned at the stake. They were strange and dangerous times for Portugal. Had Lopes, now on the island, been informed of the trials that were starting to take place, he would probably have made no comment, but there is little doubt that he had sensed the way the people had spoken after the earthquake, blaming the New Christians, and in his heart, he would have understood that nothing had changed. Many years earlier as a young man he had left Lisbon for India, carrying within him a sense of unease that all was not well in his beloved kingdom. He had then felt the anger, hidden and open, directed against him, and it is my view that perhaps his worst fears had been realised with the massacre of the New Christians in 1506. Upon his forced return to Lisbon his sense of unease would have remained undiminished. A dark and ominous shadow loomed over Portugal. But in Lopes' heart and in his silence, he would also have known that the torture and hatred which had been inflicted upon him by Albuquerque, which demanded that he accept who he ought to be, rather than who he was, was in its way a microcosm of the torture which the King of Portugal now inflicted upon the Jews.

It is tempting to ask whether, during his stay in Lisbon, there had been a reunion with his wife and son. It had been 24 years since he had last seen them. He was now disfigured and certainly very different from the young man who had set sail from Belém. His actions in India had undoubtedly brought dishonour to the family and his son would not have recognised him anyway, as he was an infant when Lopes left. The sources are silent on this matter and in many ways that is natural, for why should they record something as insignificant as the meeting of a man and his estranged wife? Perhaps she had died, for there had been many outbreaks of the plague in the years that passed. Perhaps the plague had carried off his son as well. But in our hearts at least let us ignore the silence of the sources and hope that neither had died and some form of reconciliation had taken place.

CHAPTER TWENTY-THREE

A Mysterious Kingdom

'Out beyond ideas of wrongdoing
and rightdoing there is a field.
I'll meet you there.'

RUMI

By 1532 Lopes had returned to Saint Helena. Once again, he vanishes from the records with only fitful mentions of him. An unheaded report, dated around 1531, written by an anonymous Portuguese official to João III, mentioned Saint Helena. The author argued that it should be settled so as to fortify it against French vessels which were increasingly encroaching on the island. The report went on to argue that those who settled on the island would 'find that it gives wheat of good quality and chickens and there is salt like saltpetre and gum like incense or mastic'. The official then makes a rather curious statement: 'Fernão Lopes, the hermit, asked me to remind your Highness to send him the slave'. Perhaps Lopes had been promised a slave by the King during their meeting. The next time we hear from Lopes is a few years later in a letter, dated 23 May 1538, and it is

305

the only document which bears his handwriting and signature. Once again the letter relates to a slave and is clearly dictated by Lopes and addressed to João, but since he was unable to write it is drafted in elegant handwriting by another person. Lopes writes that one of the King's ships had arrived on the island captained by a certain Lopo Vaz Vogado, with one of the King's knights on board, by the name of Gonçalo Fernandes Ferreira. Lopes continues that Ferreira agreed to leave him a mixed-race slave who was a mason, as Lopes wanted to build shelters for the Portuguese on the island and he needed help. He then goes on to say that the slave would be his 'companion on this work' and explains to the King that Ferreira agreed to leave the slave with Lopes for one year during which the work would be completed. Lopes then makes the request that the King pay Ferreira the cost of the slave for that one year. At the end of the letter, in a markedly different and jagged handwriting which is barely legible, Lopes scribbles, with his left hand, a blessing on the King and signs his name. It is an interesting letter for many reasons. For the first time, we can hear Lopes' voice. He may not have written the first part but he clearly dictated it, probably to Ferreira. It deserves to be quoted in full:

My Lord
To this island has reached a ship from Your Highness captained by Lopo Vaz Vogado in which goes Gonçalo Fernandes Ferreira, knight from your household; on my request, he [Lopes refers here to Gonçalo] left me a mixed race mason slave to do some shelter for people who arrive here, at the island, with your ships. Dom João Pereira [one of the King's noblemen who would have been present on the island] and other individuals present at the ship will tell you; and, by being here after the departure of the ship, this slave, with certain conditions suitable for God's and Your work, is going to be my companion on this work; I request Your Highness that this slave can be

paid to Gonçalo Fernandes, who left him here under the condition of returning [the slave] in a year so that, despite being yours [ultimately the slave belonged, as did all things, to the King], I can have him here, benefiting from his company, while my days last; I pray to Our Lord [God] in order to enhance your state and domains and to let you finish in His service

Island of Santa Helena / 23rd May 1538 /

Lopes addresses João in a formal but direct and functional manner with no fawning. He needs help to build some shelters (Lopes would have been nearly 60 years of age) and he is confident enough to ask that João compensate Ferreira for the use of his slave since the King knows he has no money himself. At the same time one is struck by the humility of the letter: Lopes does not say that the slave will do the work, but that he will be 'my companion with the work'. In addition, and as happened when Lopes met the King in Lisbon, he asks for nothing for himself, nor does he request that the slave remain any longer than the one year to complete the task at hand.

In between the years mentioned, the Portuguese captains would return to Lisbon and report how Lopes greeted them and how the crew fed on the oranges and other fruits that were now so plentiful that they fell to the ground in abundance, or how they had feasted on the goats and sheep and pigs that roamed freely all over the island. Lopes it seemed was everywhere, scurrying among the trees, pointing out new fruits that he had planted a few months earlier and reminding some of the crew who had visited the island previously of how big the trees had grown. And so the years passed, year by year, until 1546 when a Portuguese captain reported, in a few brief words, that Fernão Lopes had passed away on the island and that he had been buried there. Since there is no mention of any previous illnesses one imagines it was a natural death, for by then he was 66 years old, an advanced age for the period. The captain's note does not make clear whether Lopes had been found dead or had died while the ship was there. In total, he had been on the island, with a brief sojourn in Lisbon, for over 30 years, alone for most of that time, during which he had patiently cultivated the land while cultivating his soul.

It was in many ways a life of extremes. Lopes was born during the country's Golden Age, an age when it appeared, for a shimmering moment, that, in this Portuguese dawn, in this wide world, all was possible. He lived during the 40 or so years which divided Manuel's forced conversion of the Jews to João III's Inquisition, when Jews became New Christians, only for them to discover to their cost that they were neither new nor Christian. He had returned briefly to Lisbon, but that was not of his choice, and what he saw there simply made him determined to return to the island, withdrawing while events darkened the soul of Portugal. I could easily have called this book *The Lives of Fernão Lopes*. There was a life of which we simply know nothing, one where Lopes carried a different name and worshipped a different God (that it should happen once in a man's life is an extraordinary event, but I consider that in Lopes' case it had occurred twice). In his Muslim life he would carry a Muslim name (lost to us) and worship a different God. There was a life as a Portuguese squire and knight in India, one full of colour and adventure, wealth and ambition, and there was a life on a deserted island, one of solitude and reflection, self-recrimination and redemption. And yet there was only one Fernão Lopes whose mind and soul were subjected to these many fissures and fragmentations. In many ways he died as enigmatically as he lived and it is tempting to ask who the real Fernão Lopes was. Which one of the many variations was the closest to the original? This is an absurd question. In the many different stages of his life Lopes was who he was, a man searching for an identity, a soul searching for a centre.

How do we attempt to make sense of Lopes' spiritual

transformation on the island? The fact that he did not, apart from the letter quoted above, leave any writings behind or have any companions to pass on his story makes it a near impossible task as we can only view him through the eyes of others, and even then fleetingly. For Lopes the island presented an inherent paradox: it was an inescapable exile where death or misfortune could befall him at any time, a place where he was helpless. At the same time, it was a place of reconciliation, of acceptance, of life and peace. Like Plato's cave, the island was a 'conversion and a turning about of the soul', and an 'ascension to reality'. Islands have always occupied a powerful place in the imagination of men, though clearly the island as a site for such personal transformation is never encountered in so immediate a way as in the case of Fernão Lopes. The very nature of a piece of land which is separated from us by water renders it a very powerful symbol, one encountered and imagined only in folkloric literature. In *The Legend of King Arthur*, souls find their final resting place on the island of Avalon, while in *Orlando Furioso*, Ludovico Ariosto, writing in 1532, evokes an island, supposedly in the Indian Ocean, inhabited by an enchanted witch. Islands were the places where heroes retreated to rest, that drew people to them but never let them leave, where treasure was hidden and magic was found. Islands were Edens, Arcadias, bridges between one world and the other. We have already spoken about the mythical island of Antilla which was so embedded in the collective imagination of the Portuguese.

When Lopes arrived on Saint Helena he was a broken man, full of despair and anguish both physically and spiritually. As a young man, Lopes (and, I think, his traumatised soul) had made the physical journey to India. In Bijapur and in Islam he had found a peace which had acted as a balm (*I am a Muslim and I shall die a Muslim*) but fate dictated that this peace be temporarily taken from him so that he could die again before he could live. The island provided him with a place to question himself and his world and everything in which he had previously trusted and believed. It is also important to stress that Lopes was not a castaway. He *chose* to be on the island, and though one accepts that at first he may have done so out of fear or self-destruction, it does not explain why he chose to remain there for so many years. Nor of course does it explain why he chose to return. Something undetermined but certain inside Lopes made him choose to remain on the island. It was the same certainty he had felt when João Machado had offered him a chance to become Christian and save himself, and he had turned him down. If I choose to use the image of an embarkation point I do so with caution, since though in one sense one can write about the spiritual journey of Lopes, the reality was that, other than circumambulating the island, Lopes remained in one isolated place. There were of course 'lesser' journeys: from Lisbon to Goa to Saint Helena, from one faith to another, but they were in many ways ones embarked on in shallow waters, in seas of monotheism and with the shore in sight. The real voyage, the inner one, the one beyond any shore, required no corresponding physical one. It required stillness and silence. What is extraordinary about Lopes' spiritual experience was that he was exposed to total isolation for so many years, literally cut off from the world. The silence, the absolute silence, which engulfed him would have driven most men mad but in the case of Lopes it did not. In some mysterious manner, it healed him and it transformed him. The *how* is the great mystery. Contemporary sources certainly recognised the transformation: the words hermit and mystic were often used to describe Lopes. In addition, the decision of the King to see him must have been motivated by more than mere curiosity, for royalty do not grant audiences to just anyone. If the Papal meeting did after all actually take place, then this only confirms that Lopes must have possessed a spiritual quality which was recognised and respected in his day but which today we are unable to grasp or comprehend.

Today the word solitary is invariably associated with confinement, a state which often leads to hallucinations and wild mood swings as well as panic attacks and depression. That Lopes may have suffered some of these symptoms we will of course never know, although it would be astonishing if he had not, since solitude produces melancholy. And yet what we do know is that Teixeira found him lucid, as did the King of Portugal, as did the Pope. For modern man the sheer scale of isolation which Lopes subjected himself to is almost incomprehensible, primarily because today we live almost exclusively in relation to others, constantly wanting to be recognised, to be connected. Above all, to be validated. Increasingly our reality becomes dependent less on who we are and more on how we are seen by others. How many followers do I have on Twitter? How many friends on Facebook? How many Google hits does my name generate? If we dread one thing it is being cut off from our social group even for a moment, the fear of missing out. But the fear never diminishes, nor does the shadow recede. Young people today can barely comprehend the concept of solitude, nor even imagine why one should be alone. And yet they fear it: not so much the solitude, but the loneliness with its attendant anxiety and grief, and the incessant use of technology is a constant effort to stave off its shadow. There was a time when we called our friends once a day but now we call or contact them a hundred times, day and night, and in so doing we have lost our ability to be alone and our capacity for solitude. Yet there is a dignity to solitude, an opportunity to confront and meet oneself in a moment of silence and in so doing recognise that we are not just social beings, and that each of us is separate, solitary, unique, each one containing a mysterious path within ourselves, leading to a hidden treasure which expresses itself in many layers. It is precisely the scale of his solitude and its transformative nature which makes the story of Fernão Lopes so fascinating.

To attempt even a humble approach to understand Lopes' spiritual journey we first need to try to understand in what terms his contemporaries would have conceptualised his spirituality. When people referred to Lopes as a mystic, what did they mean? There can be no better guide in this task than the writings of St John of the Cross, who would have been a boy when Lopes died and who as a priest, scholar and mystic is considered one of Christianity's greatest writers on mysticism and spirituality. He dedicated his life and his writings to one aim: to transmit his own experience of God's mystery so that others might share the same experience and be transformed by it. At the heart of this experience lay the fundamental and immutable principle that silence is the language of God. In one of his most striking sayings, St John wrote that God speaks always in eternal silence, and in silence must be heard by the soul. For Lopes, one can imagine that the silence was initially terrifyingly empty, as his mind raced to fill the chasm with memories, some real but many false, and with countless prejudices, false judgements, afflictions and anxieties. Above all, thoughts and memories of revenge. But in the face of solitude all that mattered was stripped bare and rendered obsolete. Physical appearance certainly, as well as noble comportment. Ideas and thought would have lost their significance. Even the rituals of religion which Lopes had tried to hang on to all his life now appeared redundant. He had forgotten the Arabic prayers he had so assiduously memorised and though for a while he probably continued to prostrate himself, one imagines he soon ceased. To Lopes, on the island, the world and his life appeared meaningless. Days of despair where he felt that he had dropped off the face of the earth would have been woven into days when he felt he was at the centre of the universe and that he was God's sole focus.

It was the island which had saved him from madness, for surely he would have committed a sin and killed himself otherwise. The island taught him that it is not what one gains but what one loses that matters, for when one loses everything that which remains is who one is. The island taught Lopes that silence is difficult and confusing, but that it was necessary to live in the trust of God. It taught him that God is a mystery, and that silence is the key to this mystery, for only in its depth can the Absolute be heard. He was alone on the island, totally alone. For months and years he saw no one, spoke to no one, other than those who stopped at the island. He was cut off from the world. And yet in the crystalline light and the crisp air, under the scudding clouds and starry nights, probably he never felt alone. It is natural to think that isolated on the island he was somehow cut off from the world, but the reality was that there was always something to see, something to hear. He may have left the world but the world had never left him. On the island he could still love everyone he had ever loved. Whether the moon reflected on the ocean surrounding the island or the Tagus River, it was still the same moon, he was still the same man.

On the island, he would have realised that only he could save himself. He had never been a practical man but he surprised himself by how well he had managed, and though there were times when he felt he was going to die, his body wracked with fever, in those moments when he thought about death he was likely not afraid. Instead he had learned to plant and to fish, skills he would never have thought he possessed. What was it like on the island? Perhaps sometimes he sang songs he recalled from his childhood, or danced. Some nights, perhaps, he counted the stars until sleep overtook him. Many nights he surely wept. He had begun to plant.

Silence had many faces. There was the silence of listening to waves crashing on the breakers and the silence of a spider waiting for its prey. There was the silence of the mind and the silence of the heart. And then there was the most profound silence: when silence was not the surrounding and the context but the being and the content. In his long meandering walks or as he watched the dolphins out in the ocean oblivious in their joy, or even when he felt overwhelmed and crushed by the weight of the stars, Lopes would have been silent, but this silence was a positive presence, complete in itself. Do not be fooled that silence does not possess its own power, its own authority, for it has a presence that cannot be contained in words. Silence is alive and vibrant, its own mysterious kingdom. On the island, he would have felt that it was both detached from him and part of him. And it would have shifted constantly, with moments of blissful silence when it seemed like his heart was about to burst with joy and when he felt that in that moment he had all that he had ever desired. But silence would soon show him a different visage, one of an ominous terror which weighed so heavily on him that it paralysed him and he felt that he had to shake himself just to get his heart beating again. There was a horror to the stillness, one pregnant with memories which haunted him, and the despair of knowing that all that he could look forward to was its tyranny. But that moment also passed.

On the island, Lopes endured his dark night of solitude, the spiritual stages of which St John of the Cross so movingly wrote, and it was during his journey through this night that he reached the nadir of his existence, which he had been convinced was forsaken, and underwent a transformation in relation to the world and to God. Where once there was despair, he began to sense in the silence of his mind, as his memory was emptied, an inner stillness and freedom which went beyond words. He gradually came to understand that there was nothing to fear and that God was not an abstract divinity, but that He was an inexpressible mystery closer to him than his jugular vein, yet far beyond his imagining at the same time. Slowly Lopes began to comprehend that he was not lonely. He was alone. Alone in the sacred silence of God. In solitude he lived, and in solitude he built his nest, and in silence God guided his soul, purifying it quietly and secretly without the soul knowing how, and without the sound of words. This was the great mystery. The mystery of silence, the mystery of the sacred.

CHAPTER TWENTY-FOUR

'A Desert out of a Paradise'

'And the Earth discharges her burdens ...'
QURAN 99.2

The history of Saint Helena in the years which followed the death of Fernão Lopes is a dispiriting one. As I briefly recount the tragic fate of this paradise lost over the past 500 years, one can sense gathering clouds of melancholy thickening over it to such an extent that not even the hoped-for aeroplanes can dissipate them. With the airport comes renewed hope, but history refuses to loosen its grip, and even as the airport was being constructed, as late as 2014, the island's earth revealed and brought forth a further macabre reminder of Saint Helena's legacy of sorrow.

In the years following Lopes' death Saint Helena remained largely uninhabited. Ten years or so after his death, there is mention in the records that several slaves escaped there, abandoning the ships which stopped at the island, and provisioning themselves with 'half-wild cattle, goats, and swine as well as plantations of vegetables and fruit'. Another ten years or so passed before the island recorded its first permanent structure, which naturally was a chapel, on whose altar 'stood a large table, set in a frame, having on it the picture of our Saviour Christ upon the cross, and the image of our Lady praying'. In 1588 the English navigator Thomas Cavendish visited the island and came across pheasants, partridges and guinea fowl. He also recorded 'thousands of goats … are very wild; you shall see one or two hundred of them together, and sometimes you may behold them going in a flock almost a mile long … we took and killed many of them for all their swiftness, for there be thousands of them upon the mountains'. The swine, he recorded, were 'very wild, very fat and of a marvellous bigness'. For those traversing the South Atlantic Ocean the island was always a welcome sight. For Jan Huygen van Linschoten, a Dutch traveller voyaging on a Portuguese ship, there was, upon sighting Saint Helena, 'great joy in the ship, as if we had been in heaven … It is an earthly paradise.' Other than the goats, Linschoten noted that there was an abundance of fish, fruit and wood. However, not all visitors, it seems, were impressed, for a chronicler writing in 1600 blandly noted that the island 'is not an earthly Paradise, as it is reported', although intriguingly no further details are offered. Six years later, in 1606, the navigator John Davis mentioned the goats and pigs as well as a 'great store of Partridges, Turkie, Cockes and Ginnie Hennes'. Davis made one further remark: 'This island is not inhabited.' That, however, was to change, for in 1634, a report stated that besides the chapel there were about 40 or 50 dwellings which had been built by the Portuguese.

Change was already in the air, and this was noted by the more observant visitors. Although the French traveller Pyrard de Laval extolled the virtues of Saint Helena when he visited the island in 1610, writing that 'Providence has bestowed upon it all that is best of air, earth and water and nowhere in the world I believe will you find an island of its size to compare', he also noted that the once-plentiful fruit trees had all but disappeared and had to be searched for. Laval blamed the Dutch but it seems the Portuguese and the English were also not faultless, for each crew stopping at the island had endeavoured to cut down the fruit trees while they were still in flower, so as not to leave them to the others. They were acts of wanton destruction and vandalism, as noted by Tavernier when he visited Saint Helena in 1649:

> There are quantities of lemon trees and a few orange trees, planted originally by the Portuguese. For these people have one thing to their credit, that wherever they go they attempt to improve the place for those who come after. The Dutch do just the reverse and destroy everything so that those who follow after them shall find nothing. It is true that this is not due to their leaders but to the sailors who, knowing that they are not likely to return to the place, combine together to cut down the trees so as to get all the fruit with the least trouble.

It is important to mention the goats, for of all the animals which were introduced to the island they were to cause immeasurable destruction and constituted the single most effective agent of deforestation and landscape change. Goats may have been introduced when Lopes was still in situ, to provide passing ships with fresh meat, but soon they were everywhere on the island, overrunning it, devouring the young plants and the leaves of the trees which were within reach and hindering any forest regeneration. In 1588 the governor, Captain Quendol, noted that there were thousands of goats and that they 'were seen one or two hundred together, sometimes in a flock almost a mile long'. When the English navigator Lancaster made a return visit to the island in 1603 to get fresh meat and water he remarked that the goats had become very wild and difficult to manage, and in 1610 the Frenchman Laval recorded that 'it would be impossible to ascend and still more descend' the hills without trampling or being trampled by them. Not only did goats have a long and extremely destructive effect on the vegetation and on the ability of the forests to regenerate, they also constituted a direct threat to the survival of domestic stock. By the 1690s they had reached plague proportions and in 1816 official British records noted that 'to the goat is solely to be ascribed the total ruin of the forests and evil which is now sorely felt by every individual living on the island'.

The rats quickly followed the goats in spreading across the island, and soon made their distinctive appearance. In 1666, a traveller noted the 'vast quantities of rats upon which the Governor wages a sanguinary war'. They were 'sorely vexatious', and 'mischievous vermin', and in 1698 Legaut judged that 'the few inhabitants of this island might live much better, or more at ease, were it not for a prodigious number of rats that spoil their fruit and corn'. The cats it seems were uninterested, as in 1717 it is stated that the rats ate up all the grain as soon as it was sown, and this in spite of a 'vast number of cats, that went away from the houses and became wild, living among the rocks, where they found good [food] feeding on young partridges, so that they became as great a plague as the rats'. Mice were also abundant, particularly in the more barren lowland areas, where they were so slow and lazy that they might be caught by hand with ease. In the face of the rats, cats and dogs (which had been gradually introduced to the island), native land birds and the burrowing petrels were defenceless, and what took place on Saint Helena was an extermination which involved the imported animals destroying the indigenous fauna, including birds, and feeding on the plants and young trees. In addition, the impact on the native vegetation was extremely deleterious so that today the only part of it that remains, the tree fern, is confined to a small area on the high central ridge of the island and numerous endemic plant species are becoming rapidly extinct. To blame the goats or the rats for the deforestation of the island may add some colour, but it would not be telling the full story. The real culprit of the destruction of the natural habitat of Saint Helena was man. To understand this better, it is first necessary to briefly examine the torturous history of the island and the East India Company, a history of indiscriminate deforestation and burning.

Over the years, the island had become increasingly important for the London East India Company as a place where their vessels could take on fresh supplies and as a place of rendezvous for their homeward-bound shipping. Inevitably the idea of colonising the island remained uppermost for the Company, who had ambitious plans to transform it into a plantation economy. Thus, one of the Company's minutes of December 1658 noted that 400 men were to remain 'on the island, with conveniences to fortifie and begin a plantation there'. All, it seemed, appeared both promising and propitious. The Company attempted to establish a plantation agriculture model based on the North American colonies and the West Indies. However, this was in a small area of very high relief with variable rainfall. In addition, it was convinced that in the course of clearing the forests and planting crops, a 'purely beneficial process of improvement' would be achieved. But the company had not accounted for two critical factors: it was certainly not aware that forest clearance for plantation could lead to devastating environmental calamities. Not that the Company lacked information, for in 1676 it had funded the six-week expedition to Saint Helena by Sir Edmund Halley for the purpose of observing the transit of Venus, during which trip research was also conducted on the water storage capacities of bare soil and rocks on the island, although sadly with no relevant conclusions drawn.

The Company's initial concern, it seemed, was to convince those who had been sent to the island to actually do some planting since 'several persons have many times neglected the planting and improving of ye lands allotted to them and have taken the liberty to hunt and kill many of the goats'. By 1700, however, the dangers and unpredictable consequences of deforestation and drought were already beginning to be recognised. Already by the turn of the century ship crews were complaining about the shortage of water on the island. The Astronomer Royal Sir Edmund Halley himself noted the threat to the island after his second visit in 1700, when he recorded that 'the continued rains made the water so thick with a brackish mud that when settled it was scarce fit to drink'. Deforestation also meant that crops were frequently being blasted and destroyed by dry winds during drought periods and soon other issues emerged, such as the burning of large amounts of wood for the distillation of arrack which was the main island spirit. In other cases, the devastation was simply due to carelessness and neglect. The redwood and the ebony trees were destroyed by the tanners who 'for laziness never took pains to bark the whole tree but only the bodies'. Certainly, by the time of the arrival of the new governor, John Roberts, the consequences of deforestation appeared irreversible. The governor noted gloomily that within twenty years, the island would be 'utterly ruined for want of wood, for no man upon Saint Helena can say there is one tree in the great Wood, or other wood, less than 20 years old, consequently it will die of age'. Despite the governor's pronounced concerns, flat valley land was cleared to produce fruit and vegetables and further cutting of trees was carried out for lime burning and tanning skins – both these practices being very wasteful of timber. Governor Roberts' concerns were justified. By 1713 the island was in the midst of a drought which saw more than 2,000 cattle die and the Company's records noted starkly that the island 'was in a very bad and deplorable condition'.

The Company had one aim only and that was to make money. This meant that everything on Saint Helena belonged to the Company. A man who owned a pig could not slaughter it until he got a licence from them, and if he wished to sell its meat he needed another licence. Neither birds nor goats could be killed and all sea birds belonged to the Company. The inhabitants of the island worked for the governor – initially there had been 70 men and women who were the first to arrive to settle it. They had been sold the idea of a paradise to entice them to leave England and to make the crossing, but the reality was that the poverty they carried with them continued to be fixed firmly on their backs. They were little better than the slaves, and they quickly found out that if a man did not work hard enough (that is, did not generate enough money for the Company) their land was confiscated and they were returned empty-handed back to England. Those who inhabited the island considered their situation a state of exile few of them had any hopes of getting away from. Isolation normally would have brought people together for companionship and entertainment, but writing in the early 19th century, a visitor noted that most of the inhabitants 'pass the remainder of the year apart from each other'.

By 1700 Saint Helena was extensively deforested and soil erosion and deep gullying were widespread. When Sir Joseph Banks, who was later to become president of the Royal Society, visited the island in 1771, he was shocked at what he saw, contrasting it unfavourably with the situation at the Cape colony. There, he claimed, the Dutch colonists had made a 'Paradise out of a Desert', while in Saint Helena the English had made 'a Desert out of a Paradise'.

The island's most famous visitor was of course Napoleon, and part of the island's administration was temporarily transferred to the British government from 1815 to 1821, while he was exiled there. While the literature on Napoleon's exile is extensive, it ignores the island almost completely, as if it were little more than an empty stage on which the Corsican played out the final act of his life. We read that Napoleon's heart sank when he first set eyes on his future home, its appearance foreboding little but gloom ahead. He had expected the luxury of fruit trees and rich forests.

Instead he found himself in a desolate land called Deadwood Plain over which a stubborn fog of melancholy hovered. We know that Napoleon was familiar with the story of Fernão Lopes, the other exile, but for the Emperor it was little more than an amusing anecdote. In any case, he hated this isolated island on which he was imprisoned.

In the years immediately following Napoleon's death on the island, Saint Helena handled up to 1,000 ships a year. But there were fewer and fewer reasons for ships to stop there. Just as sailing ships became faster, the preservation of foodstuffs was becoming better and cheaper, meaning that there was no real cause to put in for fresh food and water. In 1834 the island was transferred to the British government when it became a Crown Colony. This not only took the ownership and administration of the island away from the East India Company but also removed the Company's financial support of the island. The results became gradually clear; the island's situation changed from that of a vibrant economy to one of poverty and virtually no economy. Visiting the island in 1836, within two years of the transfer, Charles Darwin commented on the severe poverty of the locals. He also noted how the goats had destroyed the forests, adding bleakly that as late as 1716 there were many trees but that by 1724 the old ones had mostly fallen, describing Saint Helena as 'so utterly a desert that nothing could make me believe that they could have grown there'. In 1869, with the opening of the Suez Canal, the dwindling number of ships calling fell further, and Saint Helena's military garrison was substantially reduced. Subsequently, the number of ships stopping at the island fell from 1,044 in 1860 to a mere 51 in 1910. The reduction in the number of ships soon became reflected in the population as it fell from 5,838 in 1871 to 3,342 in 1901. In 1900 the Boer War led to a temporary boost for the economy of the island when 6,000 prisoners of war, including the South African Zulu Chief Din Zulu, and their captors were stationed there. Two huge camps were built and for three years the Boers became part of island life. Many worked as builders, farmers and carpenters but very few stayed on when the bulk left around 1903. As the years passed people continued to speculate about the potential riches to be made from the island but these were largely fool's dreams. One man was convinced he had found gold but there was none on the island, just some iron pyrite. Coffee beans, sugar cane and indigo were planted but none flourished. In 1874, New Zealand flax was introduced and a small flax industry was started, only to close in 1881. Another attempt to revive the industry plodded along until 1967 when it finally shut down, an outcome it is claimed caused by the British Post Office changing from string to rubber-bands but probably more a result of competition from man-made fibres.

At present, the economy is limited to some domestic food and wood for fuel, fish for domestic consumption and export, and a few handicrafts. Napoleon's home during his exile, and his tomb, remains naturally and inevitably the island's main attraction point for any potential tourism. There are gift shops and arts and crafts for sale, and cruise ships occasionally stop at the island. In real terms gross domestic product (GDP) on Saint Helena increased annually by only 0.7 per cent on average between 1999/2000 and 2009/10, a consequence of a lack of significant export earnings, weak productivity and little investment as well as population decline. Once a flourishing community, Saint Helena is now characterised by migration, remittances and aid. Unemployment remains high and the island remains dependent on financial assistance while the historical solution to its economic problems has been migration. In 1981 the islanders even had their British citizenship rights taken away (which had been conferred on them by a Royal Charter of 1673) and lost their right of access to the UK as well as any right to a British passport. The Act was passed to prevent immigrants from Hong Kong entering the UK after Hong Kong was handed over to China in 1997 (however, it should be noted that two of the British Overseas Territories, Gibraltar and the Falklands, were exempt from the Act). Without a British passport, the islanders' long-standing option of migration was blocked and travel without a visa or permit became almost impossible for the Saint Helenians, known as the Saints. They have since had their rights returned to them, under the Labour Government of Tony Blair, and in 2002 the Saints were once more entitled to a British passport and a right of abode in the UK. This has simply led to more islanders leaving Saint Helena. In 1987 the population was recorded as 5,644; by 2003 it had been reduced to 3,900. More recent counts have estimated it to have slightly risen again to 4,030. Among the islanders there remains the strong belief that 'to better oneself, one has to leave the island'. Although there exists a genuine sense of loyalty and love for the unique quality of life and the sense of belonging, the camaraderie and security found on Saint Helena, many still feel the need to leave and appreciate this quality from afar. With the restoration of the islanders' full British citizenship a quarter of the population has gone to Britain, mainly younger men and women with skills and training. Only a handful have chosen to return.

To this day, the sense of isolation and melancholy endures. Writing in 1994 in the *Spectator*, a frustrated Ross Clarke complained, 'It is not easy to find out anything about Saint Helena. It is impossible to go there unless you have six months to spare.'* The inevitable sense of disappointment in this most isolated of tourist pit stops is almost surreal. 'The main artery, Napoleon Street, was deserted, save for a woman standing outside a hardware store and a group of passengers from the ship.' So wrote the author Harry Ritchie in 1997 in his book *The Last Pink Bits: Travels Through the Remnants of the British Empire*. 'They were walking up the street as if they were on a reconnaissance party

* The *Spectator*, 3 September 1994, 18

from the Starship Enterprise checking out a suspiciously abandoned settlement.'*

In 2016 the long-awaited and endlessly delayed airport was
finally meant to open on the island of Saint Helena, thereby
dragging one of the most inaccessible places on earth into the
modern world. The aim is to market Saint Helena as a high-value
destination and a green location, with plans for up to 30,000 visitors a year. This would naturally require significant improvements
in standards on the island and there are plans to establish local
fishing, agriculture, coffee and distilling industries. The opening
of the airport naturally brings with it a giddy sense of hope that
finally Saint Helena will be connected to the world. But it should
not simply be assumed that the airport would automatically result
in an increase in the number of tourists. It took a number of years
for tourism on Easter Island and the Galapagos to increase after
airports were built, while on Montserrat the number of visitors did
not increase, even after its airport opened in 2005. Among some
there is also a sense of trepidation that not just a way of life, but
the land itself, the water and the marine resources could be threatened by a wide range of pests and diseases. A small and isolated
environment like Saint Helena, with its limited natural habitat,
would certainly face an increased biosecurity risk. These risks
come in many forms, such as vertebrates and plant and aquatic
diseases. The loss of the natural quarantine which the island has
been afforded could make Saint Helena especially vulnerable.
Whether it has the capacity to confront and to respond quickly
to this potential environmental challenge is uncertain.

The airport has yet to open, and it is remarkable to think that
in 2017, just as it was in 1815 when Napoleon landed on the
island, just as it was in 1516 when Lopes first arrived, the only

* Harry Ritchie, *The Last Pink Bits: Travels Through the Remnants of the
British Empire*, London: Sceptre Books, 1997, 218

way to reach Saint Helena was by sea. The airport is meant to bring renewed hope to the just under 5,000 inhabitants of the island, with some hoping that it would become a niche tourist destination. One wonders, though, whether the mode of transport is sufficient to lift the thick veil of solitude and melancholy which is so deeply woven into the fabric of this ancient island whose very nature is isolation. As this book was being written, it was announced that the airport's planned opening in 2016 had been delayed indefinitely as the crosswinds made landings unsafe. It appears that the island is not prepared to relinquish its isolation easily.

The island has stopped producing its own food. There had been a time when, thanks to seeds planted by Lopes, Saint Helena was resplendent with groves of lemons, oranges, pomegranate, dates, mangoes and an array of other tropical fruit, providing enough fruit in the 18th century to provision 800 sailing ships which called annually. It now has to import its food and cannot feed its more than 4,000 Saints.

≈

In 1840 ships arriving at the island to be broken down brought the termite *Cryptotermes brevis* with them which quickly spread, causing irreparable damage to the wooden buildings. Then the wet wood termite *Heterotermes platycephalus* also arrived, killing off many of the remaining trees. At the end of the 18th century an insect imported from Mauritius, one which was so minute it was not visible to the naked eye, destroyed almost all the peach trees, the trunks of which became covered with a white crust before they withered and died.

≈

In 2008 while excavating ground for a new road that had to pass through Rupert's Valley on Saint Helena to provide access to the future airport, a grizzly and gruesome discovery was made as the earth slowly revealed its secrets – thousands of hastily buried skeletons, some of them piled in layers. In some graves between four and seven individuals were inhumed on top of each other. Archaeologists were quick to determine that what had been stumbled upon was not a cemetery but a mass disposal of the dead. Few of the bodies were deliberately positioned, although some were laid side by side, head to toe or stacked. It was estimated that roughly 8,000 to 10,000 skeletons were buried there. The question of who they were and what had brought them to die in such an isolated place reveals one of the darkest episodes in the history of Saint Helena. It should be noted, though, that to talk of a 'discovery' of burial grounds is to some extent misleading because on the island itself the existence of these poor souls has never been forgotten.

The history of the slave burial ground on Saint Helena can be traced back to the 1839 Act for the Suppression of the Slave Trade which authorised British warships to detain Portuguese vessels equipped for the slave trade. The island acted as the landing place for many of the slaves, captured by the Royal Navy during the suppression of the trade between 1840 and 1872. Initially the idea that Saint Helena may become a depot for the freed slaves – recaptives – until they were shipped to the West Indian colonies was dismissed by the British with Lord Russell, the Secretary of War and the Colonies, stating, 'it is, I trust, highly improbable that any Africans who may be captured by Her Majesty's cruisers will be landed at Saint Helena'. Events however were proving Lord Russell's words wrong. The first major capture sent to Saint Helena was in December 1840 when HMS *Waterwitch* dispatched a Portuguese vessel to the island carrying 215 slaves, many of whom were afflicted by smallpox. Next came the *Louiza* carrying 420 slaves, of whom 82 had died during the passage. The numbers continued to increase, as did the death toll. By August 1841, the island had taken a total of 1,824 recaptives of whom 467 had died.

At first the dead were simply dumped into the ocean, but by December 1840 Doctor McHenry, one of the medical practitioners who worked tirelessly on behalf of the recaptives, wrote that there were so many being buried at sea that the bodies were simply washing ashore. He also noted that the fishermen were catching fish who had fed on the corpses. The number of recaptives landing at the island continued to increase after British cruisers were authorised to capture Brazilian slavers north and south of the equator, and between 1847 and 1849, 6,258 recaptives were received on Saint Helena, dying as they came. In 1849 the Bishop of Cape Town Robert Gray described the men and women: 'they had a worn look and a wasted appearance and were moved into the boats like bales of goods apparently without will of their own ... I never beheld a more piteous sight'. Another eyewitness account described a more harrowing sight:

> I went on board one of those ships as she cast anchor ... and the whole deck, as I picked my way from end to end, in order to avoid treading upon them, was thickly strewn with dead, dying and starved bodies ... Their arms and legs were worn down to about the size of a walking-stick. Many died as they passed from the ship to the boat, and indeed, the work of unloading had to be proceeded with so quickly that there was no time to separate the dead from the living.

Only a rough approximation can be afforded of how many perished. By the late 1860s and early 1870s most recaptives had left the island and Saint Helena returned once again to its stupor. Some left for the West Indies, while others went to Sierra Leone. In total the island received over 26,000 liberated slaves and though we cannot accurately calculate the number of deaths, we can safely surmise that of the 26,000, at least 8,000 died on the island. In fact, the figures are much worse as they do not account for those who died during the journey. By the turn of the century the slaves had all left and in Rupert's Valley, which once housed thousands, a 1938 report stated, 'there is only one person on the island suffering from leprosy'.

The figures of the deaths only partly reveal, however, the heartbreaking horror of what had taken place. Of the skeletons discovered, only 5 per cent were of people who had died over the age of 45 and one in every three of the skeletons so hastily buried was that of a child under the age of twelve. The main afflictions were smallpox, yellow fever, dysentery, pneumonia and measles. But men, women and children died for many other reasons. Some died from what the doctors simply recorded as 'melancholy' which led to suicide. Other facts stick out: the skeletal discoveries confirm that a large number suffered from scurvy which, though not a cause of death, was certain one of debilitation. The presence of scurvy may at first appear surprising since it normally affected only those who embarked on long sea voyages, whereas the journey to Saint Helena took a maximum of three weeks. But what it perhaps demonstrates was not the length of the journey but the hardship and trauma of the environment in which the slaves were transported. Slave vessels were notoriously hot and many bodies on board were in an advanced state of decomposition.

Contemporary accounts could barely conceal the horror of what was taking place. In 1849 Doctor Vowell, the surgeon on the island, described 'the ferocity of the rats attacking the dying and the dead'. But contemporary accounts also help bring to life the slaves not as numbers of dead but as human beings, revealing fragile and poignant portraits of the men, women and children whose fate was to become enslaved and then perish on a remote island they never knew existed. Writing about the arrival of the recaptives at Saint Helena, George McHenry observed that although the majority were naked, many had sought some semblance of dignity by neatly plaiting their hair which they ornamented with strings of beads, and coins and pieces of metal. Some wore neck-laces and bracelets around their necks and arms while others wore large glittering copper rings around their legs for anklets. In 2008 when the skeletons were unearthed, many of the ornaments were found near the corpses. Glass bead jewellery was found scattered in the graves. It was also noted that the disarray of the limbs meant that the corpses were simply dropped into the graves. In some cases, mothers were buried with their presumed children, or sometimes the bodies were so close that one assumes they were a family clinging on to each other. No shrouds were used.

And still the island of Saint Helena continues to reveal its scarred and haunted past. On 12 December 2014, a human grave containing several skeletons was disturbed during road works. The airport contractor halted work as soon as the remains were found. Shortly afterwards an official statement was released: 'All evidence points to these being further liberated African remains'. For the locals, the unearthing of the island's tragic past did not come as news. After all, the stories and memories they carried within themselves and their community from generation to generation spoke not just of a Portuguese, English and Dutch ancestry, but also of one derived from Malay, Goanese, African and Madagascan slaves, of Chinese labourers and of Boer pris-oners of war. As an elderly local recalled, the island was a ghost island:

My Grandmother used to scare the living daylights out of us, if we wanted to go outside in the evening she would say the China man will get you. You know the place called China Lane, well that used to be a graveyard there. Well, houses were not built on there, and if we went as far as there, you'd turn round and come back just in case the China man was sitting on the grave, that's why it was called China Lane, it was a Chinese graveyard. The island can be very spooky when the clouds come down and the fog, and it all gets a bit dark and you can't see very far and it feels damp ... going from Longwood Gate, to Deadwood, they used to say that you would hear chains rattling of horses riding down there and the slaves screaming.

AFTERWORD

At what point do the two journeys of Fernão Lopes, the worldly and the spiritual, merge? We read in the story of *Hayy ibn Yaqzan*, as it is coming to an end, that Hayy is convinced to leave the island in the hope of enlightening others. He is, however, dismayed by what he sees, and fearing the ignorance of the people and their obsession with appearances, and so as not to be distracted from his spiritual pursuits, he returns to his island where he remains for the rest of his life. He understands that he had no need to travel and, having done so, he accepts that this brief voyage had been a mistake. And so it was with Lopes, for having reluctantly made the final voyage to Lisbon he rapidly came to understand that there was nothing there for him, for if the world in all its bewitchment, presenting itself in its most regal form of the King and the Pope, could not entice him, then nothing would. So, like Hayy, Lopes chose to return to the island. And this is how we need to understand that final journey, for unlike all the others which had gradually taken Lopes, via trials and tribulations, from the periphery to the centre, the one he undertook from Saint Helena to Lisbon was like a wave from the depth of an ocean in whose ebb he plunged, reaching the shore before being drawn back to where he had begun. This time there was no going back.

≈

At what point did others read Lopes' life for its symbolic meaning? We are offered a clue and once more we have to return to the story of *Hayy ibn Yaqzan*, though this time in a different guise. In the middle of the 17th century the Spanish Jesuit philosopher Baltasar Gracián wrote an allegorical tale which became one of the most influential in Spanish literature, called *El Criticón*. In this work Gracián describes the lives of Critilo and Andrenio, who meet when Critilo is shipwrecked on an island where he encounters Andrenio, who has been raised by wild animals and has never seen human beings. There is little doubt that Andrenio is the exact counterpart of Hayy ibn Yaqzan. A series of picaresque episodes with undertones of a rather sardonic and pessimistic philosophy, *El Criticón* was greatly admired by Voltaire. Certainly, *Candide* with its theme of a travelling naïf and his realist-tutor draws heavily from Gracián. But what is indisputable is that Gracián was influenced by Ibn Tufayl's *Hayy ibn Yaqzan*. He would have been familiar with the story of the autodidact philosopher since he was well versed with the writings of Pico della Mirandola, whom he refers to in his correspondence, and one assumes with Mirandola's translation of *Hayy ibn Yaqzan* which we mentioned earlier. Gracián uses the story of Hayy as a starting point for his allegorical novel and it is precisely the starting point, and our discovery of Andrenio on an isolated island, which for our purpose matters the most. If Gracián was familiar with the story of Hayy it seems that he was also familiar with that of Fernão Lopes, the Portuguese hermit, for in choosing an island on which to set the story of Andrenio, his version of *Hayy ibn Yaqzan*, Gracián chose an island which he describes as at the exact midpoint between East and West.

Gracián chose the island of Saint Helena.

A NOTE ON THE SOURCES

On All Saints day in 1755, a devastating earthquake struck Lisbon, with shock waves felt as far away as Scotland and Turkey. In just six minutes, the earthquake obliterated two-thirds of Lisbon's buildings including the Ribeira Palace, and destroyed the parish records and with it any hope of finding more documents about Fernão Lopes. Consequently, for the historian attempting to trace it, the life of Lopes is full of holes. The original sources exist and they mention Lopes infrequently, offering slight variations on the events. Before we look at these variations, it is important to list the sources.

(1) The *Corpo Cronológico* is a collection located in Torre do Tombo, the main Portuguese archive. This collection is divided in three parts, of which the first two are available online (http://digitarq.arquivos.pt/). The *Corpo Cronológico*, which was compiled by the Torre do Tombo keeper Manuel da Maia after the great earthquake of Lisbon, covers the period from the 12th century to 1699 and contains all kinds of manuscripts, for example letters from administrators of Portugal and the Portuguese Empire, King's orders, diplomatic information, financial books etc. There one finds a great deal of information regarding Afonso Albuquerque.

(2) The *Cartas de Affonso de Albuquerque seguidas de documentos que as elucidam* is a collection of documents about Afonso de Albuquerque published by Raimundo António de Bulhão

Pato and Henrique Lopes de Mendonça during the 19th and 20th centuries. This publication contains all the letters written and received by Afonso de Albuquerque, as well as all his orders and even documents simply mentioning the governor.

(3) The *Gavetas da Torre do Tombo* is a collection of twelve volumes of transcripted documents contained in the Torre do Tombo's collection of the same name. It was published by father António da Silva Rêgo during the 20th century. Similar to the *Corpo Cronológico* the documents cover all kinds of subjects including diplomatic, administrative and financial information.

(4) *Lendas da Índia* by Gaspar Correia narrates the adventures of the Portuguese in Asia between the voyages of Vasco da Gama between 1497 and 1550. It was published only in the 19th century. Gaspar Correia was born in 1492 and went to India in 1512, where he was secretary to Afonso de Albuquerque until 1515. As a result of his close contact he had access to many documents. After the governor's death, he continued to travel around most of the Indian shores in the Portuguese Crown service. It is unknown when he died, but in 1563 he was still alive in India. The importance of *Lendas da Índia* lies in the fact that Gaspar Correia was in India, so he partly witnessed some of the events he narrates.

(5) The *História da Conquista da Índia* by Fernão Lopes de Castanheda narrates the Portuguese presence in Asia and, like Gaspar Correia, the value comes from de Castanheda's having been present at some of the events. Born in Portugal, de Castanheda went to India in 1528. He was present at the attack on Diu in 1531 along with Gaspar Correia, so there is a possibility that the two men met there. De Castanheda stayed in India until 1548, when he returned to Portugal, where he died in 1559. There were supposed to be ten volumes of the *História*

da Conquista da Índia (ed. M. Lopes de Almeida, Porto: Lello & Irmão 1979, 2 vols), but the last two were lost.

(6) The *Comentários do grande Afonso de Albuquerque Capitão Geral que foi das Índias Orientais em tempo do muito poderoso Rey D. Manuel o primeiro deste nome* (Academia Real das Ciências de Lisboa, 1884–1935) by Brás de Albuquerque is also a very interesting source, which complements the *Cartas de Affonso de Albuquerque*. Brás de Albuquerque was a natural son of Afonso de Albuquerque. He wrote the *Comentários* based on the letters his father sent, to him and to the King. This source shows a more private side to Afonso de Albuquerque.

(7) João de Barros is probably the most famous chronicler of the *Estado da Índia*. Born around 1496, he was overseer of the Casa da Índia, the institution in charge of taking care of all the matters concerning the Portuguese Empire. In contrast to Gaspar Correia and Fernão Lopes de Castanheda, João de Barros never went to India and he gathered information about the Portuguese in Asia from second-hand sources, whether through the official documents from Casa da Índia or reports of men who returned from India. Barros wrote the *Dos Feitos que Os Portugueses Fizeram no Descobrimento e Conquista dos Mares e Terras do Oriente* (eds António Baião and Luís F. Lindley Cintra, Lisbon: Imprensa Nacional-Casa da Moeda, 1932–1974, 2 vols) as well as the *Décadas da Ásia*.

(8) Although Barros only wrote about the first four decades of Portuguese presence in Asia his efforts were continued by Diogo do Couto and António Bocarro, extending the book until 1617. Another example of a chronicler who never went to India was Damião de Góis. Born in 1502 he is very well known for being an important humanist and a friend of Erasmus. In 1545, he became

keeper of Torre do Tombo. Because of his ideas he was persecuted by the Inquisition. Among other books he wrote the *Crónica do Felícissimo Rei D. Manuel*.

To trace the story of Lopes through the sources mentioned above was a painstaking affair, one which threw up many variations which needed somehow to be rationalised. Below I list a few of the discrepancies and contradictions which appear in the sources.

- According to Castanheda, Lopes did not defect to the Bijapuris until after the siege of Goa when the city was in the midst of a famine and he fled together with 60 Portuguese to the Muslim side. Others, however, related that he had defected earlier.

- Correia claims that the reason Lopes refused to accompany Machado and return to the Portuguese side was because he would be dishonoured and insulted. He even goes as far as saying that Machado offered Lopes protection but that was turned down.

- Castanheda notes that when the renegades were brought in the presence of Albuquerque they protested that they should not even be punished as that went against the agreement with Rasul Khan.

- Both Barros and Castanheda write that Lopes was immediately shipped to Portugal after his punishment.

- Barros and Castanheda both write that Lopes requested to be left on the island and begged the captain to leave him there to purge himself of his sins.

SUGGESTED FURTHER READING

Boxer, CR, *The Portuguese Seaborne Empire 1415–1825*, New York: Alfred Knopf 1969

Crowley, R, *Conquerors*, London: Faber & Faber 2015

Disney, AR, *A History of Portugal and the Portuguese Empire*, Cambridge: CUP 2009, 2 vols

Earle, TF & Villiers, J, eds and trans., *Albuquerque, Caesar of the East: Selected texts by Afonso de Albuquerque and his son*, Teddington 1990

Jordan Gschwend, A & Lowe, KJP, *The Global City: On the streets of Renaissance Lisbon*, London: Paul Holberton 2015

Nayeem, MA, *The Heritage of the Adil Shahis of Bijapur*, Hyderabad: Hyderabad Publishers 2008

Newitt, M, *A History of Portuguese Overseas Expansion, 1400–1668*, London: Routledge 2005

Pearson, MN, *The New Cambridge History of India, Vol. I, Part I: The Portuguese in India*, Cambridge: CUP 1987

Ravenstein, EG, *A Journal of the First Voyage of Vasco da Gama 1497–99*, ed. and trans., London 1898

Russell-Wood, AJR, *The Portuguese Empire, 1415–1808*, Baltimore: Johns Hopkins Press 1992

Schulenburg, AH, 'Transient Observations: The Textualizing of St Helena Through Five Hundred Years of Colonial Discourse', PhD Thesis, St Andrews 1999

Soyer, F, *The Persecution of the Jews and Muslims in Portugal*, Leiden: Brill 2007

Subrahmanyam, S, *The Portuguese Empire in Asia, 1500–1700: A Political and Economic History*, London: Wiley 1993

PERMISSIONS

The epigraph to this book is from *King of the Castle* by
Charles le Gai Eaton, and is reprinted here by permission
of the Islamic Texts Society, Cambridge, UK

The lyrics that appear on page 183 are from
'Looking through the eyes of Don Fernando' and
are reprinted by permission of Ralph Peters

The lyrics that appear on page 259 are from
'Honey', © Russell Cason Music, Nashville TN

The translation of the Rumi poem on page 305 is
reprinted by permission of Coleman Barkes